THE HOMEOWNER'S COMPLETE GUIDE

By the same author:

The Complete Book of Basement Finishing

How to Make Your Own Recreation and Hobby Room

Do-It-Yourself Home Protection

Early American Furniture You Can Build

Ralph Treves is also Editor of

The Family Handyman Home Improvement Book

THE HOMEOWNER'S COMPLETE GUIDE

BY RALPH TREVES

Illustrated with Photographs, Drawings, and Diagrams

A Sunrise Book   E. P. Dutton & Company, Inc.   1974

Copyright © 1974 by Ralph Treves
All rights reserved. Printed in the U.S.A.
First Edition
10 9 8 7 6 5 4 3 2 1

Published simultaneously in Canada by
Clarke, Irwin & Company Limited,
Toronto and Vancouver

Library of Congress Cataloging in Publication Data

Treves, Ralph.
    The homeowner's complete guide.

    "A Sunrise book."
    1. Dwellings—Maintenance and repair.   2. Do-it-
yourself work.   3. Repairing—Amateurs' manuals.
I. Title.
TH4817.T73   643'.7   72-94705
ISBN 0-87690-106-2

CONTENTS

ACKNOWLEDGMENTS

The author wishes to thank the following companies for their cooperation in furnishing photographs or technical information for this book:

Armstrong Cork Company
The Stanley Works
Ridgid Tool Company
Irwin Tool Company
Down Corning Company
Loctite Company
U.S.M. Company
Bernzomatic Company
Rawlplug Company
P.P.G. Industries
Benjamin Moore & Company
United States Gypsum Company
E. I. du Pont de Nemours & Company
Product Development & Manufacturing Company
Wallcovering Council
Peerless Faucet Company
The Moen Company
Sears, Roebuck & Company
Masonite Corporation

Grateful acknowledgment is made to the editors of *Workbench* for permission to use material by the author originally published in that magazine.

THE HOMEOWNER'S COMPLETE GUIDE

INTRODUCTION

Taking care of a house can be either drudgery or an interesting and pleasant leisure-time activity. It depends entirely on your attitude. Maintenance and repair chores can indeed be a nuisance if they are approached with resentment or a feeling of boredom. Many homeowners, on the contrary, discover that such tasks are actually fun, offer opportunities for learning, provide a source of varied physical activity, and pay off in both cost savings and a sense of accomplishment.

The purpose of this book is to help you enjoy your home and to make home ownership easygoing and economical, eliminating as much as possible dependence on outside mechanics and servicemen.

The Homeowner's Complete Guide takes the mystery out of the house systems, equipment and appliances, explains how they work and how to keep them in working order, schedules the routine servicing that is necessary to avoid costly deterioration, and tells how to make many repairs when breakdowns occur. This book also is concerned with the safety of your family and keeping your home fresh-looking and attractive.

You're on Your Own. The modern home has become increasingly complex. Just push a button or set the dial, and with no further attention, the home is kept uniformly warm, regardless of winter's vagaries, and pleasantly cool through the most sultry summer day. Automation also controls our washing machine, refrigerator, water heater, freezer, water softener, flush tanks, humidifier, and dehumidifier—even watchfully adjusts the oven, just so, to turn out the roast at its perfect color and tenderness. No wonder that we have come to depend so completely on our appliances and equipment.

Occasionally something will go wrong; however, when it does, you need not wait fretfully, the entire household disrupted, until the plumber, electrician, or appliance serviceman shows up. Acting on the instructions in this book, you will be able, in most cases, to make the repair yourself.

Keep Appliances Working. Some people find it necessary to buy a new washing machine or vacuum cleaner every year or so, while others, this writer included, keep them performing in top condition for 20 years and longer, with hardly a cent of extra cost. A newspaper article described one couple's tribulations with a fairly new refrigerator-freezer that went into a long defrost cycle so frequently that the food was constantly spoiled. Repair charges mounted, but the trouble continued until a dinner guest, hearing their tale of woe, made the obvious test and found the electric receptacle contacts were so worn that the plug connection was broken by vibration when

The pleasant home is kept in tip-top condition, inside and outside, by routine maintenance that is both interesting and instructive. The knowledgeable homeowner can avoid expensive deterioration and annoying breakdowns.

anyone walked nearby. The "off" times had been incorrectly blamed on the defrost switch, but the first rule of appliance servicing is to check out the electric connection as the most likely culprit. The refrigerator was in perfect condition! Replacement of the old wall receptacle would have spared this couple much expense and annoyance.

Broadening Our Skills. In our technological society, most occupations are highly specialized, limiting a person's training and functions to a narrow field. The tendency, then, is to rely on the services of other specialists and repairmen. The early American colonists and the homesteaders who settled the West, by contrast, developed varied skills so they could build their own homes and barns, make furniture, farming tools, and almost everything else they needed, utilizing whatever resources were at hand.

The person who can do simple carpentry surely also can develop cabinetmaking, masonry, plumbing, and other manual abilities. But such efforts should not be attempted blindly. Why stumble around haphazardly when some knowledge of the equipment or process that is involved will help avoid needless damage and wasted time? A number of basic techniques involved in various home chores are specifically detailed in this book for your guidance.

Some Restrictions. You should be able to handle most of the work around the house yourself, but some operations are best left for the professional mechanic. Certain installations are restricted by local ordinance to licensed trades; others are so complex or dangerous that it is wiser to leave them to experienced workers. In the first category are electrical circuits and plumbing lines. Local regulations range widely, some requiring, for example, that electrical work *behind* the wall surface (new circuits or additional receptacle outlets, for instance) be done only by licensed electricians after a permit is issued; others specify only that the work comply with the National Electrical Code standards established by the National Board of Fire Underwriters. You would certainly want your home wiring to meet these safety standards.

Plumbing regulations also may be quite strict in order to safeguard community health, while building department rules usually require prior approval of any alteration or addition to the house structure, to make sure that the design and materials conform to local standards.

It is certainly true that much mechanical work requires special skills acquired only after many years of apprenticeship, so some work should be undertaken by a homeowner only if he is certain of his ability to do the job properly. Roofing, as an example, involves more than just nailing down shingles, sealing of flashings, pitching drains and gutters, and the ability to work on high ladders.

Adjustments of certain heating equipment controls are done with sensitive instruments and it certainly is not practical to buy these tools for one-time use. But appliance repairs that involve replacement of components or assemblies, such as motor, timer, belt, water pump, or gaskets, can usually be handled successfully by the homeowner.

Many product manufacturers make available without charge booklets or manuals containing detailed instructions on installing, cleaning, and repair of their products. These informative booklets, and catalogues describing various tools, hardware items, and other materials, can be of considerable help to the homeowner. Sources for obtaining some of this free literature are listed at the back of this book. Write for them and study the items so you will know what's available. Many of the tools are indeed ingenious, and you may find at some future time that one of them serves your particular need as no other tool can.

An intangible benefit gained by the homeowner with each task that he attempts is the experience that makes the next effort easier and more successful. This book aims to provide the encouragement, as well as the step-by-step instructions, for achieving a confident and self-sufficient home ownership.

1. THE TOOLS YOU NEED

Just having the needed tools and supplies on hand is a big step toward doing those maintenance and repair chores that crop up occasionally in every home. Most routine jobs can be accomplished with just a few basic tools—a hammer, screwdriver, slip-joint pliers, adjustable wrench, and hand saw. But the lack of certain additional tools sharply limits the scope of your efforts, makes the work much more difficult, and may cause further damage.

Very likely you know some homeowners who seem to get along with just a beat-up screwdriver and a pair of rusty pliers. You can take it for granted that such equipment produces botched jobs, continued trouble, and ultimately extra expense. As every mechanic knows, the quickest and most efficient way to do any job is with the right tools that are in good working condition. Readers of this book will, hopefully, recognize that an adequate collection of the necessary tools will assure prompt and proper repairs, thus contributing to pleasant and economical home ownership.

Quite a large collection of tools is needed for effective, cost-saving home maintenance. Fortunately, hand tools of even excellent quality are quite inexpensive; most cost just a few dollars and will last a lifetime if properly handled. If it serves your budget better, start with a small basic assortment from the primary list below, and pur-chase the additional items over a period of time, or as needed. Even the few portable electric tools that are so useful—a drill, sander, saber or circular saw—represent only a modest investment for the benefits they bring. Just think how much time and effort a drill or saw will save, year after year, at an outlay of only 10 to 30 dollars for each of these items! Other electric tools, when you are ready for them, will also vastly expand your capabilities. Considering the enormous cost of outside repair services, a modest investment in tools will be insignificant in relation to the extensive savings that will be possible, in addition to the benefits derived from avoiding dependence on the vagaries of independent servicemen.

A useful way to save on the cost of tools is for neighbors to purchase certain items cooperatively, such as a long extension ladder, a pipe threader, or belt sander. More expensive items, or those which are needed for one-time use only, such as a wallpaper steamer, can be rented for a day or two at moderate fees from hardware stores or rental outlets.

SELECTING THE TOOLS

Tool assortments needed vary according to specific conditions: whether you have a home or live in an apartment; the extent of the repairs that you intend to tackle; whether you will be doing some home improvements and workshop projects. The woodworking and mechanical enthusiast will want a complete workshop, including power tools.

As you go along, your growing need for special-purpose tools will enlarge your collection: a certain type or size of wrench, a sledgehammer, a concrete float trowel or joint-striking tool for mortar joints, hole saws, painting and wallpapering equipment, and many others.

SPECIAL-PURPOSE TOOLS

Whatever the repair problem you run into, it has been encountered before and very likely a special tool has been designed to take care of the difficulty. Why struggle unnecessarily, often vainly, when the right tool will solve the problem? Copper tubing is quickly and neatly formed to a required shape when you use a coil spring bender that costs just a few dollars for a complete set of sizes; without this tool, the tubing may become kinked and useless.

A stapling gun by Arrow Fastener shoots round-topped staples to secure low-voltage wire safely for audio speakers, doorbells, and burglar alarm wiring. Similarly, a unique basin wrench will reach up and turn the coupling nuts on otherwise out-of-reach plumbing connections, saving hours of time and skinned knuckles. Power screwdrivers, used with an electric drill, take the tedium out of cabinet assembly and boat building, while flexible steel tape "snakes" help you do concealed electric wiring like a professional.

BASIC HOME TOOLS

Drop light	with 20-foot cord
Hammer	claw type
Screwdrivers	at least three: small, medium, large, plus Phillips no. 2, and stubby type.
Pliers	slip-joint and long-nose
Wrenches	adjustable wrench; set of open end wrenches (¼ to 1 inch), and set of Allen hex wrenches
Plane	6-inch block plane
Saws	26-inch crosscut saw; hacksaw frame and blades
Rules	6-foot folding rule or yardstick
Files	one each: flat, round, and rasp
Oil can	pumper type
Electric drill	with ¼- or ⅜-inch chuck, and set of fractional size bits
Plumbing tools	coil type sink auger; plumber's force cup
Caulking gun	cartridge type
Awl	any size
Painting and wallpapering tools	including a 2-inch edging brush, 9-inch roller set
Putty knife	1½-inch width
Electric extension cords	3-wire grounded type, 20 feet
Stepladder	5- or 6-foot, wood or aluminum

ADVANCED TOOL ASSORTMENT
(*Addition to Basic Tools*)

Workbench	with vise
Chisels	set of wood chisels, ⅜ to ¾ inch; and a cold chisel
Level	carpenter's spirit level
Gun tacker	5⁄16-inch staples
Paint scraper	with extra blades
Electrician's tools	wire stripper, linesman's pliers, instantaneous soldering gun
Saws	keyhole or coping saw
Miter box	
Clamps	two 4-inch C clamps, two sets of pipe clamps
Sharpening stone	whetstone
Wallboard knife	with extra blades
Masonry tools	trowel, mortar jointer, setting tool
Trysquare	with miter gauge and spirit level
Center punch and nailset	
Electric tools	drill, with assortment of bits; sander; saber or circular saw
Extension ladder	24 feet or longer if needed
Wrenches	pipe wrench, basin wrench

EXTENSIVE TOOL ASSORTMENT
(Addition to Assortments)

Hammers	wood or rubber mallet, ball-peen hammer, small sledge
Plane	smoothing or jack plane
Propane torch and soldering tip	
Tinsnips	
Pry bar	
Plumbing tools	pipe or tubing cutter, bending springs, threader
Drill bits	carbide-tipped, ¾₆- and ½-inch bits, and set of pilot hole bits
Screwdrivers	offset, standard, and Phillips
POP rivet tool	with assortment of rivets
Power tools	bench or radial saw, router, bench grinder
Screen repair roller	double-wheel type
Electric glue gun	with glue and caulking sticks
Wheelbarrow	
Vacuum cleaner	shop type with large tank

INDIVIDUAL TOOL KITS

Instead of selecting and gathering together the various tools for each job to be done, you'll save time and steps by arranging certain tools and supplies in specialized kits, ready to go. For example, you can have a box with everything needed to install masonry anchors. Such a collection would include a star drill, carbide-tipped drill bits, various types and sizes of wall plugs or anchors, a setting tool to expand the masonry anchor in its hole, screws, a rule, and heavy hammer. The electric drill can be kept separately, taken along as needed.

For plumbing repairs, make up a kit containing a tubing cutter, bending springs, solder and resin paste, sandpaper, propane torch, faucet washers of the correct sizes, thread compound or tape dope, screwdrivers, and slip-joint pliers. The tape dope is a thin Teflon plastic that seals the pipe threads against leaks, serving the purpose of plumber's compound. If your house has rigid pipe, you may need also a pair of Stillson pipe wrenches with toothed jaws to turn a pipe, a hacksaw or pipe cutter, and threading dies.

As you encounter various tasks, the kits will expand when you discover the particular tools and supplies needed for the different work. Other special kits may include equipment for electrical work (wire stripper, linesman's pliers, wire nuts, pliers, screwdriver, electrical tape, etc.), and paperhanging (paste brush, smoothing brush, drop line with plumb bob, paint brushes, razor blades, seam roller, and edger).

Specialized kits will require duplicates of some tools, but the cost of hand tools is so moderate that the saving in time and effort will fully compensate. Small metal toolboxes are the best way to keep the kit assortments.

CARING FOR TOOLS

There are three essential rules: Protect your tools against damage; always keep them clean and sharp; store them so that you can find the ones you need almost instantly. Let these suggestions become a matter of normal workshop routine, and you'll never be concerned about the condition of your tools:

1. Provide suitable racks for sharp-edged tools, such as chisels, augers, scrapers. A simple length of 2 × 4, drilled for a series of holes of the proper size and attached to a wall, can store auger bits separately in upright position, each size marked for ready selection. Twist drills are best kept in a drill case or open-type stand that holds the drills in graduated size arrangement. Sharpened circular saws should be kept in their original envelopes, the center holes placed on a heavy wall nail. Wood chisels come with protective plastic caps, which should be retained. In any event, never store chisels haphazardly in a single carton or drawer; supply a receptacle for the graduated sizes. A cloth or vinyl strip with sewn compartments makes an excellent storage arrangement, holds a dozen or more sizes. Attach the strip to a wall or fold it when placed in a drawer.

Handy tool carrier holds stock of needed supplies in compartment tray, has ample space for various tools. Special-purpose kits can be arranged in separate tool cases or carriers like this.

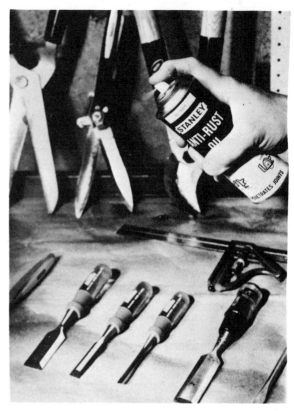

Aerosol anti-rust spray coating protects polished surfaces of such tools as saw blades and chisels. Rusted and pitted surfaces prevent efficient tool performance.

A tool carrier like the one illustrated will keep your tools in convenient array, save you much time and wasted steps returning to the workshop for some forgotten item. The handle on the tool kit eases the load, frees the other hand to carry additional items.

2. Do not toss metal tools on top of each other on a workbench or jumble them in a toolbox. Rather, take the little time that is necessary to provide the receiving holes or brackets for each type, whether in the toolbox or on the bench. A perforated pegboard wall makes an excellent adjunct for the workbench, or any place where tools are stored, as there are dozens of special hangers designed to receive the different types of tools. Always place a wood plane on its side, never with the blade on the bench top. Files and rasps do their work because they are specially tempered and hardened; as a result, the teeth will chip when thrown in contact with other metal tools. Saws, awls, and tools with sharp edges must be kept separately to avoid damage.

3. The bright polish on tools is more than just good looking. It permits smoother, more effective functioning, as with a saw blade or chisel. Tools stored in basement workshops may be subject to occasional or seasonal dampness. Protect your tools with a very fine coating of oil or other rust-preventing product. Tools that are used infrequently, like a dovetail saw, may be kept in special rust-protective bags. Saw blades that have become

rusted will meet resistance going through the work; chisel blade edges that have become rusted can break off more easily. Axes, hatchets, knives, and putty scrapers should be wiped dry and oiled after each use.

Keep your tools always in good working condition. Set aside a specific time—once a month would be just right—to straighten out your workshop or tool chests. Sharpen your chisels, plane blades, and hatchet (just a quick whetting or honing of each cutting edge, as described in the Sharpening section, usually will be sufficient to keep the edges keen). Top it off by applying a thin coat of protective oil from an aerosol can to saw blades and other tools that might become rusted. Polishing often restores tools that have become rusted or pitted.

Replace all twist drills and auger bits in their correct positions, check over your hardware supplies to see that you have the necessary washers, screws, caulking compound, and other material. Brush off or vacuum the workbench to clear away shavings, metal chips, and other debris, paying particular attention to the area under the bench vise and drill press table, if you have one. Also, empty the sawdust retainer of your table saw (with caution against fire hazard); then do a quick vacuuming of the area. All these chores contribute to the ease and efficiency of your home ownership.

ELECTRICAL GROUNDING PLUG

Nearly all the new electric tools, and some home appliances, come with a special 3-prong electric plug that has, in addition to the regular contact blades, a U-shaped grounding plug. This is intended to protect you against dangerous shock if the tool housing should become "hot," or electrically alive.

This plug requires a special grounding receptacle, which has now become standard in new installations. Adapters to permit use of the 3-prong plug in a regular receptacle have a thin green "pigtail" wire for attaching to the receptacle plate, but this step is often neglected, defeating the purpose for which the device was intended.

It's a simple matter to convert all workshop receptacles to the new type, as explained in Chapter 5. These receptacles can be used for the old electric cords as before, but they will take the new safety plugs and eliminate need for fussing with adapters.

BUILDING A WORKBENCH

For the homeowner, the most helpful single piece of equipment is a workbench—the bigger and sturdier the better. Whatever the task, from

Standing on rugged 4 × 4 legs, properly braced with 2 × 4 rails and stretchers, and with a solid top of 2 × 6 lumber, this workbench will become your standby to assist on any type of maintenance problem or for general workshop use.

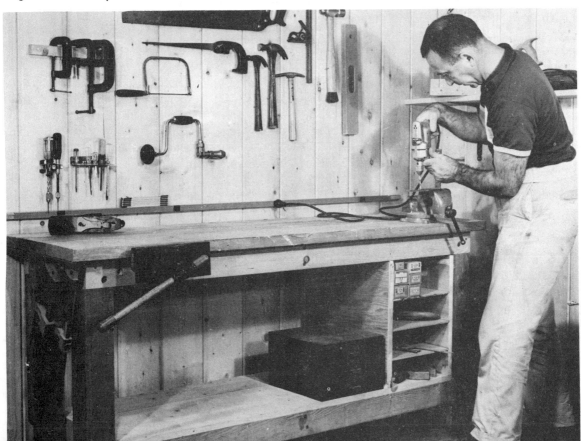

filing down a latch plate to reassembling appliance units, it will be done more easily, promptly, and efficiently when there's a suitable bench on which to work.

The workbench is also the storage center for your tools and supply of hardware, all properly arranged so you can find what you need without a time-wasting, frustrating hunt. The effort spent in assorting and labeling these items will be more than repaid by the speed with which you can dispatch the various chores that are part of home ownership.

Locating the Workbench. A separate workshop in the basement, preferably in an area with an outside window to facilitate bringing boards and other materials into the shop, will be ideal. Other possible locations are the utility or "mud" room, the garage, even an outbuilding or shed in the rear yard if electric connections are provided for lighting and power tools. In an outbuilding, an electric heater, a small potbelly coal stove, or even a charcoal brazier (with adequate ventilation) can provide the heating that will occasionally be needed.

Workbench Plan. A good shop bench has ample surface area, is fitted with a vise, and is solid enough to stand steady when you hammer, plane, or chisel. The base can contain storage shelves and drawers, while the wall space above is utilized for hanging tools within close reach.

The design of the bench illustrated here meets these requisites and might well be copied. This bench can be built entirely with hand tools, including the notched joints, although a power saw will do the job quicker and more accurately.

The bench is 6 feet long and about 22 inches deep. Standard overall height of about 34 inches can be altered for your personal comfort. You will need the following materials: 12 feet of 4 × 4 fir stock (in 6-foot or 12-foot lengths) for the legs, 36 feet of 2 × 4s for cross rails, 24 feet of 2 × 6 fir (in 6-foot lengths or multiples) for the top, and 12 feet of 1 × 10 for shelving, plus a dozen each of ¼-inch by 4-inch carriage bolts and 3-inch no. 12 screws. The bench will be worth far more than the outlay for lumber.

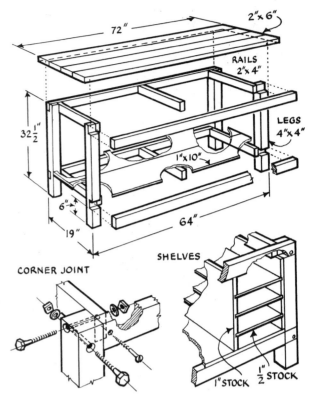

Construction of the bench is detailed in the sketch. Height should be adjusted to make the bench more comfortable for you. Convenient electric receptacles are provided by the surface channel illustrated.

Building the Bench. Construction details are shown in the sketch. Saw the four legs of the 4 × 4 stock. Cut notches at the top end and 6 inches from the bottom of each leg to lap the 2 × 4 rails, as shown. Do it this way: place the 2 × 4 over the notch position, mark its width and thickness. When cutting on a table saw, set the blade to the thickness depth and make the first cuts through the width line, then pass the stock across the blade with successive slight shifts in position to remove the inside waste stock; finish neatly with a chisel. The process with a hand saw is similar, the waste stock being removed with a chisel. Final adjusting cuts may be needed for snug fit of the 2 × 4s.

Cut the long 2 × 4 rails to length and assemble the frame, boring the bolt holes with a ¾-inch

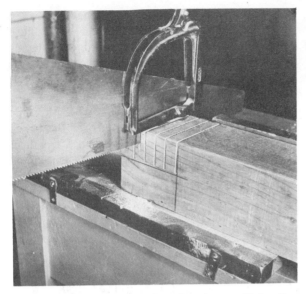

Cutting half-lap joints with a hand saw. Make first cuts along the marked outline, then saw closely spaced cut within the waste area. Saw is used here in a miter gauge for better precision.

Chisel removes waste stock down to the marked line, so 2 × 4 stretcher will fit into the lap joint. The lapping is done much more quickly on a bench or radial saw.

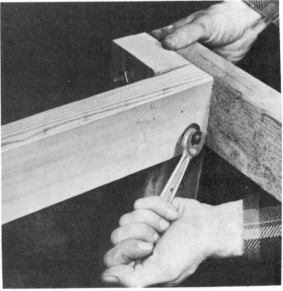

Stretchers are lapped to the legs, securely bolted in each direction. Countersinking the bolt heads takes little extra time, makes a neater job. Cut all equal-sized parts at one time to speed assembly.

Note that cross-rails are braced against both the legs and stretchers, under the top and at the lower supports. Use heavy carriage or lag bolts, no rails or wood screws, in the basic frame.

auger first to a depth of ½ inch, which will countersink the bolt heads, then using a ⁵⁄₁₆-inch drill to go through. The point of the auger will guide starting the smaller drill. Join the rails and legs, two at each end and two across the center, as shown.

The top consists of four 6-foot lengths of 2 × 6 stock, butted edge to edge, the rear board flush with the back rail, the front board overhanging about 3 inches for a clamping surface. The boards are fastened with countersunk 3-inch wood screws through drilled holes into the framing members. Attach a panel of ¼-inch tempered Masonite hardboard, which resists denting, over the bench top. If a backboard is desired, fasten a length of 1 × 6 stock across the back. The bench should stand steady on the floor; if not, adjust by sawing the required amount off the legs or attach shims as needed.

If desired, interior shelves of 1-inch stock can be added as shown in the sketch at lower right.

A WORKBENCH IN THE GARAGE

Even if you have a satisfactory workbench in the basement, an extra bench in the garage is useful when you are working on outdoor projects and require a surface for sawing, or need un-

Top of 2 × 6 lumber, fastened with counterset screws into the rails and stretchers, overhangs at front for clamping and placement of vise.

Tools arranged on pegboard wall above workbench for convenient accessibility. Special hangers are available for almost every type of item to go on the board. Not every tool in the basic list is shown here.

Shallow workbench designed for limited space in a garage will be handy for occasional use when working outdoors. Base, of 2 × 2 stock, is solidly attached to the garage wall. The 5-foot-long top is a length of 1 × 12 shelving. For greater strength, use 2 × 3s for the base, edge-butted 2 × 6 stock for the top.

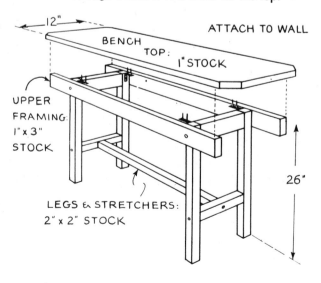

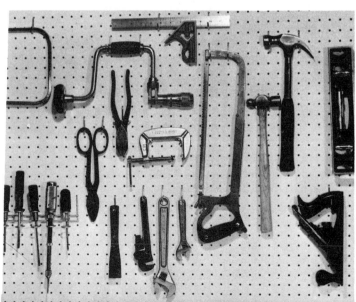

encumbered space to handle long boards and large projects. Additionally, sanding and furniture spraying should be done in the garage rather than in the house, where sawdust or paint spray can spread far and wide. And in mild weather, it's more pleasant working in the open.

The simple, easily constructed bench that is illustrated will be adequate for occasional use, although dimensions are kept to the minimum to leave garage space for the car. The length is at least 5 feet, the top only 12 inches deep. The base, built of 2 × 2 stock, is attached to the garage wall for rigidity. If more space is available the bench should be enlarged, and shelves included in the base for tools and supplies.

TIPS ON USING TOOLS

Many persons lack any experience with mechanical work and, as a result, doubt their ability to handle tools. These fears will be overcome and confidence acquired after just a little experience with several simple and routine tasks. The new homeowner, particularly, will find that learning to do the various repairs is essential both for economy and to free himself from frequent dependence on outside services.

Caution is essential until sufficient confidence is acquired. Avoid both damage to the work and possible personal injury by studying carefully the instruction sheets that are supplied with many tools; do additional reading in some of the excellent home workshop books that are available. Keep the suggested rules in mind as you proceed carefully with the work. Good lighting is an essential; one of the best aids to safe and efficient work is a drop light on an extension cord, and it should be used wherever the normal lighting is inadequate.

Specific suggestions are provided below on working safely with several of the most commonly used tools.

Screwdrivers. While these are possibly the simplest of tools in design and function, there are some important rules to keep in mind for safe and proper use. But first, you will need a sufficient assortment of screwdrivers—they're not all the same, as many people think, and you may need half a dozen or more to take care of the routine jobs.

The standard screwdriver has a wide, tapered blade at the working end, a secure handle of wood, rubber, or plastic at the top of the shaft, or rod. Blade width and thickness are two essential dimensions, overall length of the rod is another. A minimum assortment would include four sizes, as follows:

Point Width, in inches	Point Thickness, in inches	Overall Length, in inches
¼	.040	8
⁵⁄₁₆	.045	10
⅜	.050	12
¼ (shorty)	.032	3½

You will need a similar assortment of Phillips type screwdrivers, which end in four crossed points, rather than a straight blade. They are used mostly on appliances, electrical parts, automobile work, and toy assembly. Point sizes are related to the screw sizes that they will fit.

Phillips Point Size	Fits Screw Sizes
1	4 and smaller
2	5 to 9
3	10 to 16
4	18 and larger

Several additional screwdriver types are useful to own. One is an offset, in which the handle is at a right angle to the blades for closeup work where clearance is insufficient for a regular screwdriver. These offset types have a standard blade at one end, a Phillips type on the other. Also valuable in the tool collection is a heavy screwdriver with a square rod on which an open-end wrench may be used to provide additional power for loosening stubborn bolts and screws. Electricians' and appliance service screwdrivers, similar to the standard ones above, are used for fine work, have square tips but generally narrower and thinner blades.

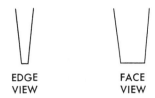

EDGE
VIEW

FACE
VIEW

Correct grinding of screwdrivers: the blade faces are
slightly tapered, the end ground square and flat.

The tips of screwdriver blades are not sharpened; rather the sides are slightly tapered, the tip
ground square to fit snugly in the screw slot. If the
tip of a screwdriver becomes slightly rounded, it
can be restored by holding the edge flat against a
grinding wheel. Screwdrivers are frequently used
as handy pry bars; this will bend the rod. The
condition sometimes can be corrected by rolling
the driver on the workbench to determine the
high spot, then carefully tapping with a hammer
to straighten it. Make it a rule to avoid abusing
the screwdriver, as it is not tempered for the kind
of work that the pry bar or pinch bar can do best.

Rules for correct, safe use of screwdrivers:

1. Select driver of proper size for the screwhead, blade thickness just fitting the slot, its width
slightly narrower than the screwhead diameter.
A blade extending beyond the screwhead will rip
the adjacent surface. Rod length is also important
as it enables you to apply the force that is needed
—a driver that is too long, however, may cause
the screwhead to break off.

2. Pre-drill pilot holes for screws to prevent
splitting the wood. Countersink pilot hole drills
make it possible to turn the screwhead down flush
to the cabinet surface or below the surface, so the
screwhead can be countersunk and covered with
wood putty.

3. Fit the driver blade all the way into the slot;
hold the handle down firmly. A common cause of
difficulty is attempting to twist while the driver
is not fully seated; the blade may slip out and
jab the hand.

4. Start with a slow and steady pressure to get
the screw started, then it can be turned in or out
more quickly.

Hammers. The type of hammer most commonly
found in the home is the claw hammer, which is
helpful for withdrawing nails from wood. Hammers are so versatile and simple in form that they
are used for almost every task that requires
pounding. The trouble that arises from this practice is that when used on stone or other masonry,
the tempered head of the hammer may become
chipped or otherwise damaged. Then when used
to drive nails, those distortions prevent hitting
the nailhead squarely.

The newer hammers with integral steel handles
are excellent. Select the type and weight that feel
best in your hand after checking the balance of
the hammer. Several other types of hammers are
useful in the home shop. For masonry or other
concrete work, use a stonecutter's adze; for
gluing and other cabinetry use a mallet with a
soft plastic or rubber head; for metalworking,
select one of the ball-peen or machinist's hammers of the required weight.

Care of the hammer should not be neglected.
Wipe the handle frequently to remove dirt and
grease; check the hammer heads to be certain
that they are securely wedged onto the handle,
the wedge deeply inserted and tight; replace any
cracked or split handle; avoid incorrect use that
will damage the hammer head.

Pliers. Any type of pliers will do in a pinch, but
you'll make out a lot better with the right kind
for the job at hand. Many a homeowner still relies
on ancient dime-store pliers, and surprisingly,
they do the job quite well most times. But on
occasion, those pliers are responsible for more
damage than they cure—because they scratch and
dent finished surfaces, fail to tighten a part sufficiently, and may round off the corners of a nut
so it can no longer be gripped even by a proper-
size wrench.

The point is that while most pliers can handle
a wide range of work, the proper pliers for a
particular job will help avoid wasteful fumbling,
damage, and possible injury.

Changing faucet washers, for example, involves
turning out the chromed cap nut and other
polished parts. This should be done with pliers
having smooth-surfaced jaws set parallel, similar

to the jaws of a monkey wrench. Toothed-jaw pliers are effective on pipes and irregularly shaped surfaces.

The famous "linesman's" pliers has flat jaws with a powerful grip and side cutters that can snip electrical and steel wires. A special notched type also strips insulation from electrical wires. Two other useful types are the "long-nose" pliers and the diagonal cutter. The slim long-nose serves for delicate jobs such as repairs of costume jewelry, chains, and other fine metal work. If you go in for more extensive home projects, or do some work on the car, the diagonal cutter is perfect for pulling cotter pins, cutting wire, etc. End-cutter nippers are used also for chipping ceramic tile to size.

The size of pliers can work with you or against you. It's not smart to use tiny 5-inch pliers on large work that would be done easier with an 8-inch size that gives extra leverage. But you can't work properly on small items held between massive jaws that get in the way.

Pliers can be damaged when incorrectly used. Twisting loosens the pivot pin, throws the jaws out of alignment; hammering can chip the jaws, while cutting too-large nails will burr the cutters. Pliers need almost no attention to give long, dependable service aside from occasional lubrication of the pivot pin and protection against rusting.

Planes. Many home chores and repairs are accomplished most easily and successfully with a plane. Typical uses are trimming the edge of a sticky door, smoothing uneven surfaces of wood flooring, and for fitting cabinets, benches and other home improvement projects. To achieve the objective of long, thin shavings, the blade must be sharp, the cutting edge set at the right depth, the plane held correctly.

The smoothing or bench plane, 8 to 9 inches long, is most versatile for general work in home or shop. It is held with both hands, the left hand on the front knob applying downward pressure at the start of the cut, the right hand pressing down hardest on the heel of the plane near the finish. The smaller block plane, 6 to 7 inches long, is held in one hand for cutting. Accurate smoothing and fitting of long boards is best done

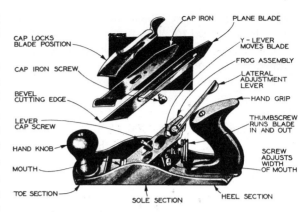

The smoothing plane is assembled with the beveled edge of the blade on the underside, extending not more than 1/16 inch beyond the base sole. The cap iron stiffens the blade, while its arched end serves to spiral out and break off the shavings. The front lever is used to adjust the blade so its edge is extended evenly.

with the jack plane, which has a base 11 to 22 inches long.

Another tool that serves the purpose of a plane is the Stanley Surform, made of thin metal with hundreds of tiny, razor-sharp edges for fast cutting of wood, plastics, and soft metals. One style is in the shape of a plane, with double handles to be

This is the Surform plane, a new type of tool that comes also in file and rasp shapes.

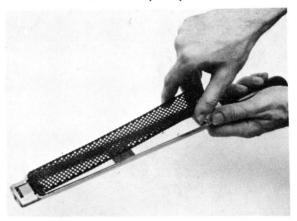

held by both hands. Others are round, curved, even drum-shaped for use in an electric drill.

The early planes were simply chisels firmly embedded in blocks of wood. The modern plane, with its cast iron body and comfortable grip, has many refinements that permit more precise adjustments and facilitate its use. Cutting is done with a chisel-like blade, as before, but there's also a cap iron, also known as the chip breaker, arched at the bottom to deflect and break off the shavings, and a locking cap to hold the blade securely in position. An adjustment knob raises or lowers the blade edge through the bottom slot, or throat, and a large lever is used to adjust the edge laterally so it is straight across. Even the size of the throat opening can be adjusted for deep or shallow cuts by turning a screw.

Assembling the Plane. The cap iron and blade are first joined with a short screw, the cap iron

uppermost and its arched end close to the unbeveled edge of the blade. When inserted into the plane body, a lateral slot in the cap iron fits over a bar leading from the adjustment screw. A heavy metal plate, clamped on by snapping a cam lever, locks the assembly in place. The blade's bevel is facing downward, the edge projecting very slightly through the plate slot.

Adjusting the Blade. Hold the plane in one hand, bottom up, the forward end away from you, and at a level with your eyes; sight along the projecting blade edge. Move the large frog lever to right or left until the blade edge is uniform, that is, it extends equally at both ends.

Now turn the adjustment screw to retract the blade edge so it is only $\frac{1}{32}$ to $\frac{1}{16}$ inch beyond the bottom, depending on whether the wood is soft or hard. The projection should be just enough so it can be felt with the fingers. A sharp blade, squarely set, will produce long thin shavings of uniform thickness, without gouging the work.

Always move plane from edge of wood toward center to avoid splintering.

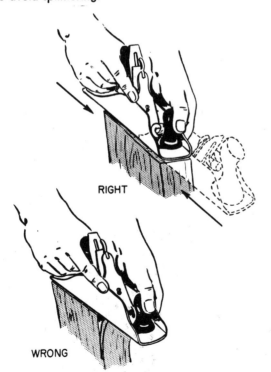

RIGHT

WRONG

Wrenches. Though the "left-handed monkey

Collection of wrenches, all useful around the home. From the left: Socket in ratchet handle; socket in T handle; socket in L arm; group of Allen hex wrenches; Big Mouth; small open end, open end plus box; open end; 2 adjustable; small Stillson; Stillson; monkey; vise-grip; chain sprocket; and basin. At upper left, a group of sockets with swivel coupling.

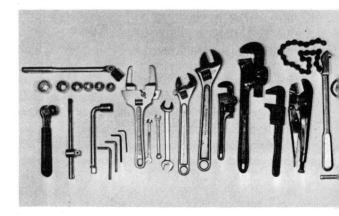

wrench" is a gag intended to fool the unwary, using the "right" wrenches around the home definitely makes sense. Of the dozens of types, each is designed to best accomplish certain tasks.

The jaws should fit exactly, to retain their grip, and the handle should be long enough for leverage. If the jaws slip or spread, the nut will become rounded so that it can't be gripped, or worse still, the wrench will pull free and cause injury to the user. Adjustable wrenches, while highly useful in many cases, are not entirely reliable for breaking tightly locked nuts, as any auto mechanic can attest. Socket or open end wrenches of the precise size should be used.

For the home workshop, an assortment capable of handling most situations would include a large adjustable or monkey wrench, a set of open end, socket, and Allen hex wrenches, a basin wrench, Stillson pipe wrench, and a vise-grip wrench. A necessary adjunct is a can of penetrating oil, often helpful to release "frozen" joints.

Saws. Practically everyone is familiar with the typical handsaw, the basic woodcutting tool. There are many other types of saws, each for a different purpose, all variations on the theme of tiny teeth that gouge or slice out bits of wood with each pass of the blade.

The two basic wood saws are the crosscut and rip. You can tell the difference by examining the teeth. Those of a crosscut saw are sharpened at a bevel like a knife blade, while those of the rip saw are square across the tip like a chisel, to chip rather than cut. Rip saw teeth are larger than those in a crosscut, and the set is closer together; that is, there is less bend from the center line. Handsaws are measured by the length of the blade, from tooth edge to tooth edge. Common sizes are 24 and 26 inches. The coarseness or fineness of cutting depends on the size of teeth; the larger the teeth, the fewer "points" (teeth) there are to an inch, and the coarser but faster the cut. Smooth cutting saws have 10 to 12 "points" to an inch.

A new stainless steel hand saw has a mirror finish for exceptional cutting smoothness and won't tarnish or rust.

Miter and Dovetail Saws. The miter saw, sometimes referred to as a back saw, has a rigid steel channel along the top to prevent flexing, for accurate miter cuts. The dovetail saw is the same, but is much shorter and has finer teeth for precise cutting of moldings and other small cross-sections.

Hacksaw. Highly tempered, the blade of a hacksaw will cut through almost any metal. The blades come in various tooth sizes, are interchangeable in the hacksaw frame. Around the home, the hacksaw is used for cutting pipe, electric BX cable, bolts, and other metal items.

Coping Saw. One of the lowest-priced tools, the coping saw consists of a steel or wire frame forming an open square or rectangle, holding a very narrow blade across one end. The saw is used mostly for cutting irregular shapes in thin wood,

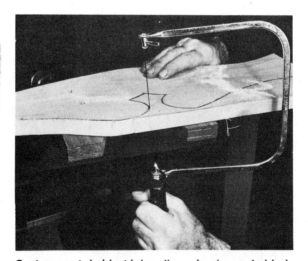

Coping saw is held with handle under the work, blade cuts on either up or down stroke, following guide line in any curve radius. Work here is supported in bench vise.

including circles, and for shaping the backs of mitered crown moldings. Cutting is done with the work suported on a simple wood frame with a large V-shaped opening at the top; the saw action is vertical with the handle held below the work.

Keyhole and Compass Saws. The tapered point of the blade permits starting the cut within a drilled hole, or cutting in close quarters for trimming and shaping. A thumbscrew tightens or releases the blade, which is interchangeable with a dozen or so lengths and tooth variations. The keyhole blade is the shorter of the two.

Power Saws. When much woodcutting is to be done, or precision fitting required, one of the power saws will do the work most quickly, easily, and accurately. The bench saw and radial saw are the backbone of any advanced workshop, but considerable skill is required for safe operation, and the homeowner who obtains one for the first time should go about using it very slowly and carefully, after studying the instructions until he has become familiar with the procedure.

The easiest to use, and safest, of the power saws is the portable saber saw. This is a small tool, comfortably held in the hand, that operates a narrow blade in a short vertical stroke. The saw is guided along a marked line to make straight or irregular cuts in wood, with or against the grain. There are a dozen or more types of blades, including a hacksaw-type blade to cut steel and all non-ferrous metals.

Portable circular saws are widely owned, especially by carpenters. They cut rapidly through wood up to 2 inches thick, and can be quite accurately controlled with the aid of a guide. The blade is tilted to make various bevel and compound miter cuts. While the self-positioning guard covers the blade quite safely, the user must be always alert to the possibility of dangerous kickback, which happens when the blade becomes jammed in its cut, known to carpenters as the kerf.

Portable circular saw has self-setting safety guard.   Base can be tilted for various bevel and angle cuts.

Chain Saw. This saw rapidly cuts tree limbs, logs, and beams regardless of thickness or shape. Powered by either a gasoline engine or electric motor, the saw can be dangerous to any but an experienced and cautious user, as the sprocket chain that does the cutting is fully exposed. As the saw is held with both hands, accidents occur not so much from contact with the blade itself as from sudden shifting of the log or wood being cut.

Rolling Stand for Bench Saws. Few workshops have sufficient space for efficient use of a stationary bench saw—fore and aft when ripping, on both sides for cross-cutting. A free-wheeling saw stand, on large casters, enables you to swing the saw around to obtain needed clearance, and to roll the saw completely out of the way when not in use.

The base cabinet shown has a forward compartment that serves as a sawdust collector; the rear section stores extra blades, adjustment tools,

Base is made entirely of ¾-inch plywood. Bottom panel is full size of stand. Sizes have setback to clear the motor. All parts are securely attached with counterset screws.

Practical circular saw stand has lock-type casters so saw can be rolled around to obtain clearance. Compartment at front collects sawdust from chute; one at rear holds accessories. Switch is conveniently located.

Front panel is cut for access door, while cutout is made for gem box to hold motor switch standard toggle. Additional receptacle is wired with BX cable from the 3-wire grounded cord.

Top panels cover both sections with about 1-inch overhang at front. Opening is located under the sawdust chute in the saw housing.

Bar clamps are similar to pipe clamps, but lack the versatility as to length. The clamps shown have swivel-type head stocks, are used mostly for cabinet assemblies.

dado cutters, and so on. The on-off switch is conveniently located at the front, extra receptacles are at the side to plug in portable tools. The base, wide enough to support the saw when the table is enlarged by adding extension sections, is made of ¾-inch plywood, mostly small pieces. You may have enough scrap on hand to do the entire job.

Vises and Clamps. A good bench vise, and a basic collection of clamps, are essential for even a minimum level of home maintenance. The machinist's vise is more versatile than a woodworker's vise, although both will be useful for the homeowner who does cabinetmaking and similar projects.

A machinist's vise with 3-inch jaws will be adequate for most homeowners. Replaceable jaw faces and rubber jaw covers are desirable features, the latter particularly as it permits using the vise for chromed and polished items that would otherwise become badly marred. Portable vises, with vacuum mounting cups, may be useful when working away from the shop bench, although a solidly mounted vise is superior.

A woodworking vise is wider, attached to the edge of the workbench, rather than on top, to hold boards for planing and grooving. Size selection will depend on the extent of woodworking that you anticipate. The smaller 4-inch sizes are under 5 dollars, the largest 15 to 25 dollars.

Clamps are like additional hands and can apply the required pressure for gluing and other purposes. Their cost is quite nominal, so it is surprising that many homes have not a single clamp, or perhaps only tiny ones that are of limited value.

Pipe clamps, consisting of a "head" at one end, a turnscrew at the other, are assembled with lengths of ¾-inch steel pipe, threaded at one end. Used iron pipe is suitable. Keep on hand several different lengths, ranging from 18 inches to 6 feet —the clamp heads and tail blocks are easily shifted from one pipe to another, so you can select the most convenient length for whatever work you will be doing.

Other types that will extend your workshop capability are bar clamps, large C clamps with 4- and 8-inch openings, spring clamps, 2- or 3-inch

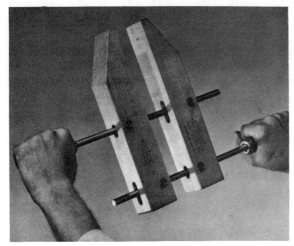

Screw type wood clamp.

excess supply may come in handy. But hardware is of little value if you can't find what you need. An investment of 5 to 10 dollars gives you a workshop cabinet of up to 48 small drawers, with clear plastic see-through fronts for orderly storage of many small items. An alternative is to keep screws, nails, and similar items in plastic prescription jars and metal Band-Aid boxes—a good many will fit into a single drawer. The "flip-top" cigarette packages also are suitable—you can collect dozens without cost, labeling the contents on a strip of masking tape over the lids.

Nails and screws are designated by diameter, length, head shape, and type of threads. The following sizes of screws and nails comprise a basic assortment to which you can add as needed.

Flathead screws	no. 6, ¾ inch; no. 8, ¾, 1, 1½ inches; no. 10, 1, 1½ inches
Sheetmetal screws	no. 6, ¾ inch; no. 8, 1, 1½ inches
Nails	common, 4d, 6d, 8d; finishing, 4d, 6d, 10d; also small brads
Iron washers	assorted sizes

size, for light gluing or soldering, and a couple of 1- or 2-inch C clamps for small items.

Gluing of mitered corner joints for picture frames and other projects always is difficult; a 4-piece set of corner clamps will help produce neat, well-bonded joints.

Lubricate the screw threads of your bench vise and clamps so they will operate smoothly, but make sure that oil does not go on the jaws where it can come in contact with the work.

Double-screw wood clamps, in various sizes with openings to 10 or more inches, are a favorite of old-time cabinetmakers. They adjust to irregular surfaces, have wide contact on the surface, won't twist when tightened. There's a certain skill to tightening the clamp properly, so that the jaws remain parallel.

HARDWARE SUPPLIES

Efficient home maintenance requires that you keep on hand at least the basic hardware items: screws, nails, rivets, staples, sandpaper, glue, caulking compound, masonry fasteners, faucet washers. The collection grows as you go along; it usually pays to buy a larger quantity each time than just the amount you need because the cost usually is the same or just a little more, and the

Nail Sizes

Penny Size	Length in Inches	Wire Gauge No.	Wire Diameter in Inches
2d	1	16	0.0625
3d	1⅛	15½	0.0672
4d	1⅜	14	0.0800
5d	1⅝	13½	0.0858
6d	1⅞	13	0.0915
7d	2⅛	12½	0.0985
8d	2⅜	11½	0.1130
10d	2⅞	11	0.1205
12d	3⅛	10	0.1350
16d	3¼	9	0.1483
20d	3¾	7	0.1770
30d	4¼	6	0.1920
40d	4¾	5	0.2070
60d	5¾	3	0.2437

No more guessing! Chart tells what you need to know about common nails—the length in inches for "penny" size, the gauge, and diameter.

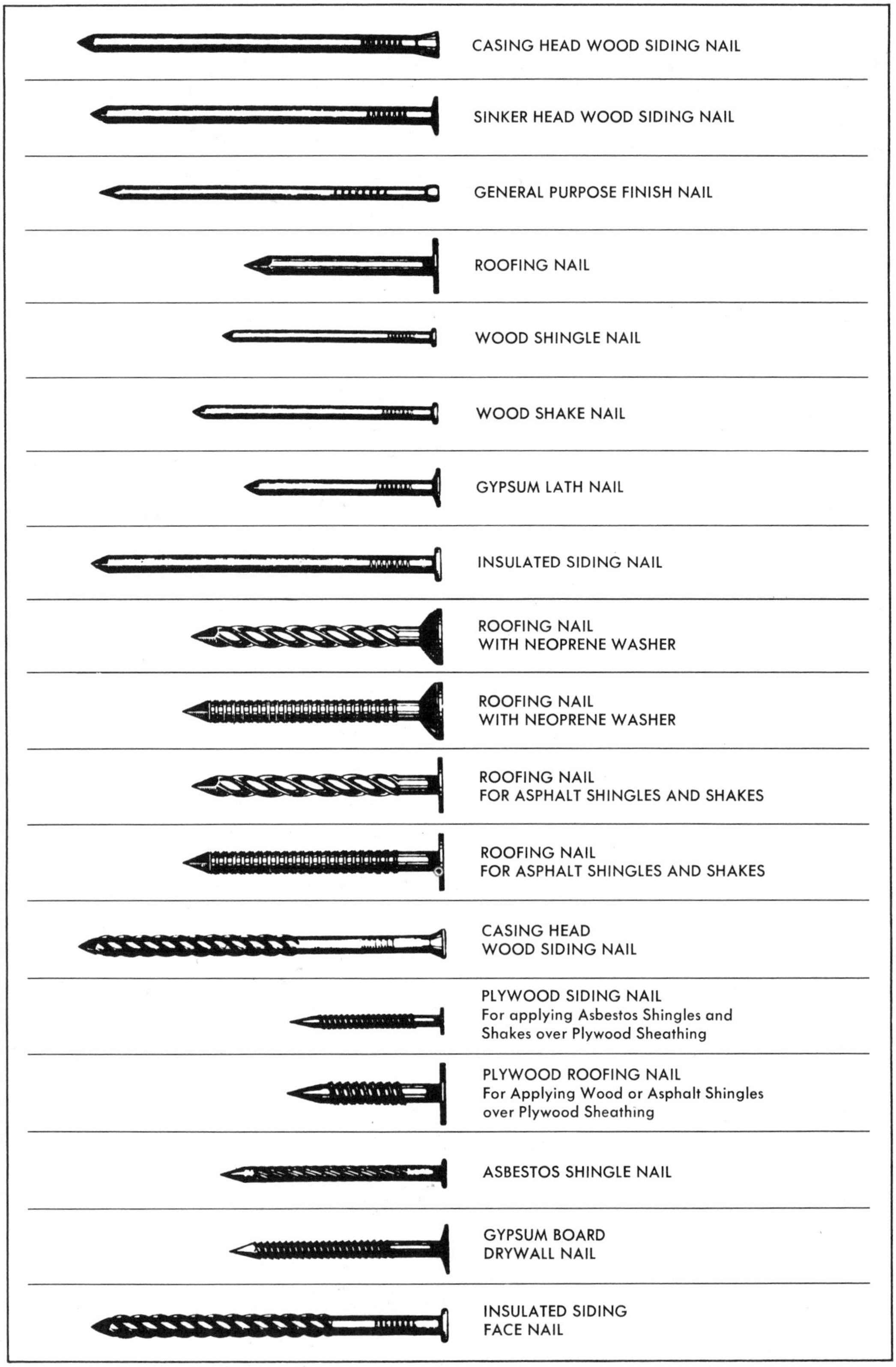

CASING HEAD WOOD SIDING NAIL

SINKER HEAD WOOD SIDING NAIL

GENERAL PURPOSE FINISH NAIL

ROOFING NAIL

WOOD SHINGLE NAIL

WOOD SHAKE NAIL

GYPSUM LATH NAIL

INSULATED SIDING NAIL

ROOFING NAIL
WITH NEOPRENE WASHER

ROOFING NAIL
WITH NEOPRENE WASHER

ROOFING NAIL
FOR ASPHALT SHINGLES AND SHAKES

ROOFING NAIL
FOR ASPHALT SHINGLES AND SHAKES

CASING HEAD
WOOD SIDING NAIL

PLYWOOD SIDING NAIL
For applying Asbestos Shingles and
Shakes over Plywood Sheathing

PLYWOOD ROOFING NAIL
For Applying Wood or Asphalt Shingles
over Plywood Sheathing

ASBESTOS SHINGLE NAIL

GYPSUM BOARD
DRYWALL NAIL

INSULATED SIDING
FACE NAIL

The success of a repair or construction project depends in large part on selection of suitable nails for the material that is used. Illustrated here are the various types for home use.

Rivets. Though often overlooked, rivets frequently are more suitable for certain assemblies than screws or nails. They may be used effectively to join sheet metal, attach hinges to boxes, reinforce railings, join flue pipe sections, repair luggage and handbags. Rivets are peened flat so there are no projections on either side—a decided advantage in certain materials that are to be handled, like garden tools. Most riveting can be done with ordinary tools.

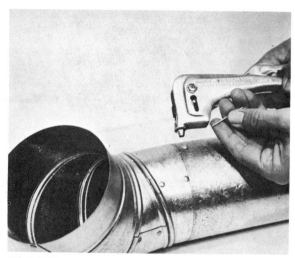

Blind POP rivet can be used even where back is not accessible for peening, as with this flue pipe section. Rivet has pin through the mandrel which is put into drilled hole.

An invaluable addition to the home workshop is the unique POP rivet, which does "blind" riveting—placing a rivet where the back cannot be reached for peening. The joint is pulled together by a special type of pliers more tightly

and neatly than can be done with the usual peening method. The rivets consist of aluminum or copper pins projecting through a short, tube-like aluminum mandrel. The mandrel is inserted into a hole drilled to correct size from the outside, or face, through the parts to be joined, and the pin is gripped by the pliers. Squeezing the pliers pulls the pin against the back of the mandrel, which expands on the back of the joint until the joint is so tightly compressed that the pin shears off flush with the surface of the material.

Pliers pull up pin so the mandrel is compressed at the back, pulling the join tightly; then the pin shears off neatly, close to the work surface.

POP rivets are excellent for assembling roof gutters, attaching the end caps, drop outlets, and corners, and sections of the downspout. They also make it a cinch to securely join metal flue pipe, for example, and the exhaust pipe of clothes dryers, on which the inside cannot be reached for peening.

These rivets come in three sizes, short, medium, and long, and in three diameters, $\frac{1}{8}$, $\frac{5}{32}$, and $\frac{3}{16}$ inch. A complete outfit, including the setting pliers and an assortment of rivets, costs about 4 dollars.

Other types of rivets come in soft steel, copper,

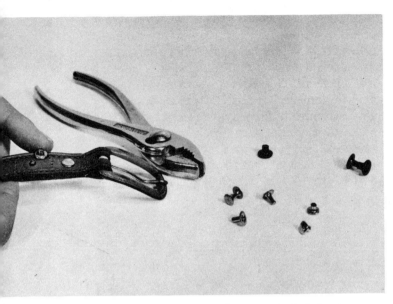

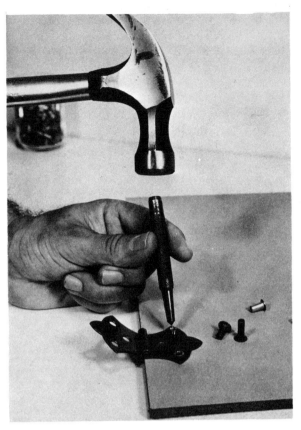

(Above) Two-piece cinch rivets repair belts, luggage, and other items where holding strength need not be very great. Hole is punched just large enough to receive thicker half of rivet.

(Right) Hollow core rivets are applied with a center punch, do a creditable job of fastening. Rivet should extend only 1½ diameters beyond work surface.

or brass. Cinching is done with the rivet head backed up against a metal plate while the open end is peened with a rounded hammer. When a number of rivets are to be placed in a material, uniform spacing of the drilled holes is important for good appearance. Split shank rivets lack strength, but are more easily installed. They are used largely for repairs of luggage, belts, and household articles, the split ends merely bent over to stay in place.

2. USEFUL "HOW-TO" TECHNIQUES

The ability to handle various tools is a major step toward a homeowner's independence and self-sufficiency. Knowledge of certain manual techniques is another. Much of the work is done by following specific procedures. Those procedures that are directly related to particular areas of work will be found in their related chapters, and the index will help you locate the one you need. There are, in addition, various manual techniques that have much broader application, and a selection of those which might be most helpful to the homeowner is presented here.

Techniques differ from skills in that they do not require years of apprenticeship or study, as is the case with stonecutting, plastering, or brick-laying, for examples. Rather, they are applied by following specific instructions, step by step. These procedures have been thoroughly tested for practical results, but the newcomer to manual tasks might well try them out first on scrap material, to gain some familiarity with the procedure.

Such a preliminary trial should certainly be made when first using plastic laminate sheeting, now so widely adapted to surfacing and finishing of counters and furniture. The material is fairly expensive and an entire panel can be spoiled just by chipping an edge slightly while drawing a file in the wrong direction, or failing to provide sufficient support when sawing, and thus allowing the thin sheeting to rip apart.

LUBRICATION

Elbow grease is one way to keep things moving around the house. A drop of oil or touch of tallow in the right place, however, is effective in keeping equipment in good operating condition and helps prevent annoying, costly breakdowns. Lubrication once was a frequent routine in the home and shop, but with the development of sealed bearing motors in appliances, and nylon anti-friction surfaces, oiling has become neglected, although still very necessary on some equipment. Refrigerator and washing machine motors keep going for many years without lubrication. Other equipment, however, and many items of the house structure itself need regular attention. If forgotten, shrill grinding noises or balky operation will bring them to attention, but then it's often too late—the bearings are burned out or other damage is done. A suggestion: study the service manual when you buy tools and appliances, keep a chart listing the lubrication specifications: locations of bearings, frequently of application, and the type of grease or oil. Keep in mind, also, that excessive lubrication, or use of a type other than the one recommended by the manufacturer, can jam the mechanism, cause deterioration of rubber or other components, or become solidified with grit. Seasonal factors may be also involved, as weather often determines the type and viscosity of lubricant.

Lube Equipment. Keep on hand a small trigger-type oil pumper of 6-ounce capacity; an aerosol silicone can (but guard against inhaling the spray); a grease stick and tube of powdered or liquid graphite. Certain tools and appliances, such as the saber saw, require specially formulated greases obtained from the tool manufacturer.

Garage doors have complex hardware that is subject to extreme stress. Oil the hinges at overhead door sections and the rollers that ride in the channel tracks.

Several grades of oil and grease, and various types of oil cans, should be kept on hand. A pumper can with a long spout, as shown, reaches the oil cups of motors without spilling.

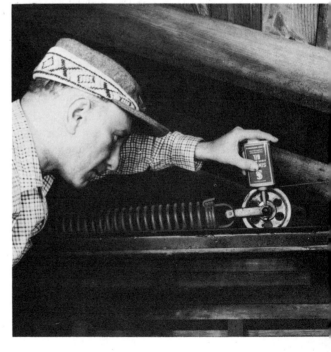

Overhead Garage Doors. These heavy doors have ball-bearing rollers on each section that ride in a channel track. A dry roller may jam the door and pull the sections apart. The hinges and locking mechanism (but not the lock cylinder, which receives only graphite) need regular oiling. Frequency of lubrication depends on how much the door is used—generally, once every few months will be sufficient. Use a light machine oil. If the bearings seem to have accumulated considerable grit, flush first with varnoline or other minerol solvent, wipe the surface clean, then allow the solvent to dry before applying new oil.

Window Rotors. Casement windows will open more smoothly if the rotor gears and swing arm guide are cleaned and lubricated seasonally. Remove the mechanism by loosening the rotor case screws, push out the sash until the swing arm can slip out of a slot in the side of its guide track under the sash. Clean off old grease and grit with a cloth dampened with varnoline. Put a bit of light grease (Vaseline is satisfactory) on the rotor gears and inside the sash track. After reassembling the window opener, place a drop of oil on the hinge pivots.

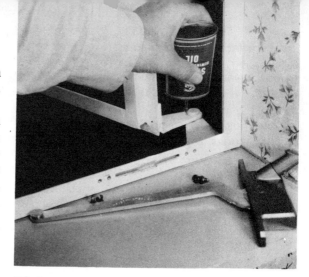

Oil the casement pivot hinges and lock handle, also the opener guide that rides in a metal channel at the bottom of the sash.

Window rotors become difficult to turn when the gears are clogged with grime. The entire mechanism is removed with a screwdriver for cleaning and greasing.

Motorized Equipment: All electric motors, except those having sealed bearings, should be lubricated occasionally with just 2 or 3 drops of light oil, placed into the oil cups at each end of the motor shaft. Do not overlubricate, as the oil will flow

Some electric motors have oil cups to lubricate the bearings. Apply just 1 or 2 drops, infrequently. Too much oil will damage the commutator.

onto the motor commutator and gum up the brushes. Frequency of oiling depends on amount of use. For example, an attic fan motor needs to be oiled just at the start of the warm weather season; motors used continuously can be oiled every 2 or 3 months. The universal motors of most portable tools and appliances, such as the drill and vacuum cleaner, need no oiling although other working parts may require periodic lubrication.

LUBRICATION CHART

Item	Part	Lubricant
Attic fan	bearings	no. 30 oil in fan bearings, 1 or 2 drops of no. 30 oil in motor shaft cups
Auto wheel jack	rachet	silicone lubricant
Baby carriage	wheel axles suspension springs	light grease drop of oil
Band saw	blade guide	solid grease stick
Bench saw	tilting arbor (never oil radial saw arm carriage)	light grease on gear
Bicycle	wheel bearings, sprocket chain, fork bearings	all light grease
Car door lock	cylinder, latch	graphite
Casters (furniture and tool)	stem, wheel bearings	no. 3 oil
Chain saw	chain sprockets	oil and gasoline mixture (or as recommended by manufacturer)
Door hinges	hinge pins	tallow grease or silicone
Door spring latch	latch	graphite
Drill press	quill	no. 3 oil or silicone spray

Drill press quill is cleaned and lubricated with single spray of silicone from aerosol can.

Item	Part	Lubricant
Electric portable tools	mechanical parts	as recommended by manu-facturer
File drawers	slides, bearings	light grease or silicone
Furnace	air cleaner fan	no. 30 oil
	blower fan bearings	no. 30 oil
	oil burner motor	on service
Garage doors (sectional overhead)	hinges, rollers, track	oil
Garden shears	pivot screw	oil

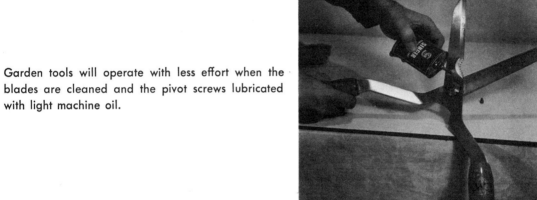

Garden tools will operate with less effort when the blades are cleaned and the pivot screws lubricated with light machine oil.

Hair clippers	cutters, pivot screw	sewing machine oil, no. 3 oil
Lawnmowers (hand)	blade gears	light grease
Lawn tractor	as specified by manufacturer	grease in pressure fittings
Locks	cylinders	graphite
	latches, bolts	graphite
Paper cutter	knife edge	wax
	pivot screw	oil
Patio door	track, rollers	tallow wax or silicone
Roller skates	wheel bearings	oil
Sewing machine	Singer oil	refer to instruction booklet
Sump pump	impeller shaft	oil
Swivel chair	tilt springs, rotation plate, casters	no. 3 oil
Tinsnips; pliers; scissors	pivot screw	oil
Toilet tanks	trip lever	oil
Typewriter		refer to instruction booklet (avoid oil on paper roller)

Item	Part	Lubricant
Windows (casements)	rotor opener and guide strip	light grease
Windows (double-hung)	guide track	light grease
Zippers (metal)	closure tab	special wax (stainproof) or petroleum jelly

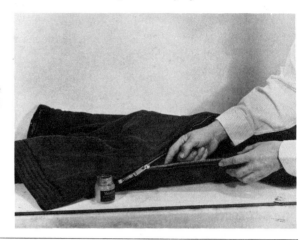

Zippers snagged? A touch of light grease will make the slide move more easily. Apply grease to the metal tabs only. Nylon zippers need no lubrication.

DRILLING

Electric Drills. The electric drill, an essential and highly versatile tool around the home, is quite safe and easy for almost anyone to use. The drill should either be the double-insulated type with a plastic housing, or have a 3-prong plug to be used in a grounded receptacle. Be sure that for the latter type, extension cords include a third grounding wire and have matching connectors to maintain grounding continuity.

A portable drill with $\frac{1}{4}$-inch chuck and 2-ampere power rating is satisfactory for average home chores. A $\frac{3}{8}$-inch drill with $2\frac{1}{2}$-ampere rating, variable speed, and reversible motor features is more versatile and sturdier, less likely to burn out, so is more economical in the long run. A separate bench stand with pressure applicator lever, into which the drill is clamped, permits more accurate work and is desirable for the home shop that lacks a drill press.

Drill Accessories. Various special-purpose tools used with the drill include small wire brushes for cleaning metals and rust spots, small grinding wheels, power screwdriver, percussion drill for masonry fasteners, sanders, and polishing buffers. The drill is not really suitable, however, for certain "combination" tools such as a saw or router.

Types of Bits. A standard assortment of high-speed twist drills, starting with $\frac{1}{16}$ inch, and including all sizes graduated by $\frac{1}{32}$ inch to $\frac{1}{4}$ inch or $\frac{3}{8}$ inch, will be adequate for the average home. Drill sizes are designated by three systems: numbers, letters, and fractions. Except for advanced shop work, the homeowner would do well to stick with fractional sizes, keeping the assortment always complete by replacing worn or broken drills.

Carbide-tipped drills are used for masonry, plaster, marble, and ceramic tile. Standardizing on no. 8 and no. 10 Rawlplug fiber fasteners will require just two carbide bits—the $\frac{3}{16}$- and $\frac{1}{4}$-inch sizes. More details are provided in the discussion of masonry anchors.

Drilling Larger Holes. Although the drill may be rated for up to $\frac{1}{4}$- or $\frac{3}{8}$-inch sizes, larger holes can be drilled in wood with special bits. The wing borer, sometimes called a spade drill, fits the ¼-inch chuck and comes in sizes from ⁵⁄₁₆ inch to 1¼ inches. The same sizes are available in twist

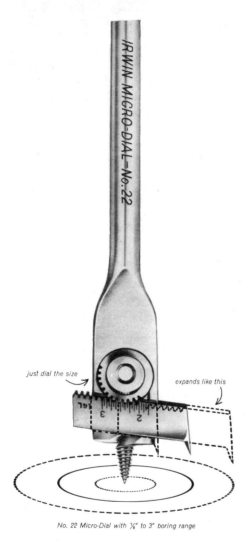

just dial the size

expands like this

No. 22 Micro-Dial with ⅞" to 3" boring range

Expansive bit with Irwin micro-dial permits precise adjustment to hole sizes up to 3-inch diameter.

type bits, resembling augers, and hole saws, with mandrels to fit the ¼-inch chuck. In addition, there are expansive bits that adjust to any diameter, such as the Irwin bits, with ranges from ⅝ inch to 1¾ inches or ⅞ inch to 3 inches.

Pilot Holes for Screws. Driving a screw into wood without first boring a pilot hole may split the wood, and unless the stock is very soft, the screwhead won't go in flush with the surface. Formerly two steps were required for pilot holes —boring to the needed depth, then countersinking with a separate bit. Now the process is speeded with the pilot hole bit that fits a ¼-inch chuck, drills and countersinks simultaneously to the correct depth, the taper mated to the screw diameter. There are a dozen sizes, and the correct size should be used for the screw. Five popular sizes are included in the Stanley Screw-Mate kit, as follows:

No. 8 screws, ¾ inch, 1 inch, and 1¼ inch lengths
No. 10 screws, 1¼ inch length
No. 12 screws, 1½ inch length

Holes for starting smaller screws may be made with an awl, or better still, with the new Irwin screw starter that is illustrated.

Tips on Drilling. Attach the chuck key with a special elastic band directly on the electric cord

Auger tip of Irwin screw starter threads the hole so screw turns in faster and straighter. Use for small screws in cabinet work.

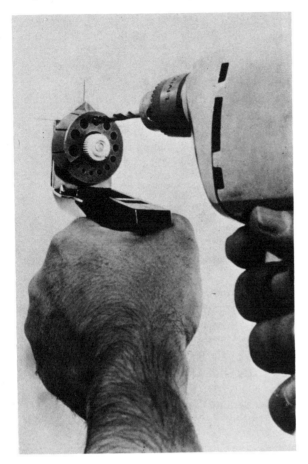

Drill guide by Stanley assists more accurate boring with electric drill. Dial is rotated to size of drill selected, up to ¼-inch diameter. No need to center punch—a non-slip rubber base keeps the drill in position on any flat surface. A storage compartment holds assortment of drills.

so it is always available. Put the drill shank as far as it can go into the chuck, tighten firmly, remove the chuck key immediately. Set the drill point on the mark, sight it at a right angle to the work, hold steady while drilling to avoid wobbling that distorts the hole out of round. If you're going all the way through the work, back up the hole with a clamped wood block to avoid splintering the other side. On metals, start the hole with a center punch, apply cutting oil or other lubricant for heavy drilling. When drilling small pieces of metal, use a hold-down clamp to prevent spinning of the work as the drill pierces through.

Straight and accurate drilling with a portable drill has been simplified with the development by Stanley Works of a drill guide accessory. A dial is rotated to the size drill selected; a non-slip rubber base keeps the drill in position, permits starting on a marked dot without centerpunching, and holds the drill at right angle to the work. A compartment in the guide holds an assortment of drill bits. Price is about 3 dollars.

Guard Against Drill Backlash. When using the electric drill in close quarters, keep your face well away from the drill housing to avoid injury if the bit jams. What happens is that the entire drill swings around forcefully and can deliver a tremendous wallop. Jaw and nose bone fractures have been caused by such drill backlash.

Drilling of plaster, concrete, and ceramic tiles is discussed in the section on masonry anchors, pages 43-46.

GLUING

There are many types of glues, each with special characteristics that meet certain requirements, so the first step in bonding any materials is to select the right glue for the job. The various categories, and their applications, are described below.

White Resin Glue. This polyvinyl acetate emulsion, the most commonly used glue for furniture assembly and other wood joinery, is suitable for almost everything from wood joints to mending or joining leather, fabrics, paper, and other semiporous materials where a waterproof bond is not necessary. It sets under clamped pressure in about one hour or less. Though the glue is white, it dries clear, without staining (but squeezed-out glue should be wiped off with a damp cloth before it hardens on the surface and interferes with finishing).

Brands include Elmer's Glue-All, Weldwood White Glue, Sears White Glue, and Glue-Bird by Wilhold.

Epoxy Cement. Formerly when the handle broke off a cup, no dependable repair was possible that would keep the cup in normal service—which meant a decline in your set of dishes. With epoxy glues, you now can permanently bond chinaware, metals, glass, porcelain, and most plastics; also concrete, brick, and small wood joints. The nearly transparent bond, when properly cured, is not affected by boiling water or the dishwasher, freezing, most acids or solvents, and when properly applied will withstand stresses up to a ton per square inch—making the glued joint stronger than the materials that are bonded.

There are two types: the basic epoxy cement that "sticks to anything" and the metal compound containing powdered aluminum which is used

Epoxy and resorcinol glues come in two parts: the resin, and a catalyst or hardener, mixed in equal amounts. Do not mix until ready to use.

Use a matchstick or wooden tongue depressor to blend the two components. Gluing must be done at room temperature, 70 degress or more.

Apply to either of the parts to be joined, press the parts together and hold for several minutes. Allow to cure at least 12 hours before using.

both for bonding irregular surfaces, particularly metal-to-metal sections, and for patching purposes, such as filling dents in automobile fenders. The metal compound is so dense that it can be drilled and tapped like the original metal.

The cement comes in two tubes or cans, one containing the resin, the other a hardener chemical. Mix just enough for the repair, placing equal amounts from both tubes on a disposable surface, blend thoroughly with a wood spatula, apply immediately to the joint, and press the parts together. Wipe off the squeezed-out excess.

Clamping pressure is not necessary, but the parts should be held together, properly fitted, with a rubber band, weight, or cord. Setting time, normally about 2 hours, can be speeded by applying heat from a photoflood or infrared lamp, or in an oven heated to 150 degrees. If the glue gets on the hands, remove at once with denatured alcohol or nail polish remover.

Brands of epoxy glues include Weldwood, Franklin Epoxy, *ZAP,* Woodhill E-Pox-E, Masonite's Holdol, Wilhold's Epoxy, and Loctite Fast-Cure Epoxy, the latter packaged in separate small plastic cups, each containing sufficient glue for individual repairs after mixing with the hardener.

Synthetic Resin. A urea-formaldehyde glue, usually in powdered form for mixing with water, also available as a liquid, provides a very strong bond for tightly fitted cabinet joints, for furniture repairs, and veneering. This requires clamping for at least 18 hours. The glue joint is highly water-resistant. A similar resin cement is used for exterior plywood and boat joinery. Temperature at time of application is a critical factor—both the room and the parts to be joined should be at normal room temperature of about 70 degrees Fahrenheit.

Glues in this category include Weldwood Plastic Resin Glue and Everite Resin by Franklin.

Contact Cement. A synthetic rubber cement, for fast bonding of almost everything, including non-porous materials, requires no clamping. It is the adhesive for laminating plastic sheeting (Formica, Micarta, Piolite) to a plywood base for countertops, and for applying wall panels such as Marlite to an existing wall surface or to studs. It is also suitable, in a special form, for installing ceramic tiles, bonding glass to metal (as with automobile rear mirrors) and repairs of luggage, rainwear, boots, handbags, and wallets.

The cement comes in both a water-emulsion type that is not flammable, and one with a highly volatile solvent (acetone) that must be used with adequate precautions against fire. An extra-strong neoprene cement applied with a caulking gun, for attaching exterior wall paneling without nails or screws, is resistant to moisture, temperature, and weathering.

When using contact cement, both surfaces to be joined are fully coated with the cement, which is allowed to dry. When the parts are brought together, they bond immediately on contact. Because it is not possible to shift the parts into alignment, special "slip sheet" techniques have been developed for this application, described later in this chapter in the section on plastic laminating. The process for wall panels is somewhat different.

Contact cements, both flammable and water-base types, are made by a number of companies, including the Weldwood brand, Duratite by DAP, Duro-Plastic by Woodhill, Fire-Safe by Wilhold,

Holdol by Masonite, Elmer's Contact Cement, and Tru-bond by Franklin.

Plastic Menders. No single adhesive or compound will satisfactorily bond all types of plastic. The epoxy glues can be used successfully on many plastics, but others require a special "welding" compound. Vinyl adhesives for patching seat covers, pool liners, shower curtains, and similar items are transparent, require no clamping, and set quickly after the parts are held together for a moment or so.

Plastic cements include several types of Weld-wood, Duro-Ply by Woodhill, Plastic Patch by Magic American, No. 7 by Du Pont, V-Bond by Wilhold, and Super Bonder 94 by Loctite. The containers specify which plastics can be bonded or repaired by each type of adhesive.

Silicone Rubber Adhesives. Certain silicone sealers rival epoxy adhesives in ability to securely

Patching of tents, luggage, or fabrics is easy with silicone rubber adhesive. Apply bead all around patch, place patch in position; press down. The patch is fully cured in 24 hours, will withstand moisture, weathering, wide extremes of temperature.

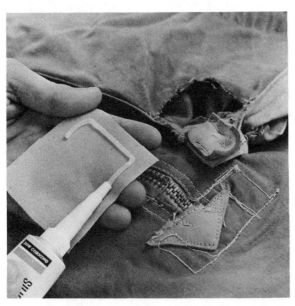

bond glass, ceramics, wood, metals, fabrics—the list includes most of the porous and non-porous materials. Use silicones for installing wall panels, mending fabrics, attaching brackets to tile or cement walls. A touch of the rubberlike sealant on doors and ceramic surfaces such as the flush tank cover, when allowed to harden, serves as a bumper to eliminate rattles and prevent breakage. Use the putty-like silicone also to insulate electrical connections and to renew the insulation on electric cords, to waterproof automobile sparkplug wires and repair torn audio speakers.

The silicone rubber adhesive is applied directly from a flexible tube, requires no pressure except on tightly fitted joints, is rated not to fail under extremes of temperature ranging from minus 65 to 500 degrees Fahrenheit, and can withstand repeated washings and dry cleanings.

The adhesives include General Electric Silicone Seal and Dow Corning's Silicone Adhesive.

Instant Gluing. A remarkable tool that bonds practically every kind of material, and does it in just 60 seconds without clamping, is the electric glue gun. A short solid slug of a polyethylene adhesive is warmed in 3 minutes by the electric current sufficiently for the plastic to flow out of the nozzle onto one of the parts to be joined. The parts are immediately pressed and held together for just a moment, and the bond is completed at near maximum strength.

The gluing gun weighs just half a pound, is 7 inches overall in length, and is operated by pulling a trigger switch. It can be plugged into any electric line, as it uses just 70 watts of current, about as much as an average light bulb. The joint is said to be unaffected by temperatures up to 150 degrees. The glue, in the shape of 1 inch slugs, can be stored for an indefinite time before use. Uses of the electric glue gun around the home may include repair of wicker furniture, attaching torn straps on golf bags and other sporting goods, tacking down loosened linoleum, bonding wood parts of iregular shape that are difficult to clamp, and repairing pottery.

Slugs of caulking compound also are available for use in the electric gun, which is sold by all hardware stores and Sears, Roebuck.

pressor, to both surfaces that are to be joined. Wait a minute or so until the glue becomes tacky, then press the parts together. Place wood blocks under the clamp heads, and tighten until the glue squeezes out, but avoid excessive pressure that may cause distortion. On large items, such as a bookcase or similar cabinet, apply two or more long pipe or bar clamps at opposite sides, the pressure evenly distributed by spanning boards to avoid twisting. When gluing boards edge to edge, apply clamps across both the top and bottom to prevent "bowing" of the boards in one direction. After the clamps are tightened moderately, check the assembly carefully to see that the parts are properly aligned before final tightening, then wipe off excess glue with a damp rag.

Do not shift the clamps until after the time

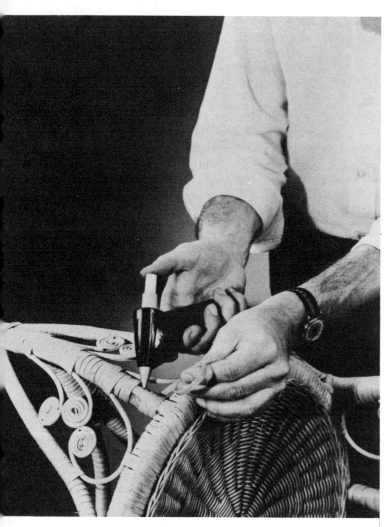

Broken wrappings of rattan outdoor furniture should be mended before they unwind. A small amount of hot-melt polyethylene-based glue applied at the break with an electric glue gun will result in an almost immediate, strong, waterproof bond.

Gluing and Clamping. Before applying the glue, make sure that the parts fit correctly, that the joining surfaces are thoroughly clean, and that they are at room temperature, about 70 degrees. Old glue must be removed, using sandpaper or scraper. When using fast-setting glue, have the clamping blocks handy. Apply the glue with a small brush or flat stick, such as a tongue de-

Bar or pipe clamps of various types make shopwork more professional and productive. Chair repair requires clamping pressure on glued joints.

required for the glue that is being used—some need only an hour or two, others, such as resin and hide glues, about 18 hours.

There are some useful tricks of the trade that will be helpful in household gluing problems. Loose chair rungs may present a problem when the leg stretchers cannot be pulled apart to reach the tenon. In that case, drill a tiny hole at an inconspicuous side of the joint and squirt in glue with an oil can or hypodermic syringe. When wood parts to be joined include an end grain, apply a preliminary coating of the glue and allow it to become very tacky before brushing on another coat—the first coat will prevent a starved joint resulting from absorption of the glue by the end grain. When joining irregular parts that cannot be handled by your clamps, such as a chair with splayed legs, use a heavy rope to bind the legs, then with a screwdriver between the rope strands, twist like a tourniquet to apply pressure. Let the screwdriver catch on the chair rail and thus maintain the rope tension.

LAMINATING PLASTIC SHEETING

Has your sturdy kitchen table become drab after long use? Make it even better than new, almost instantly, with a new plastic top in the most attractive pattern and colors. Tired of your desk or dining room buffet? In a couple of hours, you can make it more attractive than ever with a new surface of the rarest wood grain, or one that is almost indistinguishable from the finest marble.

Plastic laminate sheeting (brand names Formica, Micarta, Consoweld, Piolite, Textolite) is truly the miracle home material. The extremely hard surface of melamine plastic stands up under considerable abuse, resists scratches and dents, won't stain or fade, and cleans like new with a swipe of a damp cloth. Just cement it down, and it's there to stay for years and even decades. Widely used for kitchen countertops, furniture surfacing, wall paneling, cabinet doors, and bathroom cabinets, the plastic eliminates a main stumbling block of home workshop projects—it needs no further finishing. The pattern and color you choose in the panel is what you get in the finished cabinet.

Marlite, by Masonite, is a similar plastic on a thicker and less flexible hardboard backing. It is used most widely for wall paneling, but can be applied also as a laminate for furniture surfacing and countertops. It comes in many attractive wood grains and marble styles; also in various solid colors and patterns that produce the most delightful and almost indestructible finishes.

The sheeting is laminated to any rigid backing with quick-setting contact (rubber) cement. No clamps are needed. The plastic panels come in sizes from 2 by 5 to 5 by 12 feet, priced by the square foot.

Countertops with integral rounded fronts and backsplash are made by the heat-forming method; this is usually done on large industrial presses, but can be done also with heater wires. You can obtain such ready-made countertops for the kitchen, doing the installation yourself at a considerable savings, or construct your own counter with "self-edge" of the same material as the top, or with metal edge moldings.

Tools Needed. The panels can be cut with a fine-tooth hand saw, a saber saw, portable circular saw, or a bench power saw. A special laminate cutter by Stanley, similar to a wallboard knife, also does the job quickly and neatly. Cutting is not to precise size; instead, a small overlap is allowed for final trimming after the laminating with a block plane and fine file, or still better, a router using a special carbide bit. A small serrated trowel for spreading the cement is supplied. You will need also a sheet of heavy kraft wrapping paper, as large as the panel that is to be laminated, as a "slip sheet."

Preparation. The plastic can be applied over an old wood surface, like a desk top, if it is clean, smooth, and sound. It's best to remove any old paint or varnish; old enamel should be sanded to cut the glaze. New countertops, lavatory cabinet, and similar surfaces must be of ¾-inch plywood or particle board, the underside coated with ⅛-inch hardboard, also applied with contact cement, to balance the "pull" of the top plastic

The plastic sheeting and the panel or furniture to which it will be bonded must be conditioned to the temperature of the room for at least 24 hours. Use contact cement, preferably the non-flammable type, as described in the previous section on gluing, spreading the cement with a serrated metal trowel, or just any piece of hardboard.

Cutting the Plastic. Measure and mark the panel, allowing about ⅛ inch excess for file trimming, ¼ inch for router trimming. *Caution:* Always cut with the saw teeth feeding down into the plastic surface, to avoid chipping, which could ruin the

Contact cement is used, spread with a specially notched trowel that controls amount of cement applied. Apply to both the panel and the counter, seeing that every spot is covered with cement.

Plastic laminate sheeting is cut with hand or power saw, or with special laminate cutter. It is essential that blade teeth cut into the surface of the work, rather than through its backing, to avoid chipping the brittle plastic.

Allow cement to dry. Cover the counter top with "slip sheet" of heavy kraft paper; place the panel and align with edges.

entire panel. Thus, the panel is face up on a bench or radial saw in which the blade teeth turn downward from above the table. But with saber saws and portable circular saws, in which the blade cuts from below, the panel is placed face down and the guide lines are marked on the back. With a hand saw, the panel is placed face up but the cutting is done only on the down stroke of the saw. Make sure the panel is adequately sup-

Lift one end, fold back part of the slip sheet, then lower the panel, which will bond on contact. The rest of the sheet then can be pulled out and the full panel pressed down.

Roll the panel, or tap with wood block over entire surface, to obtain good adhesion.

Trim excess on front edge with file or plane, cutting on the downstroke. A laminate trimmer in a router does quicker, neater job.

ported; otherwise it may start to rip because of the weight of the partially cut section. If the countertop or cabinet is to have a self-edge of the same plastic, the edging is applied first and trimmed flush before the top panel goes on. Precut strips usually are available to match the panel colors and patterns.

Application. Assuming only the top surface of a counter is to be laminated, proceed as follows: Spread the adhesive with the serrated trowel over the back of the plastic panel; set the panel aside, apply cement over the surface to be covered. Make sure every inch is covered; touch up any skipped spots with more cement. Allow the cement to dry, which will take 20 minutes, more or less, depending on the room temperature and humidity. Test with a piece of kraft paper; if the cement is dry, the paper comes away without sticking.

Now spread the large kraft paper over the entire surface, set the plastic panel on top and align the edges in final position (the excess plastic overlapping the front edges). Lift one end of the panel while holding the rest in position, fold back

about a quarter of the paper underneath, then press down the panel which will bond immediately in correct position. The other end of the panel now is lifted enough to withdraw the paper, so the full panel becomes bonded. Use a roller, or wood block with hammer, pressing down on every inch of the plastic surface for good adhesion.

Self-edge applications are done similarly, the excess overlapping at the top where it is trimmed flush. The slip sheet, if the edge is long, can be held in place with masking tape for about two-thirds of the length, leaving only a short section to be aligned with the fingers.

Trimming. A block plane, cutting only on the *downward* strokes at a bias angle, removes excess material close to the final edge, then a fine file is used for final smoothing. Be careful to avoid chipping. Both top and edge form a uniform bevel that shows as a narrow black line at the joint. A router with a carbide trimmer bit (by Rockwell, Skil, Stanley, or Black & Decker) does

Student desk resurfaced with plastic laminate is neat and colorful, easily maintained.

the job more neatly and quickly. The router is guided along the plywood backing by a broad plate, or shoe.

An excellent way to protect a plastic counter from knife cuts and scratches is to keep a square of ⅛-inch clear Lucite handy to use as a cutting board.

SWEAT SOLDERING

Sweat soldering to join copper tubing and fittings is a useful and interesting process that is easily mastered. The only tools required are a tubing cutter, which includes a reamer, and a propane gas torch. Materials needed are sandpaper and emery cloth, wire solder, and paste flux. The entire process is further simplified by using a combination solder and flux in paste form, such as the Swif solder paste made by Hercules Chemical Co., or no. 50-50 solder by Mueller Brass Co.

For good solder joints, the tubing must be cut square, burrs removed with a reamer, the joining surfaces sanded to a bright metal cleanliness. Clean both the tubing (to a distance of about 1 inch from the end) and the inside of the fitting with fine sandpaper or emery cloth until the metal shines brightly, all oxidation removed. Blow out any sand or grit.

Preparing the Joint. Coat the tubing end with the flux paste using a soft brush. (Do not brush paste into the fitting itself, as it will thus get into the water line!) Push the tubing all the way into the fitting so it seats against the inside flange. Rotate the tubing a bit so the flux is evenly distributed.

With the propane torch, heat the joint, playing the flame on the shoulder of the fitting. When the metal is hot, *remove the flame* and apply the wire solder to the rim where the tube joins the fitting. If the metal is sufficiently heated, the solder will melt and run into the joint.

Good solder joints can be made regardless of the position of the tube or fitting, even upside down as it would be if the fitting is vertical and the joint at the bottom; the solder is drawn up all around into the joint by capillary attraction, over-

MAIN OPERATIONS IN SWEAT SOLDERING OF COPPER TUBING FOR WATER LINE

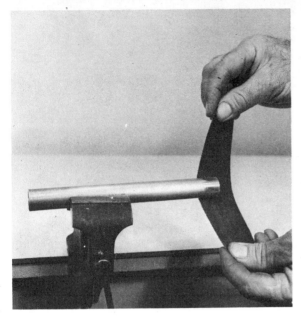

Copper tubing is polished with emery cloth in preparation for sweat soldering into a fitting. The copper must be cleaned right down to bright metal. Clean the inside of the fitting in the same way.

Brush flux on end of tubing, immediately insert into fitting and rotate several times so flux is evenly distributed. Push tube all the way into the fitting.

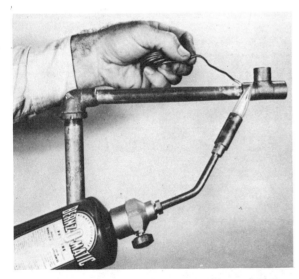

Play torch flame on shoulder of fitting until it becomes hot enough to melt the solder, then remove the flame and touch solder to the collar of the fitting. The melted solder is drawn into the fitting by capillary action.

coming gravity and forming a strong, leakproof seal.

Getting a Neat Finish. Do not apply the flame directly to the solder. If the solder does not melt rapidly when it touches, reheat the fitting until it is of proper temperature and try again. As soon as the solder has run, and while the joint is still hot, wipe off excess solder and flux on the outside with a cloth, for a neat appearance and to prevent corrosive action by the flux.

Do not heat after the solder has run, as this will weaken the joint. If the solder shows neatly all around the edge of the joint, you can be sure there is a good seal. If at any time it is necessary to disassemble the tubing lines, just heat each joint with the torch and the fittings will separate.

To use the paste form of solder-flux, just brush it onto the tube end. No separate solder is needed, but the parts must be exceptionally well cleaned. Heat the joint with the torch until the resin begins to bubble around the outside of the joint. Immediately remove the flame and wipe off the dark residue with a cloth.

When the tubing to be soldered is inside a wall or near wood framing members, place an asbestos tile between the flame and the flammable material. Keep a pail of water or fire extinguisher handy, and check carefully to see that you do not leave any smoldering embers.

DRESSING PLYWOOD EDGES

When plywood is used for built-ins or other projects, the edge grain must be dressed for good appearance and to prevent snagging of the surface veneer by clothing.

Thin wood tapes, ¾ inch wide, are available with a coating of contact adhesive for easy application. Care must be taken to align the tape properly as it is put on, as it sticks on contact and cannot be shifted—slide the fingers of one hand along the top and bottom of the plywood and tape to guide the tape uniformly along the edge of the plywood. After application, tap down along the entire length to assure good adhesion.

Wood strips may be sliced on a bench power saw from solid stock that matches the surface veneer, then applied with regular wood glue under clamp pressure. Place a straightedge board, at least 1 inch thick, all along the plywood edge, use sufficient C clamps so the pressure will be uniformly distributed. Wipe off squeezed-out glue quickly with a damp cloth.

A practical edging for kitchen counters and similar projects is the hard plastic sheeting that is used for laminations. This self-edge application is described elsewhere in this chapter. Also used for edge trim are specially shaped stainless steel and aluminum moldings, decorative tapes in various metallic colors and textured patterns, and plastic T-shaped strips that lock into a center groove cut along the plywood edge. The latter are made by Pioneer Plastic.

LOCATING WALL STUDS

When installing bookshelves, large mirrors, and

Thin wood strips used for bonding plywood edges are flexible enough to conform to curves. Contact bond cement is brushed on the veneer and on plywood edge, allowed to dry for half an hour.

Regular wood veneer to match plywood surface is available in rolls. Tape is slightly wider to allow for sanding after strip has been cemented in place.

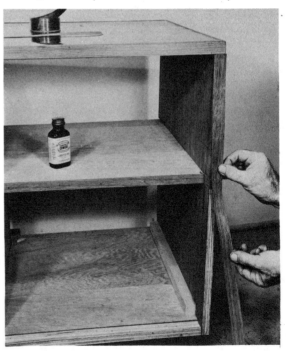

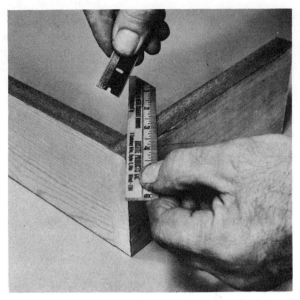

At corners where tapes meet, they are overlapped and mitered, then cemented down. Use sharp blade to cut through both veneers for a perfect fit.

New on the market: metallic-colored tape embossed in decorative designs. Paper-covered back has pressure-sensitive adhesive, is self-adhering.

other heavy objects on a plaster or gypsum wall, it is safer to anchor the hangers or brackets with screws directly into the wood wall studs, if they are in the desired location, rather than relying on fasteners that grip just the thickness of the plaster or wallboard.

Locating the Studs. Many stud finder devices are available, but none so far is entirely effective. The magnet type is probably the most reliable, working like a compass to show where nails have been driven through the lath or wallboard into the studs. If the finder reveals a vertical line of nails, it is safe to assume that a stud is at that position.

A more certain method uses a thin awl or ice-pick. Drive the point into the wall just above the baseboard, placing a hole every inch. When a stud is struck, the adjacent studs will be approximately 16 inches apart on center from the one that has been located. Drop a plumb bob to align the shelf bracket with the bottom stud position. A bit of soft plaster applied with a fingertip will effectively refill all the awl holes.

WALL ANCHORS

With close attention to details, you can quickly install fasteners on plaster and ceramic tile walls, for curtain and drapery rods, shelves and other articles. There are many types of wall anchors: plastic, fiber, metal. It is advisable, however, to stick to just one type and size of wall anchor, at least at first.

The fiber Rawlplug with lead core is recommended for plaster walls on a solid lath base, and for double-thickness gypsum board walls. The plug, hole, and screw must all be the same size number. A no. 10 Rawlplug requires a no. 10 ($\frac{3}{16}$ inch) drill and $\frac{3}{16}$ inch metal screw, the type that is threaded its full length. The screw should be just long enough, taking into account the thickness of the fixture bracket, so that the part that enters the plug will be somewhat shorter than the plug itself, and thus will not exit at the rear of the plug.

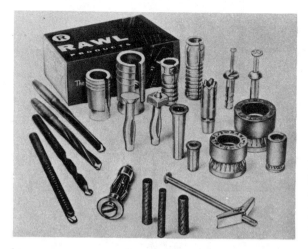

There's a type of wall fastener to meet any requirement. Shown are fiber Rawlplugs, toggle bolt and hollow core Mollys (at bottom), expansion bolts and slotted drive-ins (center), 2-piece and flush anchors at top. Several drills are at left.

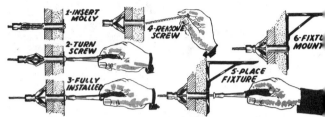

How a Molly is installed in hollow wall. Tightening of bolt causes ribbed sides to spread, forming legs that fold flat against the inside wall surface. After fastener is drawn up tight, the bolt is removed and put through the bracket hole.

Holding Power of Rawlplugs
(Columbia University Test)

Size of Rawlplug	Size Hole	Size of Screw	Kind of Screw	Length of Screw Engaged	POUNDS PULL	
					1:2:4 Concrete	Brick Masonry
No. 12	1/4"	No. 12	Wood	1½"	1525	660
No. 14	9/32"	No. 14	Wood	1½"	1590	900
No. 16	5/16"	No. 16	Wood	1½"	2150	1400
No. 20	3/8"	No. 20	Wood	2	2830	1750
No. 3/8	7/16"	3/8"	Lag	2½"	3700	2980
No. 7/16	1/2"	7/16"	Lag	2"	6670	3200
No. 1/2	5/8"	1/2"	Lag	3"	8900	3900
No. 5/8	3/4"	5/8"	Lag	3"	12700	6150

Use a carbide-tipped bit for drilling. This costs no more than an ordinary carbon drill, which would be instantly dulled if used in plaster. It is important that the hole be perfectly round and true. (The Stanley drill guide, described in the section on drilling in this chapter, will be very helpful.) Wobbling of the drill enlarges the hole or makes it go out of round, prevents proper grip of the plug.

Drill just a bit deeper than necessary to fit the plug flush with the surface. (Use an awl point to check the depth if necessary.) When ready, insert the plug carefully so as not to break off any plaster. If it does not go in smoothly, bevel the end slightly with a razor blade or dowel sharpener. Before inserting the plug, spread the core center at the outside end just a little with an awl so that the screw point starts easily. When the plug is fitted snugly in position, turn the screw part way to start the thread and tighten the plug in place, then remove the screw.

Leveling Shelf Brackets. Place the shelf bracket in position and turn the first screw through the bracket. Mark the position on the wall of the second hole in the bracket. If the bracket hole is large enough, drill right through it, insert the second plug and tighten both screws. If not, remove the first screw, drill and install the second plug in the manner as before. Now the bracket can be permanently attached with both screws. The lead core of the Rawlplug, once it is firmly seated by expansion into the hole, becomes threaded and permits removal and reinsertion of the screws. These plugs can be removed any time they are no longer needed by gripping with needle-nose pliers and yanking them out. The hole is patched easily with plaster.

For shelves, there must be two or more support brackets. After the first bracket is installed, rest one end of a shelf on it, and place a spirit level on the other end. Raise or lower the shelf until the spirit bubble shows it is exactly level, then place the second bracket underneath and mark the hole positions with an awl. Drilling must be quite precise to keep the shelf level. Now you can complete the installation by attaching the second and additional brackets, if any.

Here are some related details. The screw must be driven in really tight; any play in the bracket mounting will result in further loosening of the screw and finally of the wall plug. If the screw does not pull up tightly when first installed, it is because there is inadequate compression of the plug, or the screw size is too small. Use either the next larger size screw, or pack the plug with one or more wood matchsticks. If this method fails, it is possible the hole is out of round and may have to be abandoned. In that case, the hole can be patched with plaster, a new one drilled close by. When you have developed the necessary skill, there will be very few times when such mishaps occur.

Single-panel gypsum or composition walls will not hold compression anchors very well. The most effective alternatives are Molly fasteners or toggle bolts, which are illustrated. Installation is easy.

Concrete Fasteners. As a general rule, anchors in concrete have to be of larger diameter than those suitable for plaster walls. The ½-inch expansion bolt is usually adequate for such purposes as attaching a laundry sink stand to the floor, or fastening garden hose reels, lanterns, and ladder hangers to walls. The anchor used for this purpose may be a fiber Rawlplug, same as used for plaster walls but of larger diameter, or one of the metal expansion bolts. The hole is drilled with a hand-held Star drill by repeated hammer blows during which the drill is slowly rotated to prevent binding. Except when the concrete is exceptionally hard, drilling usually takes three to five minutes for a hole 1½ inches deep.

After the concrete dust is blown out, the anchor is inserted and expanded by tightening its bolt. Another type of anchor, which has a lead ring outside a tapered center of harder metal, requires tamping with a special setting tool.

Percussion drill with protective rubber holder is used on concrete wall. Turn the drill constantly to prevent jamming. Crossed lines show center position for drilling.

Two-piece anchors require tamping of a drop-in sleeve with special tool shown, thus compressing the threaded cone of the anchor. Bolt is then turned into the cone, as illustrated.

The tamped 2-piece anchor holds heavy bench bracket. Machine screws are turned tightly to prevent slippage that would dislodge the anchor.

Carbide-tipped bit in drill is held straight and steady to make perfectly round hole for fiber plug. The bit, screw, and fastener are all the same size.

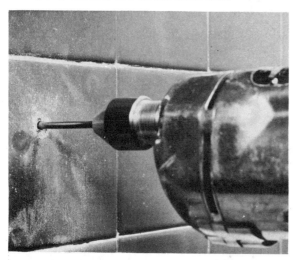

Ceramic Tile. Holes can be drilled into ceramic tile for wall anchors to mount tub grips, towel bars, and cabinets. First scratch the glazed surface with an awl at the point where the drill is to start, to keep the drill bit from sliding on the smooth tile. Drill with a carbide-tipped bit, applying only light pressure to avoid cracking the tile. Use lead-center fiber Rawlplugs, as on plaster walls described above.

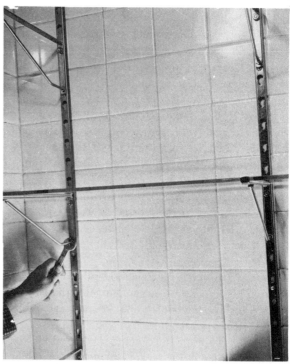

Glass shelving on ceramic tile wall is supported by brackets secured with screws into fiber plugs. These plugs serve almost all household purposes.

SHARPENING

Knives and tools become dull when the thin cutting edge bends or rolls over, forming a "wire edge." You can feel this by moving a thumb along the bevel, encountering a hump of metal where the cutting edge should be entirely smooth on both sides. Keeping knives and tools sharp requires removing this edge by honing on an oilstone, drawing over a specially hardened steel rod, or stropping on a leather strap. Tool edges that have become nicked, such as a plane blade after striking a nail, need to be ground to form a fresh edge. Saw blade teeth are sharpened with a file, then "set" by a tool that bends the teeth alternately in one direction or the other.

Keeping Knives Keen. As a slicing tool, high carbon knives are sharpened by moving the cut-

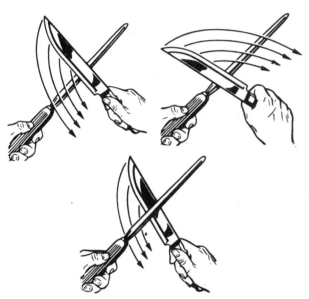

Honing on a whetstone or hardened steel sharpener will keep knives keen. Draw the blade, with its edge foremost, downward toward the handle on the first stroke, then reverse the knife to draw the blade outward. An alternative method is to draw the blade always to the handle, reversing positions at each stroke so both sides of the edge are whetted equally.

ting edge into, or forward on, the stone and alternating for an equal number of strokes on each side. Small knives are moved straight forward on the stroke, larger knives are given a rotary motion, making small circles starting at the tip

of the knife blade and moving forward up to the handle. You can test sharpness by placing the edge against a fingernail—if it slides downward instead of catching, continue stropping. Honing on a leather strap (the kind used by barbers) produces a razor edge.

Nicks in pocket and hunting knives usually can be removed on a coarse oilstone; larger kitchen knives may have to be lightly ground on a wheel to clean the edge and restore the bevel. Always be careful to avoid overheating, which draws the temper from the blade.

When using a sharpening steel, hold the steel in the left hand, the knife in the right. Draw the blade along the steel toward the handle, the bevel edge foremost and tilted at about a 20-degree angle so only the bevel touches, and stroke the blade the full length of the steel. Turn the blade over, and the bevel edge faces forward as the stroke moves the other way toward the end. Another way is to sharpen only on the instroke, the blade positions reversed above and then below the steel, so that both sides of the blade are done. Just one or two strokes on each side should be enough to restore the razor edge. Knives with a rippled edge, such as bread knives, require considerable experience to follow the original bevels.

Axes and Hatchets. These are sharpened differently in that instead of the tool moving across the oilstone, the stone (in small sizes and convenient shapes) is moved across the cutting edge. Another difference—while a knife blade is sharpened by pushing the cutting edge forward into the stone, in the case of the axe the stone moves from the bevel outward, toward the edge.

Burrs on axes can be removed with a file. Grinding on an electric wheel is not recommended as the heat would ruin the tool's temper. A hand or foot-turned grinder, however, is slow enough and produces a keen edge on these tools.

Scissors. As they do not cut the material, but rather shear it by the squeezing action of the blades, scissors do not have a keen bevel. Sharpening, instead, means removing any burrs and truing the edge from end to end. A common fault of scissors, excessive bending of the blades so they do not meet properly, can be corrected by tapping on an anvil or steel bar. However, scissor blades are quite brittle and may break when hammered, so it may be wise to leave straightening to a craftsman. Another important detail is adjusting and peening the pivot screw or rivet so that the blades come together with the right

When sharpening plane blades, hold blade at the proper angle to retain the original bevel. Special plane sharpening jigs are useful for this purpose. Several strokes on the oilstone should suffice to keep edges keen.

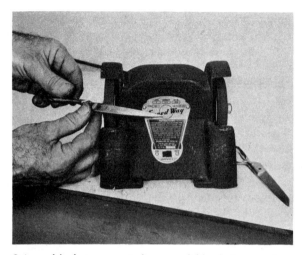

Scissor blades are not sharpened like knives; rather, the original bevel is retained and the edges ground to remove burrs and retain the proper alignment for shearing action caused by crossing of the blades.

When sharpening chisels, be careful to avoid rounding off the corners, which should be kept perfectly square. If the blade edge is knicked, grinding will be necessary to restore a true edge.

shearing action, yet are not too tight for comfortable use.

Chisels and Plane Blades. Use a flat silicone carbide stone. Hold blade at the slope of its bevel against the coarse side of the stone, stroke back and forth, or in a figure-8 movement, so the stone scrapes and rolls the steel particles until the wire edge that is formed breaks off.

Follow up by stropping the flat side of the blade. This leaves a smooth and strong edge that will stand up in cutting. Nicks on the edge must be removed by grinding; otherwise the chisel or plane will leave ridges in the work. A special sharpening jig, in which the chisel or blade is clamped at a specific angle for moving across the

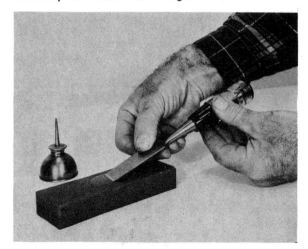

oilstone, produces a keen edge and retains proper bevel.

Power Mower Blades. Before removing the blade, mark the face with crayon to guide replacing the blade right side up. If blade ends are bent, flatten with a hammer on an anvil before grinding. Grinding can be done with an abrasive disk, such as the Stanley no. 143, chucked securely into an electric

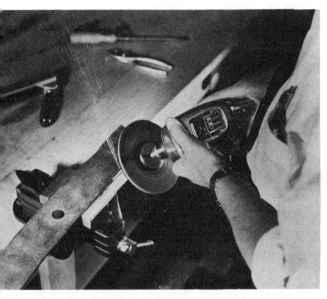

Power mower blades need occasional sharpening for efficient performance. A sanding disk in an electric drill will do the job efficiently. Draw the disk slowly and evenly along the cutting edge so it remains uniform throughout its length. When locking the blade in a bench vise, place a piece of wood under the vise jaws to prevent nicking the blade.

drill, using only the edge of the disk. Start at the inner end of the blade, and sweep the disk along the bevel toward the outer end, maintaining a uniform angle. Grinding is done at a minimum drill speed of 1,700 rpm, and maximum speed of 5,000 rpm for this disk.

Screwdrivers. Though they are not "sharp," screwdriver blades do need attention after extended use. The purpose is to keep the blade tip square, the edges parallel. Touching the blade tip lightly against the grinding wheel usually is sufficient to accomplish the purpose. Further details on screwdriver adjustment are given in Chapter 1.

Auger Bits. Burrs on the spur, the part that starts cutting after the screw point enters the wood, dull the auger bit. Sharpen by drawing a fine file just a few strokes across the inside edge. Never file off the outside edge. The cutting lips, which are just under the spurs, are also sharpened with a file, on the upper edge only and with the same number of strokes for each cutter.

The auger must be straight to bore true. If distorted, roll it on a flat surface to locate the high spot of the bend. Straighten by tapping with a hammer on a block of wood to avoid breaking off part of the spiral edge. Remember to store the auger bits upright in a length of 2 × 4 drilled for a series of deep holes, each marked for its size, to prevent chipping of the cutters.

DOWELING

Dowel joints are strong, do not tend to split the wood as nails and screws often do, and they contribute to the better appearance of cabinets and other furniture. Jointing with dowels isn't tricky, as it may appear—a low-cost jig locates the dowel hole positions and guides the drill for straight boring.

Dowels are commonly made of birch or maple, sold in 36-inch lengths and diameters from ⅛ inch to 3 inches. Most convenient, however, are dowel pins, 2 inches long, tapered at the ends for easy insertion, and with spiral grooves to prevent air lock in the glued holes.

Open-end doweling is easiest—the parts are clamped together, holes drilled through the center of the outside edge, glue brushed in and the dowels driven in as far as they can go, then the excess is sawed off and the end sanded flush with the surface. At least two dowels at each joint are needed.

"Blind doweling" is used when the dowel ends are to be concealed. In this method, the holes in the parts to be joined must be drilled internally in perfect alignment so the dowels will fit when the parts are drawn together under clamp pressure. Blind doweling can be done on mitered, curved, tapered, or other material, but the parts must match exactly.

Another method of lining up the dowel holes uses small metal plugs fitted with sharp metal pins at the center. One set of holes is drilled first, the plugs inserted, and the parts brought together so that the center pins indent the opposite side for positioning the drill. This method is more difficult and the results not as accurate as with the jig.

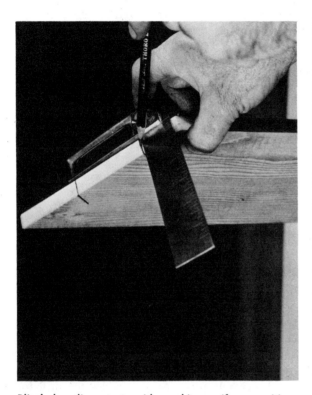

Blind doweling starts with marking uniform positions on each of the parts to be joined. Use a trysquare to assure straight lines.

Drilling is guided by a deep collar in the doweling jig, which is set at the center position of the boards to be joined so that each part is uniformly drilled.

Blind doweling is done with the aid of a dowel jig (Stanley tool no. 59) with guide tubes for six common drill sizes. The jig is adjusted to the thickness of the wood stock, or locked on lines drawn across both parts with a trysquare. The jig thus determines the position for drilling, the guide tubes hold the drill straight and at right angles to the work.

In blind doweling, the holes must be drilled deeply enough so that the precut dowels will go in far enough to permit bringing the assembled parts fully together.

In edge-to-edge doweling, as when two boards are joined to make a wider one, the thing to watch is any warping or uneven bellying of either board, as it would be difficult to assure that the

Another method for locating the dowel holes uses dowel centers, which are set into holes drilled in one of the parts. The parts are then pressed together so that the pins mark the opposite hole positions.

Holes must be precisely matched and drilled straight for perfect fit when dowels are joined for gluing.

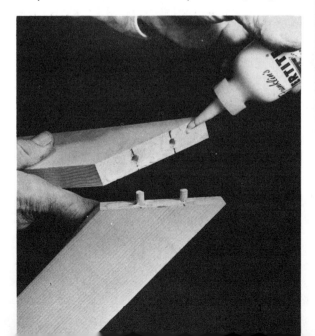

surfaces will be flush all the way. A slight misalignment may be overcome by placing weights or clamps to flatten the boards.

THE ROUTER

A portable router is useful for various home repairs and general shop work. It cuts dado grooves and rabbets for cabinet jointing, including the shelf support grooves of such projects as the floor-to-ceiling bookcase that is described later. Numerous cutter bits are available for shaping the edges of cabinets, routing hinge mortises on doors, carving decorative designs in panels, and for other purposes such as grooving kitchen cabinets to install compartment dividers.

The router consists of a high-speed motor with a chuck to hold the cutter bit. The depth of cut is

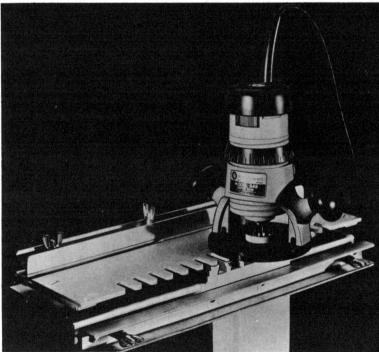

Router shown with dovetail jig, for making drawer joints. The high-speed router is used also for carving decorative designs into wood surfaces and shaping edges of cabinets.

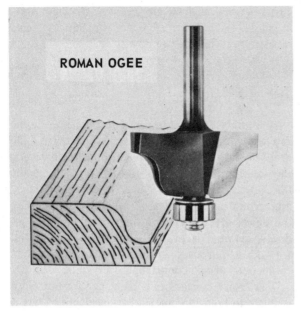

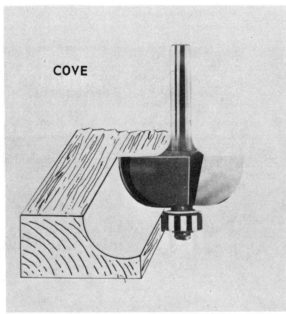

Two of the common bits used with a router to shape cabinet edges and moldings.

between two sections of an adjustable wood fence against which the work is moved. In this position, however, the router functions as a shaper, and must be used with extreme care to prevent the work from flying out of hand.

A special laminating jig with a carbide cutter is used with the router for edge trimming the plastic laminate surfaces (Formica, etc.) of countertops, desks, and other furniture, as described previously, and a dovetail jig permits accurate cutting of drawer parts.

Several practical accessories may be used with the router serving as the power source. These include a sander and planer, although it is usually just as economical and certainly more convenient to own separate tools of these types.

LOOSENING RUSTED BOLTS AND SCREWS

An exasperating problem that arises occasionally is that of a rusted bolt in which the nut has "frozen" in position and cannot be turned out. Various methods are used by mechanics to overcome this problem.

First try penetrating oil, which may well loosen the rust sufficiently so that the nut can be turned out. Patience is necessary as it may take several hours for the oil to penetrate.

A next step, if that fails, is to try cutting partway through the nut with a hacksaw, then splitting the nut apart with a cold chisel. Rarely will the nut be in position to permit using a regular hacksaw frame, so it may be necessary to work with just the blade itself—in that case, cover the blade teeth at one end with several layers of electrical tape to provide a comfortable handle. It won't be necessary to cut all the way through—usually the nut can be cracked apart with the chisel when the cut is halfway through.

Where space clearance does not permit use of the saw blade, it may be possible to split the nut simply with blows of the chisel, a process that may loosen it enough so it can be turned.

Another possible approach is to saw the bolt itself just above the nut. Should the bolt rotate

adjustable. The edge against which the cutter's guide bar moves must be smooth and clean to avoid deviations in the cut. The router can be mounted in a table, the bit upward and exposed with the blade strokes, it can be held in place with a screwdriver at the head. Internal bolts, those that are not locked with a nut, sometimes are driven in so tightly that they cannot be turned by ordinary means. Avoid careless treatment that will distort the bolt slot and make removal still more difficult; use a screwdriver with a square shaft so that a wrench can be applied to increase the torque pressure. This can be done also with a Stillson pipe wrench on a screwdriver with a round rod—but be certain that the screwdriver blade is of correct size to properly fit the bolt slot so it won't slip.

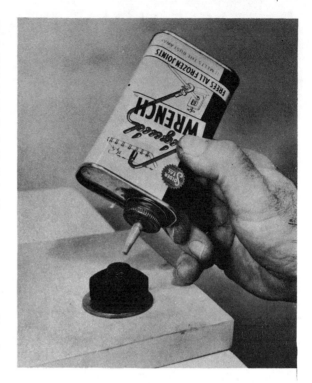

A can of penetrating oil doesn't look like much of a tool, but it has served many a time to loosen frozen nuts that a wrench couldn't turn. It's smart to keep it handy.

3. BASIC HOME REPAIRS

A list of things that can go wrong around the house would be sufficient to make any homeowner feel harassed. Doors squeak, sag, bind, swell, and warp. Window sashes become stuck, drafts develop, panes crack, moisture condenses and water streaks the sill paint. Faucets drip, toilet tanks operate erratically, drains become clogged—to mention a few routine events.

Fortunately, these incidents do not occur very frequently, and hardly ever simultaneously. Repairs usually are quick and easy, when you have the right tools and know what to do. Prompt attention when these difficulties arise, never allowing the defects to accumulate into an oppressive backlog, is the way to keep an easygoing stance.

The material in this chapter can help you deal more easily and successfully with the problems that you are likely to encounter. Not every condition can be discussed here, of course, but the selection includes those which are most common, and the instructions offer clues to tackling many other situations.

DOOR TROUBLES

Routine lubrication of the hinge pins, once or twice a year, will eliminate annoying squeaks and encourage softer closing of doors. Tap out the hingepins one at a time, wipe clean with a solvent-dampened cloth, then spread on a bit of petroleum jelly or light grease. Drive the pins back and the job is done.

While you're at it, carry along a medium-size screwdriver. Tightening any screws that might be loose removes extra strain on the remaining screws and prevents sagging of the door. Making the rounds of all doors in the house should take just an hour or two, unless you run into some difficulty that must be corrected.

Removing Hinge Pins. Most hinge pins can be lifted out easily with the fingers. Any that have become "stubborn" can be driven out, using a rather heavy screwdriver placed at an angle under the ball at the top of the pin. Tap the screwdriver sharply with a hammer until the pin becomes free and is lifted sufficiently so it can be pulled out. Some hinges have a similar ball at the lower end which is merely for decorative purposes and need not be disturbed except when the pin is "frozen" and cannot be easily removed. In that case, tap out the lower ball, exposing the bottom end of the pin. Use a heavy nail or a center punch to drive the pin upward until it loosens. When replacing the pin, see that the hinge leaves are lined up properly so the pins can slip through the loops. With only occasional application of grease, the door should swing quietly—that is, if there

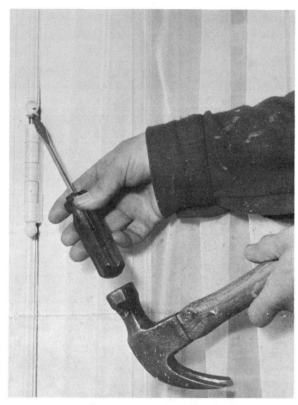

Hinge pins are removed by tapping upward against a screwdriver blade set under the ball-shaped top of the hinge pin. Bottom knob need not be disturbed, unless the pin is solidly frozen in place and must be driven upward with a center punch or similar tool.

is no other cause of friction, such as binding at top, bottom, or side.

Reinforcing Hinge Screws. Any hinge screw that continues to turn after being driven in all the way isn't doing its job, leaving the weight of the door to be carried by the remaining screws and thus making it likely that those other screws will subsequently loosen and cause the door to sag. Free-wheeling screws should be turned out, the screwholes packed with a wood matchstick dipped in glue, and the screw turned back in partway before the glue sets. After the glue has hardened, turn the screw all the way in and it should hold properly. This method works in almost every instance except when the door jamb itself is split,

a rare possibility that might require reconstruction of the frame, a job for the professional carpenter.

Some additional details regarding hinge screws should be noted: when substituting a longer screw for one that fails to hold, use flathead brass screws of the same size head (diameter) as the original, so that the screwhead will countersink flush into the hinge leaf. Prop up the opened door to ease the weight when tightening hinge screws. Replace any screws that are missing.

Binding Doors. Binding usually is caused by the door frame becoming slightly tilted out of square as a result of settling of the house. Close the door until it just touches the jamb, to observe the location of friction, whether at the top or bottom, or at some point on the lock side of the jamb.

Binding at the side is cleared up by shimming the hinge at the end opposite to the point of friction. Thus, if the door is binding near the top, the lower hinge is shimmed out sufficiently to square up the door in its frame (if the door has three hinges, two must receive the shim treatment). Do it this way:

Open and prop up the door with papers or a book, sufficiently so it won't drop but not enough to put any strain on the hinge pin. Draw out the pin of the required hinge, remove the screws from the half of leaf that is on the door frame. Cut two shims from thin cardboard to fit the hinge recess (a plastic playing card is perfect for this) set one shim in place, punch the screw holes, replace the original hinge leaf. Try the door. If it still binds somewhat, repeat the process to set in the second shim. Deepen the mortise a bit in the frame, if necessary, and be sure to tighten the hinge screws properly. Binding at the jamb near the lower edge of the door is, conversely, corrected by shimming out the upper hinge. But shimming in a sense "turns" the door, sometimes to the extent that the binding now is at the top of the door frame or at the threshold. Usually, the degree of contact resulting from this is minor, and a bit of planing or just sanding can accomplish the needed clearance.

Swelling or other cause may make the door so tight that it can be closed only by slamming, and tugged to get it open. Planing down the door edge may be necessary, rather than a simple hinge adjustment. Remove the door and support it on its long edge. Only the hinge side of the door is planed, as you won't want to disturb the lock setting. Use a long jack plane if available, shave down just enough so the needed clearance is obtained—resetting the door several times (without replacing the hinge leaves) until you get it right. Then deepen the hinge mortise sufficiently so the leaf goes in flush, replace the screws and rehang the door.

How to Take Down a Door. Passage doors have two hinges, exterior doors usually have three. Pull the hinge pins, as described earlier (the lower hinge first so the door won't topple), then pull the door forward just a bit by grasping the lock knob, to separate the hinge leaves, so the door drops clear. The door can be carried upright a short distance, then lowered at one end so it can be turned horizontally. Be careful not to strike the walls or furniture. Support the door in position with a couple of chairs, or make a crude brace out of scrap wood. After the door is trimmed and properly fitted, deepen the hinge mortise with a sharp chisel or router bit, so the hinge leaf lies in flush, as described above.

Binding at Top or Bottom. This condition calls for planing the cross grain of the door tiles (upright members)—a slow and difficult operation if much stock is to be removed. Use a block plane, stroking always from the edge toward the center; otherwise the edge will become splintered. You may find that, instead of a standard plane, the work can be done more easily with a Surform rasp, which has hundreds of razor-sharp protrusions that chop off the wood fibers. This rasp has double handles for comfortable working and control, but is less likely to produce a uniformly level surface than a plane.

The slight swelling of the door bottom that causes friction with the threshold may be overcome by swinging the door back and forth over a sheet of coarse sandpaper. Another approach is to lift off the wood threshold and trim down its bottom edges to obtain the needed clearance.

Excessive gap at door edge perils security. Clamshell molding on door frame is removed for access to frame studs, to shift the jamb closer to the door. About 1/16-inch clearance is sufficient.

Narrowing the edge gap also assists weatherproofing of the door. Place wedges against the wall framing stud to hold the jamb in corrected position.

Door Too Narrow. Spreading of the door frame may create a wide gap at the latch side of the door. This may be due also to improper fitting to begin with. A gap of more than ⅛ inch in an exterior door can cause a draft, and makes the door vulnerable to jimmying by a burglar. The condition can be corrected by fitting a strip of wood of the right thickness along the hinge side of the frame. The new strip will have to be mortised for the hinges, and the original mortises packed with plaster or wood filler. It is possible to close the gap also in some doors by shifting the jamb on the lock side inward, wedging it farther from the frame stud, a procedure involving removal of the clamshell molding trim on the door frame.

Rattling. A door rattles when the latch is not closely held in the strike plate because the plate opening has been made too large or the outside stop molding is not correctly placed. Moving the strike plate the tiny distance required for correction isn't usually possible because the screw holes offer no adjustment—better, if necessary, to obtain a new strike plate, the cost of which is nominal, filing it down for more precise fit.

The exterior stop molding probably cannot be removed without splintering it. A strip of felt tacked against the molding may take up the slack, or better still, install new foam-edged strips alongside the original stop molding, pressed lightly against the closed door. The foam weatherstrips are mitered at the top corners for neatness and better draft control.

Latch Doesn't Catch. A common fault is failure of the spring latch to snap into the strike plate on the jamb when the door is closed. The usual cause is that the door has sagged slightly, putting the latch out of alignment with the plate opening. A flat or triangular file is used to enlarge the opening just enough—but not too much—so the latch engages. Remove the plate and clamp it in a vise for accurate filing. When replacing the plate, see that its screws hold securely—if the holes have become enlarged, use longer screws of the same diameter so that the screwheads drive in flush. Make sure also that the mortise depth

at the plate openings is sufficient for the latch to go in all the way; if necessary, deepen the mortise with a ½-inch auger bit or a chisel.

Strike plate is clamped into vise for filing to widen the bolt opening. Use a flat or triangular file to enlarge strike plate opening. Avoid taking off too much metal, as that will result in failure to hold the door latch tightly.

Clearance for Carpeting. The easiest way to cut the bottom of a door to clear new carpeting is with a carpenter's hand saw or a portable circular saw. The door must be taken down, placed flat across sawhorses or similar support. Mark the cutting line, being careful not to remove too much stock, for a hand saw, or clamp a guide strip along the bottom for a portable circular saw, allowing for the width of the saw base. One or two tries may be necessary before you get the right floor clearance. See that the door completely clears the carpeting without rubbing, otherwise the carpet will wear quickly.

WINDOW GLASS

Replacing Broken Glass. Wearing gloves and eyeglasses or goggles, break out the remaining glass.

Place glass on blanket for cutting. Hold guide strip tightly along the cutting line. Dip the cutter into kerosene, draw it quickly along the entire strip, pressing firmly. Avoid skips.

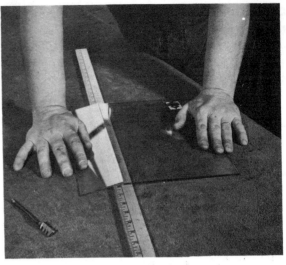

If the line is scored properly, the glass will snap easily. Place it over the ruler or along the table edge, press uniformly on both sides.

If the shards are large, apply masking or cellophane tape to minimize shattering. Sling an open carton underneath to catch the fragments; make certain all the scattered glass shards are recovered and safely discarded.

With a small chisel, chop out all old putty. If the putty has become extremely hard, heating with a photoflood lamp or special electric tool may soften it. Pull out the glazier's points with pliers. (In metal sash, remove the retainer clips, or unscrew the metal beading.) The sash has a rabbet—or recess—to hold the glass. This rabbet, when exposed by removal of the glass, should be given a protective coating of quick-drying paint.

Use a wood folding rule, not a tape, to measure the opening for the glass. Your hardware dealer will cut the pane to size, allowing a clearance of ¼ inch on both sash dimensions—or you can cut the glass yourself (see photos). Use double-thickness glass in metal sash and large windows.

With a broad knife, place a bed of putty on the sash rabbet all around. Insert the pane, press it gently into the putty cushion, adjust for equal clearance at each edge, then drive in glazier's points, at least two to each side, while holding

Wear work gloves and long sleeves when removing broken glass, have a carton or sack handy to receive the pieces. If necessary to break out the glass, apply masking tape so the pieces won't scatter.

the glass in position. These small diamond-shaped "points" are pressed into place with the end of a screwdriver blade riding against the glass; do not attempt to use a hammer. (In metal sash, replace the spring clips or glazing strips.)

Glass is cut ¼- or 3/16-inch shorter than the height and width of the opening. Apply putty all around as a cushion for the glass, forming a weatherseal when glass is pressed in.

Glazier's points are driven with right-angled tool. After putty has formed a surface skin, paint with a narrow sash brush to match the frame.

Clean out old putty thoroughly, remove the glazier's points with pliers. Old putty may be extremely hard, require slow chopping.

Knead a wad of putty until it is soft and smooth; roll it into rope-like strands about the thickness of a pencil. Lay the strips around the sash one side at a time, press smooth with the putty knife so that the putty slopes toward the outside edge of the frame. Remove the excess, using it to fill corners and missed spots. The putty should not extend above the sash mullions.

Smudges of the putty compound can be re-

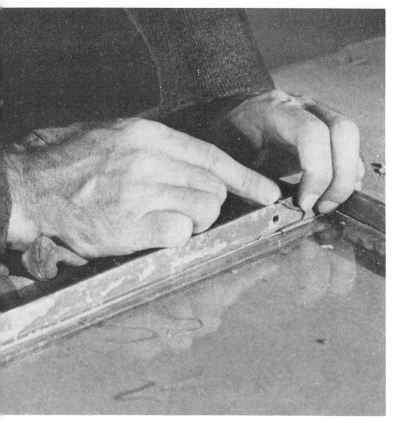

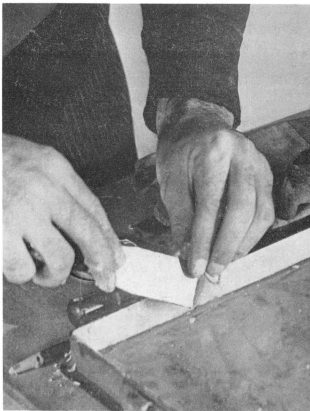

Steel sash has spring strips to hold the glass. Replace after the glass has been set into a cushion of putty. Use special compound for steel windows.

With putty knife, smooth the compound so it slopes neatly toward the sash edge.

moved at once with water applied with a soft brush, or after the putty dries, with turpentine. After the putty has set, apply a coat of paint using a narrow sash brush.

As a substitute for glass, you may prefer to install transparent acrylic plastic sheeting at vulnerable locations for burglarproofing. Plastics such as Lexan, by General Electric, and Plexiglas resist smashing even with a hammer. This plastic can be cut to size with any type of saw, and is particularly useful in doors having panes that could otherwise be broken for access to the lock. The plastic weathers well and will not easily become abraded. However, its transparency can be affected by certain cleaning chemicals.

MAKING A GLASS CUTTER RACK

Experts run a glass cutter along a ruler, and presto! There's a piece of glass cut to required size, square and neat. But most homeowners don't manage as well—at least two or three sheets of glass go to waste before the needed pane is obtained. One could learn the trick of cutting glass by constant practice, though glass replacement is quite infrequent and the skill is apt to be forgotten betweentimes.

A satisfactory solution is provided by this self-measuring cutter rack. No more hit-or-miss attempts—the piece of glass you get will be the precise size you need, every time.

CONSTRUCTION OF WALL-MOUNTED RACK FOR EASY AND ACCURATE CUTTING OF GLASS

Cut glass like a pro, to perfect size and without wasteful breakage, in this self-measuring homemade rack. Steel plate at side locks glass in position and serves as straightedge for glass cutter. Yardstick is tacked permanently in place.

Glass is moved to the desired size as shown by yardstick, seen through the glass so there's no guesswork. Cutter scores the glass straight and clean, waste piece snaps off.

Join 1 × 6 boards, one 24 inches long for the side, the other 30 inches for the bottom. Attach with steel plate and screws at the back. Cut ¼- by ½-inch rabbet along edge of the side piece, and a groove for the yardstick. Drill holes in side piece and in the flat steel plate, 30 inches long and 2½ inches wide, for the ¼-inch glass retainer bolts.

As shown in the illustrations, the rack consists of a simple wood frame with spring-pressure steel plate and a fixed yardstick. Behind the plate there is a strip of brass, ⅛ inch thick. Make the rack with two pieces of straight 1 × 6 board, one 30, the other 24 inches long. Join them, the shorter one butted to the other to form a right angle with both arms now about 30 inches long, making sure that the pieces are truly square. On one outside edge, cut a rabbet recess ½-inch and ⅛-inch deep for the brass strip. On the inside edge of the other arm, cut a groove for recessing part of a yardstick. Add a 1 × 4 brace diagonally across the two arms of the rack.

Drill ¼-inch (oversize) holes centered 1½ inches from the outside edge and 1¼ inches from both top and botton in the 2½-inch wide steel plate. A coil spring, washer, and thumbscrew go on the lag bolt in each hole.

The yardstick is placed to show the distance from the cutting edge—that is, zero, at the outside edge of the steel plate, but adjusted to compensate for the width up to the cutting wheel.

When using the device, place your sheet of glass on the wood cleat along the bottom, slide the glass behind the steel plate to the size you want as indicated by the yardstick, tighten the thumbscrews a turn or two to secure the glass. Dip the cutter into kerosene, then run it firmly along the edge of the steel plate; there's no need for heavy pressure if the cutter wheel turns freely.

Hold the cutter so the handle is at a right angle and the prongs ride flat against the glass. Move the cutter quite quickly along, all the way to the end in one stroke. There should be a clear whistling sound, no grinding or gritty noise. The waste end of the glass will snap off neatly. Loosen the thumbscrews and take out the main piece of glass, which should be just right. Additional construction details include attaching a narrow wood strip 1½ inches from the bottom for the glass slide, and drilling the steel plate for a handle.

Keep the glass cutter immersed in kerosene so the wheel turns freely. A good place to keep the cutting rack is in the garage, mounted on a wall where it's out of the way, takes up no space, and is always available for use.

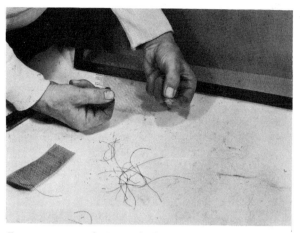

Emergency patch is made by stripping some of the screen wires on all sides and weaving them into the original.

After removing the decorative molding, pry up this spline all around, then pull out any tacks or staples to free the cloth. Smooth this material flat to measure it, cut the new screening several

SCREEN REPAIRS

A hole or rip in a screen can be patched temporarily with a piece of old screening material, held in place by several short pieces of wire through the screen strands, twisted tightly with pliers. A neater and more permanent job can be done by weaving the patch into the original screen. Very small holes usually can be bridged and sealed by coating with a colorless nail polish.

Replacement screening is better, costs about the same for enameled aluminum and the better grade of fiberglass material. Tools needed are a hammer and a small pry bar or screwdriver, wide-jaw pliers for drawing the material so it is taut, and for some types of frames, a spline roller. Screening comes in various widths, ranging by 6 inches.

Wood Screens. These usually have a narrow groove around the frame into which the screen cloth is compressed and gripped by a wood spline.

Not very pretty, but patch will hold until new screening can be put in.

BASIC HOME REPAIRS | 63

inches oversize so it can be gripped. Arrange the material so that the strands are aligned with the sides of the opening. Start at one long side, driving the spline into its groove. At the other sides, use a narrow wood strip to press the screening into the groove while holding the material fairly tight, then tamp the spline flat into the grooves. The pull of the splines should bring the screening taut. A slight "give" in the screening before you drive the splines is necessary to avoid tearing it. Drive a few thin brads into each spline before replacing the surface molding.

If the wood frame has a divider strip along the center, it is not necessary to replace the entire screening. Remove the strip molding, staple or tack the center screening tightly, then cut along the edge of the part that will be discarded. The new material is fitted into the grooves at three sides and stapled onto the center stretcher, which is covered with molding.

Aluminum and Steel Screens. The screening is retained in a channel by a spline, which is a thick

Screening is held in steel frame by metal spline which can be pried out with screwdriver. Aluminum frames may have a rope spline.

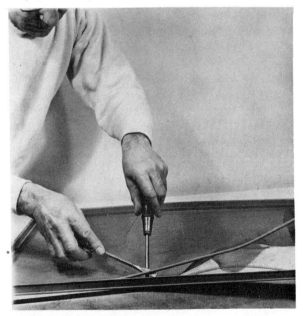

cord in aluminum frames, a steel rod in steel screens. With a pair of screwdrivers, gently pry up this spline. Pull out the screening and press flat to obtain the size, cut the replacement to fit. Installation goes quickest and most neatly with a spline roller having a small wheel at each end— one wheel rim is convex, the other concave. Press the screening into the channel all around with the convex wheel, watching to see that material is fairly taut and the wire strands parallel to the frame.

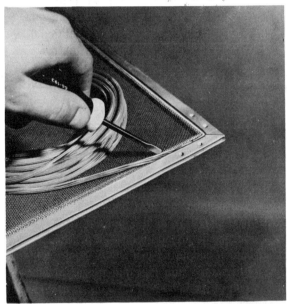

Tiny metal miter box cuts perfectly fitted corners, which are joined by right-angle corner fittings. The retainer spline to hold the screening material is purchased separately.

At the fourth side, stretch the cloth just enough so that it becomes fairly tight when the spline cord is inserted. Don't roll the wheel too vigorously or the screening may tear—rather, apply just enough pressure so the material bends over the edge into the channel. Use the second wheel to roll the cord deeply into place. Finally, trim the excess material, if fiberglass, with a razor

Replacement screen frame made with aluminum strips, available at hardware stores. Special fitting locks mitered corners.

blade. Projecting ends of aluminum wires can be eliminated by withdrawing the retainer cord, clipping off the excess with scissors or diagonal pliers, or bending the wire ends back over the channel, and replacing the cord.

width. Measure the width at both ends of the room to find the center. Snap a short chalk line across the center. Place a few tiles at the center position to get a right angle marking. Use this guide to snap a second line across the room.

Lay out a row of tile without adhesive along both lines, starting from the center, to see the width of the last tile at the end. If the tile is less than half its width, shift the center positions the width of ½ tile, to equalize the side strips, and rechalk the new line.

Use the specific adhesive recommended for the particular tiles and for the surface on which they will be laid. Applicator trowels also vary according to the width and depth of the notches; use the

FLOOR TILES

Installing Tiles. While recent advances in adhesives have simplified floor tile installation, the project is not as easy as some advertisements would indicate. However, many homeowners and housewives have done handsome installations after proper attention to details. The new adhesives are indeed less difficult than former ones to apply; some are water soluble, can be spread with a brush instead of a notched trowel, and there are now self-stick tiles that entirely eliminate handling of adhesives. Armstrong's Place 'n Press Tiles have latex-type adhesive on the back, can be installed even in the basement, and seem to be the ultimate for do-it-yourself installation.

There are two main requirements for accomplishing an attractive, practical floor job. One is that the base surface be smooth, sound, and free of wax, grease, or dirt. Armstrong guarantees the self-adhesive tiles will bond firmly to tightly affixed linoleum, old tiles, or sheet vinyl, and to painted floors. On wood floors, it is better to put down a well-nailed underlayment of ¼-inch hardboard (but not the tempered type) to assure a smooth surface. While you're at it, put longer nails into the joists to correct any squeaks in the old flooring boards. On concrete floors, trowel on a latex-type underlayment, available from flooring dealers, to fill in any dips or cracks in the concrete.

The second essential is that the room be squared off so that the rows of tiles will be parallel

Self-adhering tiles permit recovering an old floor in just a few hours of interesting work. The Place 'n Press tiles come with adhesive backing. The tile can be installed over an existing floor covering.

Find the center of the room, lay out the tiles to see whether the end tiles will be of even size; if not shift center a half-tile. Avoid placing new tiles so joints are directly over the joints of existing tiles.

one recommended by the manufacturer. Press down hard on the trowel so only the proper amount of adhesive remains on the floor—if too much adhesive is left, it will ooze up along the joints and cause a messy situation.

Start laying in the tiles at the center, working first toward one side of the room. Rolling or tapping the tiles will make certain they are down firmly. Vinyl tiles are easily trimmed to fit with large scissors or a sharp linoleum (hooked tip) knife.

Replacing Damaged Tiles. Individual floor tiles that have become cracked or otherwise damaged can be replaced. It is essential that the new tiles be of the same gauge (thickness) as the originals, and preferably of the same material—vinyl, vinyl asbestos, asphalt, linoleum, and so on. The color and pattern should match, but this is a matter of choice.

Pry up a corner of the damaged tile with a knife, then push a putty knife underneath to loosen the rest. Remove the old adhesive to provide a flat surface. Linoleum paste can be softened by soaking with hot water; some mastic adhesives soften when heated (use a photoflood lamp or sunlamp). Clean the area, particularly the corners. Test that the replacement tile fits snugly before spreading adhesive, trim the new tile edges slightly if necessary. Conditioning the new tile to the room temperature for a couple of days will assure better fit. Spread adhesive carefully, just enough to cover the area thinly, and ease the tile into place, then tap with a hammer on a block of wood so that the edges are all flush.

LINOLEUM REPAIRS

Floorcoverings are very durable, the better grades standing up under constant wear and tear for numerous years. An experience shared by many families, however, is that premature wear at just one or two spots, such as at the kitchen sink or an entrance door, makes an entirely new floor necessary.

If you've saved a piece of the original material, there is an easy way to place a neat patch. The process involves laying the new material over the damaged spot, then cutting through both old and new simultaneously with a hooked knife (a linoleum knife). The knife must be very sharp, pressed down hard to cut through both surfaces. The damaged section of linoleum can be lifted out after prying up one corner with a penknife.

The patch will fit the area perfectly, but may not go flush with the surface because of old linoleum paste. Remove the paste by scraping, steaming, or soaking sufficiently to soften it. Paste down the patch with rubber contact cement, or any of the common household glues. With the latter, apply pressure with weights over the patch for a few hours.

TOPS FOR STAIRS

Wooden stair treads wear quickly and unevenly unless covered with durable material such as linoleum or vinyl sheeting, or 9- by 9-inch vinyl tiles. A permanent and attractive installation can be achieved with some attention to details.

The installation includes metal molding (of the correct thickness to match the gauge of your sur-

facing material), lining felt, and linoleum paste. Tools needed are a linoleum knife, a notched trowel for applying the paste, a calipers-scriber, and heavy shears.

If the stair treads have badly worn spots, they can be leveled with floor mastic, applied with a trowel and allowed to harden completely before proceeding with the linoleum installation.

"Nose molding" is attached to front edge of steps to protect and help hold down stair covering. Get right size for the gauge of your material.

Cut metal moldings to length with a hacksaw, attach them to the front edges of the treads with screws. Measure carefully for a good fit, using an extension rule if you have one. Next, cut felt pieces for each step, slightly undersize. Check the thickness of your surface material plus the felt against the clearance of the molding edge. If they are flush with the molding, lay the lining only to the butt edge; if too low, place the lining over the molding lip to increase the thickness. Cement the lining on each step with the paste.

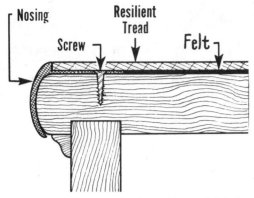

Sketch shows tread nosing with positions of felt liner and surfacing material. In this case, the liner extends only up to the molding edge, not all the way to the butt-edge lip, so surface is flush.

Fitting Linoleum Treads. The linoleum should fit snug at each step, otherwise dirt will accumulate in any open spaces. The professional way is to start with somewhat oversize strips. Place the factory cut edge against the step riser at the back, lifting the ends of the strip for clearance. Move

Linoleum hooked knife used for cutting the linoleum to size.

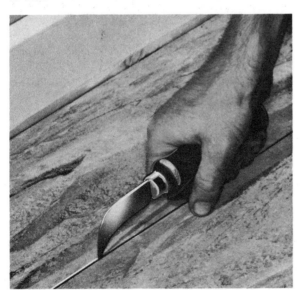

the strip so one end is flat against the stringer, which is the side support of the stairs, run a scriber along the stringer wall to mark the end contour. After cutting and placing that end snug against the stringer, mark a line near the center of the strip, both on the linoleum and on the riser at the back. Shift the linoleum slightly toward the side that has already been fitted, open the scriber to just the width of the gap between the two marked lines, and scribe the second end for cut-

Oversize linoleum strips are laid on step and scribed for edge contours.

ting. The strip will then fit the tread precisely at both ends. The front edge is similarly scribed to fit neatly against the metal molding lip. Spread paste with the trowel, either on the step lining or directly on the back of the strips, lay in the linoleum, and apply pressure for adhesion with a roller or by tapping on a wood block. Standard floor tiles may be used instead of sheeting, installed in essentially the same manner except that the center tile is cemented in first, then the tiles at both ends are fitted and cut.

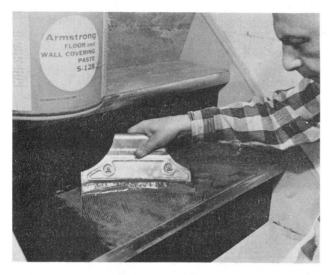

After fit is tested, apply adhesive and lay out the strips by fitting one edge tightly against side. With rolling pin, press down before adhesive hardens.

Chromium or plastic molding is attached into the corner joint of tread and riser.

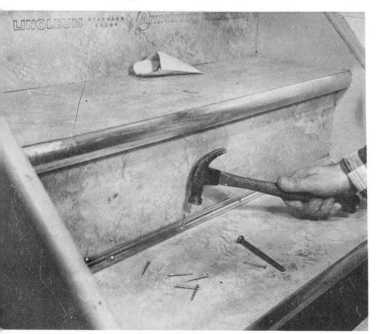

INSULATION

The time to do a correct job in insulation is, of course, when the house is being built. Supplementary insulation may be of limited effectiveness, but still very necessary and worthwhile. Older houses, though solidly built, mostly were deficient in insulation because heating costs at the time were not a significant part of home upkeep, and because the advanced materials were not available.

There are several ways, however, that you can improve the insulation and weatherproofing of an existing home, in addition to storm sash and doors.

Attic Joists. If there is no insulation at present in an unfinished attic, insulation can be installed from above without damage to the interior walls. The insulation blankets or batts are stapled between the joists, the vapor barrier facing down toward the heated room below, preventing moisture from entering the insulation wool. Edges of the batts are peeled back a couple of inches for use as a flange to be stapled to the wall framing, but be careful not to block air circulation through the hollow section of a veneered wall.

Selection of the proper insulation batts will make a considerable difference in results. For an attic ceiling, the material should be rated R-19, or at least R-13 (the numbers represent the resistance to heat flow—the higher number has greater insulating value).

In place of the stapled blankets, a granular fill can be a satisfactory substitute. This consists of vermiculite granules, poured between the joists to a depth of 3 or 4 inches. The vermiculite may be spread also over existing insulation batts to improve the heat resistance, and to fill voids at the eaves and around obstructions such as plumbing pipes and structural bracing.

Side Walls. The only practical access to the side walls for improving the insulation is by blowing in special wool with a powerful pump through a series of holes drilled in the wall sheathing. The problem here is to get the wool into every space inside the wall, overcoming the inside framing members and fire stops, for a specified density of the insulation. The drilled holes are covered by replacing the shingles or siding. This type of work is done by firms with the specialized equipment that is necessary.

Finished Attic Room. When an additional room is finished in the attic, the walls and ceiling require insulation even though the original floor area is insulated. In this case, fiberglass or mineral wool batts or blankets are installed at the walls between studs, and overhead between the ceiling beams. The vapor barrier coating of the blanket faces inside the room. An open, ventilated area must remain above the finished attic room, with louvers of sufficient dimension on opposite walls for ventilation near the roof peak to permit escape of humid air.

Crawl Spaces and Concrete Slabs. Insulation of the outside perimeter of an existing concrete floor slab or crawl space will result in warmer floors and considerable saving in fuel cost. A dense insulation board, $1/2$- or $2^{5}/_{32}$-inch thick, is cemented to the outside surface of a slab footing with asphalt mastic, and protected against the backfill earth with asbestos cement board. Similar waterproofed insulation board is installed on the exposed undersurface of floors over a crawl space.

Shingle Backers. Sidewall insulation is improved considerably when fiberboard shingle backers are

crash into a heap of debris is, fortunately, not common. Loosened tiles can be detected by the slight movement when pressed. Tile failure of this type is usually caused by excessive slamming of a door or moisture penetrating the wall. Cementing of a few tiles when this occurs may save the entire wall from collapse.

Resetting Loose Tiles. Remove the loose tiles one by one, while bracing the others temporarily against collapse of the entire section. Center tiles cannot be taken out intact; it will be necessary to start at a top or bottom row, and work toward the loose section. If the wall has portland cement backing, clean out all debris and crumbled plaster, particularly at the corners, using a brush and vacuum cleaner. Scrape old grouting off the tile edges, and remove any cement on the backs, so they are perfectly smooth. Tiles with mastic cement may have some of the hardened adhesive on the backs, which must be scraped off. Try the tiles in place to be sure there's no impediment to going in flush.

Reset the tiles with special "loose tile" cement, unless you have some of the original setting mastic. The tiles and wall must be completely dry. Apply a blob of cement to the back, slide the tile into place, and press hard. Make sure all tiles line up, their edges perfectly flush with the adjacent tiles; otherwise remove and clean out any obstruction. Do not let cement dry on the face of the tile— clean with a solvent-dampened cloth as you go.

installed in conjunction with new house siding. The insulating material comes in 4-foot-long strips that fit behind aluminum or steel siding panels. Some cedar and redwood shake shingles are made with this insulating material laminated to the backs.

CERAMIC TILES

Ceramic tiles are made to last, and that's one of the reasons they're the favored wall material for bathrooms and other installations. So it is the more dismaying when a tile wall literally falls down on the job.

The harrowing experience of hearing the tiles

Grouting the Tiles. After the cement has set for a full day, apply the grouting cement. Mix white grouting cement with water to the consistency of heavy cream, or use prepared tile grout. Apply liberally over the entire surface, working the grout deeply into the tile joints with a rubber squeegee or with your fingers. Before the grout has hardened, remove the excess with a damp sponge. Inspect the joints for any gaps or skips; fill with fresh grout.

Replacing a Cracked Tile. Removal of an individual tile in the wall or floor is extremely difficult, unless it is at the top or end of a row. A badly split tile may sometimes be chiseled out in small

Grout cement is applied with sponge or squeegee, worked deeply into the joints with a stick or the fingers. After partial setting, the grout is "struck" along the joints, residue washed off.

pieces, otherwise the rest of the row must be lifted out to reach the tile that is to be replaced, as described earlier. The latter course is preferred; it does not involve much more effort, since it will be easier to set in the new tile. Also, the replacement tile may be of somewhat different shade than the rest and would be less noticeable at the outside border than at a center, so one of the original tiles should be moved over to become the replacement. Follow the procedure described for resetting the tiles.

Cutting Tiles to Fit. At irregular surfaces, such as plumbing pipes and fixtures, the tiles are shaped by chipping small pieces with an end-cutting pliers or nippers. Cutting tiles to size is done by scoring the glaze with a glass cutter and applying pressure on both sides. More details on ceramic tile cutting are given in Chapter 2.

(Left) Fitting tiles around irregular obstructions. Use pliers or end cutters to chip corners as needed. Do not aim for tight fit—the openings are covered with escutcheon plates or other means.

(Left below) Bathroom accessories come in modular sizes to fit spaced openings. Use the same adhesive for attaching soap holder and other items to wall.

Cleaning Tile Walls and Floors. Ceramic tile is best cleaned by washing with detergent and warm water. Ordinary soap in hard water forms an insoluble film that builds up and makes the tile look dull. A soapless detergent or common washing soda, thoroughly rinsed, will keep the tiles sparkling clean whether the water is hard or soft.

Soiled grouting can be cleaned by scrubbing with a fiber brush and mild household scouring powder. The grouting tends to darken slightly with age and the homeowner should not expect to completely alter this condition. Harsh abrasives should not be used on glazed tiles.

Tile floors are best cleaned with soapless detergent. When an electric scrub brush is used, avoid leaving the brush in one position while the motor is running, as that will cause rapid wearing of the cement grout. Research reports by the Tile Council of America stress that expensive waxes, compounds, and polishes are not necessary to clean tiles, and may actually detract from the tile's performance. Whenever a tile floor seems slippery or greasy, a vigorous scrubbing with detergent and hot water will restore the original appearance and good traction.

Regrouting. The white joint cement usually lasts as long as the tile installation. Certain circumstances, however, may require regrouting, such as when the grout has broken out as a result of pounding from a nearby door, a mildew attack, or an excessively greasy condition that resists cleanup.

The grouting cement is available in various types; a recommended commercial preparation consists of white portland cement with a latex additive, which is suitable for all installations, including floors. A mastic type, premixed for direct use, does not require damp curing, as with regular cement grout.

Scrape out all old grout with the point of an awl or similar tool. With a wet cloth, wipe the tile surface, allowing the cloth to dampen the edges of all the tiles. Mix the grout with water, as described on the package, to obtain a creamy consistency. Apply the cement paste along the joints with a putty knife or other convenient means, spreading with a squeegee. Use the fingers to work the grouting into all joints. Allow the cement to set a bit, then strike the joints (compress and shape their mortar) with the edge of a wood spatula (a physician's tongue depressor is fine for this) or with the handle of a toothbrush.

The wall will have to be washed a number of times to completely remove the cement residue, but this is fine because it also serves to cure the joint grouting. Space the washings several hours apart the first day, after the grout has fully set, repeating once each of the following three days.

New Installations. An average homeowner can do a creditable installation of ceramic tile on

Dry-set organic and latex adhesives simplify ceramic tile installation. Apply as directed on container with special trowel. Cover only small areas with adhesive at a time.

splashed from the shower.

Set the tiles neat and flush. The adhesive permits truing or leveling to about ¼-inch thickness.

Bathroom needs a new floor to replace cracked asphalt tile that has permitted seepage of water

Ceramic tiles, pasted to a coarse cotton mesh, are applied flush over an approved vinyl adhesive. Grout is spread with squeegee.

Rejuvenated floor is smooth, colorful, and waterproof. The tub edge is soundly caulked, wall edge trimmed with wide rubber strips.

walls and floor. The installation has been simplified by direct application of the tile with mastic adhesive onto gypsum board, hardboard, or plywood wall panels, eliminating the former mortar base. A plaster wall may be tiled if it is smooth and square, otherwise the wall should be overlaid with new wallboard to form a better tiling surface.

The wall is prepared by coating with a moisture sealer recommended by the adhesive manufacturer. In wet areas, at the tub or shower, use water-resistant gypsum panels, all openings carefully sealed with compound or a plastic membrane. Plan the installation so that the end wall tiles are not very narrow strips that will be difficult to insert—if necessary, start the opposite side with tiles cut in half so both ends are of adequate width. Make use of rounded cap tiles, and preformed inside and outside corner tiles, for a neater job.

Tile may be installed over other existing wall surfaces or floors if they are in good condition; that is, perfectly smooth, sound, and tightly bonded. Examples are paint, wood paneling, asphalt tile, wood floors, plastic laminates. A badly cracked wall should be resurfaced with firmly attached gypsum wallboard or plywood to form a solid base for the tiling. Dry-setting latex or organic adhesives may be used. Epoxy adhesive is especially suitable for speedy installation over any sound wall surface.

4. PAINTING AND WALLPAPERING

Drop cloths protect shrubbery, also relieve you of endless cleanup of paint splatters on the walks and driveway. Large canvas cloths are best for outdoors, but plastic sheeting will serve the purpose if weighted down with stones.

Homeowners who do their own painting and wall-papering save substantial sums while keeping the house always attractively fresh-looking and protected from deterioration. This is one field in which the individual can actually turn out a job that is equal to or better than that of a professional because of more patient attention to the preparation and greater care in doing the work.

Latex paints make all the difference. You can paint a room in stages during your free time, so there's no rushing the job to get it done all in one day, or even a weekend. If you're interrupted while in the middle of a wall, drop the brush or roller into a pan of water, just shake it out when you're ready to resume where you left off. Touch-ups of the painted surface can be done later, blending neatly into the completed sections.

After you've acquired a little experience and have accumulated the necessary equipment, you'll regard redoing a room, perhaps just for a change of color scheme, as no big deal. The cost, just for the materials, will be a small fraction of what you would have to pay a painter; each effort you make will be easier and will achieve a better result than the one before. Exterior siding and trim also can be kept in top condition by a routine program in comfortable stages.

(Above left) Before starting to paint, take care of the caulking and puttying so all joints are sealed. The caulking compound should be allowed to harden somewhat before it is painted.

(Above) Preparation before painting includes removal of blistered and alligatored paint by burning and scraping. Any irregularities or other defects will be visible on new coating.

(Left) On house siding, always work from top down, completing an entire section before moving to next. Gutters and downspouts, if not previously painted, should be given coat of primer before the finish coating.

SELECTING THE PAINT

Latex water-thinned paints are excellent for nearly all purposes—interior walls, ceilings, and woodwork. In various formulations, they are also preferred for exterior applications on siding, shingles, masonry walls, porches, and decks. They go on easily and evenly, splatters wipe up cleanly with a damp cloth, the better grades cover satisfactorily with one coat. Latex paint is not flammable, contains no toxic solvents, there is no unpleasant odor, and brush and roller cleanup with soap and water takes just minutes.

Latex dries in half an hour, permitting the room to be used again, although a full day is needed for hardening, after which it can be washed, even scrubbed.

Flat latex paint is used for most interior and outdoor applications, woodwork, siding, even bathrooms and shower stalls. Acrylic enamel, in glossy, semi-gloss, or satin finish, is tougher and more durable than the PVC (polyvinyl chloride) type, so generally is preferred for bathrooms, kitchens, and playrooms, where there may be moisture conditions or the walls require more frequent washing.

The traditional oil paints are still preferred by some for exterior doors and wood trim, because of better adhesion, resistance to weathering, less chalking. On siding, however, the latex paints have the advantage of porosity, or "breathing" so moisture is not trapped behind the paint and there is no blistering. Almost all masonry surfaces are best painted with PVC latex emulsion, a specially formulated variation of the type used for home interiors, that resists cracking and peeling. Applications include brickwork, stucco, cinder and concrete block, poured concrete foundation walls, and asbestos panels. Newer acrylics are made for patios or porch decks requiring greater abrasion resistance.

Of special interest to the amateur home decorator are the dripless latex paints, which have a thicker consistency that clings to the roller, reducing the tendency to splatter. Claims for one-coat coverage are generally justified, but count on a second coat when covering a very dark surface with white.

For interior painting, do the closets first, then the ceiling including the crown molding, if any, the walls next, then the doors and windows, finally the baseboard. If you're planning any changes or additions to the room, such as wall-to-wall tackless carpeting, or wall-mounted bookshelves, the time for repainting is before the new items make redecorating more difficult.

TOOLS FOR PAINTING

A good quality brush makes a considerable difference in both the painting effort and the result. The brush carries the paint to the wall and spreads it smoothly. Use a wide 3½- to 4-inch brush on walls, a 3-inch width for doors and other woodwork, a 2-inch size for wood trim and moldings. A narrower sash brush is helpful for narrow strips like sash mullions, the strips between the glass panes. Length and density of bristles are important, too, since longer bristles have more "flex" for smoother action, while more thickly packed bristles carry more paint and produce a smoother spread.

Synthetic brush bristles were developed at about the time that water-thinned paints started to become popular. Nylon brushes are considered superior to natural bristles for these latex paints, since the synthetic filaments do not tend to become waterlogged. The newer Orel bristles by Du Pont are a further improvement, retaining their springiness even after hours of use.

Paint Rollers. Select the roller with the correct nap for the job you are planning. Make certain the roller core spins smoothly without binding, the cover slips on and off without difficulty. A 9-inch roller width is generally preferred, but you may want a 7-inch width as a starter. The ¼-inch nap is best for interior walls and ceilings, ⅜-inch for rough and textured walls, and up to ¾-inch for stucco, brick, or foundation concrete. There are various roller shapes for special purposes, like clapboard, siding, and cedar shakes.

A wood pole that screws into the roller handle enables you to paint ceilings and upper sections of walls while standing on the floor. This provides many advantages: it speeds the work, reduces need to shift a ladder around, provides better visibility during the painting so "skips" can be retouched immediately, and perhaps not least, helps avoid accidental spilling of the paint.

The roller pan should be of ample width to receive the roller; its slope sufficient to drain excess paint back into the reservoir section, and it should have clips for safely attaching the pan to the ladder shelf.

Pad Painters. The newest advance in painting is provided by applicator pads with tiny nylon bristles, used just like a brush or roller with all types of paint. The flat pad is considered by many users to be faster than a brush or roller, and less likely to drip or splatter paint. Suitable for walls, ceiling, woodwork, doors, and trim, the pad method is particularly satisfactory on shake sidings, shingles, and rough surfaces such as masonry walls. The sizes range from 3½-inch width to 5-, 6-, 8-, 9-, and 11-inch lengths.

An efficient 3- by 5-inch pad is used for edge trimming in conjunction with a roller. A special Ruff Painter with 1¼-inch nap works like a broom on stucco, brick, and concrete block. There also is a lambswool pad, useful for application of clear stains and sealer compounds on wood shakes. A special applicator for acrylic latex has a sharply beveled 1¼-inch nylon pad for cutting in the paint at difficult spots. Among the trade names for pad applicators are Speed-Brush, Shake Painter, Pad Painter, and Hyde Paint-zum.

PREPARATION

Clear the Room. There'll be no savings from do-it-yourself painting if any of your furnishings become splattered, stained, or otherwise damaged in the process. The first step is to move as much furniture as you can out of the room. This is space beyond the room doorway, as splattered paint often carries that far.

Take down all draperies, curtains, and pictures, including the rods and brackets; remove also any bric-a-brac and glassware so you won't have to be concerned about breakage. Empty the closets, remove all door knobs, electrical plates, and wall fixtures. Lower the canopies on ceiling light fixtures. The more completely you clear the room, the easier the work will be, and cleanup time reduced to a minimum.

Prepare the Surface. Paint does not bond properly to dirt or grease. Sponge down the ceiling, walls, and baseboard with a detergent or special wall cleaner to assure good adhesion of the paint and eliminate the possibility of unsightly and troublesome flaking months later. Enameled surfaces should be sanded lightly or treated with a gloss-removing chemical, unless you are using a paint that specifically states that it has a special bonding primer. New plasterboard (dry walls) should receive a base coating of oil paint, regardless of the final paint used. This painting is essential also before hanging wallpaper on gypsum wallboard, so that the paper may be stripped off later without damaging the wallboard coating.

STRIPPING OLD PAINT

Completely stripping off chipped siding paint,

important also to give you maximum working clearance. Gather the larger pieces that remain in the center of the room, cover carefully with drop cloths. Do not depend on spreading lots of newspapers for protection as they slip around and fail to cover properly. Instead, get a few large plastic drop cloths in the 9- by 12-foot or larger sizes, selecting the heaviest quality. The thinner, less expensive type, similar to the polyethylene grocery bag, tends to rip and become entangled. The better covers can be washed and folded flat into a small bundle for use again and again, so are worth the extra cost.

Protect the entire floor area in the room, spreading the drop cloths flat and neat, overlapping where necessary. Place the sheeting also in the or multiple layers of paint that threaten to break free off the wall by sheer weight, is advisable in order to get a fresh start. Removing old paint is always a rough and messy task, but the like-new finish it assures usually justifies the effort.

Paint removal is accomplished by several methods: soaking with a commercial paint remover preparation or a caustic solution consisting of 1 pound of lye in 5 pints of water; by "burning," in which the paint is softened with a gasoline or butane torch, or an electric heater, and scraped off with a putty knife; and by mechanical means, using a disk or belt sander, and sand or emery paper of varied grits to obtain the smoothest possible surface.

Many commercial removers require use of a

flammable mineral solvent, but there is a non-flammable water-wash type that is safer for home use. When using any of these caustic chemicals, exercise proper caution. Wear rubber gloves, eye-protecting goggles, and old clothes. Avoid prolonged inhalation of the fumes. Apply the chemical with an old brush that can be discarded, as the brush won't again be suitable for painting. Spread a fairly generous quantity of the chemical, allow it to remain in place until the paint shows signs of softening, indicated by a wrinkled appearance, then scrape off the old paint.

You may be confronted with the problem of applying the remover to a vertical surface. How does it remain in place for the required time? You'll find that the chemical comes in several forms: liquid, which serves very well for horizontal surfaces; semi-paste for walls on which the paint responds to the treatment fairly quickly; and paste form, which is used where the chemical must remain on a vertical surface for an extended period of hours. Paste cannot be spread properly with a brush; use a piece of hard felt or a strip of cardboard for this purpose.

After the paint has been scraped off, wash the surface thoroughly, using a mineral spirit like turpentine or varnoline unless the chemical is specifically stated as the "water-washable" type, in which case clear water will neutralize the paint remover chemical completely. Make sure that the surface is fully dry before painting, except in the case of latex paints to be used after a water-washable remover.

Using the "burning" method (actually just softening the paint by heat) involves an obvious risk of fire, and every precaution should be taken for safety. Avoid playing the flame on one spot for too long a period; never lay the torch down on a surface while the flame is going. Keep a can of sand or an attached garden hose with trigger spout handy, to quickly extinguish any fire. But most important, check thoroughly after you've finished for smoldering sparks that could flare up hours later if left undetected. Work with both torch and scraper together, applying the flame and following right up with the scraper as you go. An electric heater, however, is quite efficient on small areas and presents less of a fire hazard.

Sanding of old, brittle paint on a large surface is tiring and tedious at best, even with the power sanders. These machines must be handled with care to avoid gouging and streaking the wood siding. The disk sander is designed primarily for use on metal surfaces such as automobile fenders, as the disk tends to form semi-circular markings across the wood grain. The belt sander cuts very rapidly; it must be kept moving to avoid under-cutting. If a long electric extension cord is needed, make sure the wires are of sufficient size.

After the old paint has been removed, the surface may show small dents, wood cracks, and other blemishes. These should be packed with wood filler compound, which is allowed to dry and sanded smooth, before proceeding with the painting.

Plaster Patching. Your redecorated room will look neat and brand-new if all wall blemishes—dents, cracks, and other imperfections—have been patched. Luckily, this is quite easy to do with plaster, known also as plaster of Paris. The plaster is very inexpensive and is sold at hardware and paint stores. A 5-pound bag will go a long way, and any remainder can be kept on hand for an indefinite time in a tightly sealed container.

Plaster sets up very fast, so mix small batches at a time, enough to be used in 10 minutes or so. Discard any plaster that has begun to set and stiffen; mix a new batch. However, if you're not yet adept at handling the plaster, the setting time can be slowed by adding about 10 percent lime. A prepared patching plaster containing the lime can be purchased instead.

Spackle plaster also is slow-setting, but can be applied only in shallow depth, about ¼ inch. You will do best using both types—the plain plaster of Paris or patching plaster to partly fill large holes or dents, the Spackle for final smoothing after the plaster base has hardened sufficiently.

Wall preparation usually involves the use of a scraper to smooth bumps and widen cracks, which creates a mess unless the drop cloths are in place and the plaster dust vacuumed quickly before it scatters around the house. Scrape the surface of fine hairline cracks to remove any projecting plaster; widen larger cracks with a pointed bever-

Patching plaster sets very quickly, so mix only small amounts at a time. Spackle is slow-setting. Add only enough water for a fairly stiff batter.

All but very fine hairline cracks must be widened for better grip of the plaster patch. Use a pointed beverage can opener or scraper.

Chief stage ir. preparation for painting is smoothing of any dents, cracks or nailheads, or other imperfections in the plaster wall. A quick stroke of the putty knife will fill small indentations.

age can opener or a triangular wall scraper; clean out the plaster dust with a vacuum hose or damp sponge.

Make the patch by picking up some of the wet plaster with the putty knife, turn the blade toward the wall and draw the flat of the blade along the crack, pressing down hard. Don't repeat by going back and forth—just once over and let it be, the blade scraping off all excess plaster. Most likely there will be "skips"; leave them and wait until the new plaster has hardened before repeating the stroke to fill in.

Larger Wall Patches. Larger wall openings in hollow walls, sometimes resulting from plumbing repairs or electrical line installations, will need backing for the patch. One way is to pack the hole with crumpled newspaper. The best means is with wire lath, cut with shears to somewhat

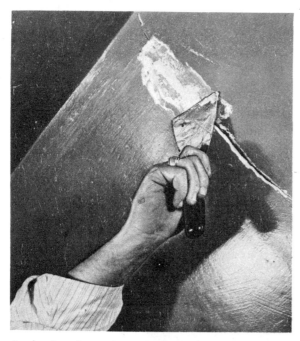

Apply the plaster in a single stroke, pressing hard to remove any residue. If crack is not completely filled, wait until plaster has set, repeat with the broad knife.

Another way to finish the plaster hard and smooth is to sponge it after it has set, but before plaster has fully hardened.

Use sandpaper on a wood block to cut down and smooth plaster bulge.

Large holes or openings in wall can be patched, but need backup for the plaster. Metal lath serves this purpose well. Cut with heavy shears, an inch or so larger than hole on each side.

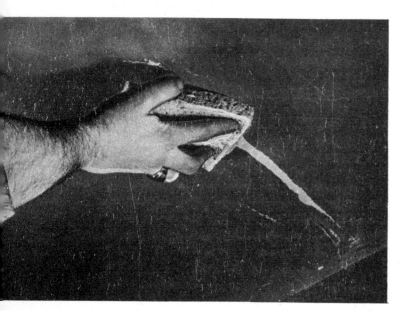

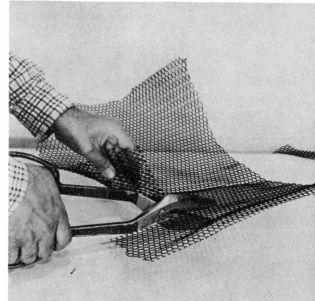

larger size than the opening. Undercut the edges of the opening slightly to slope inward for better grip of the plaster patch, fold the lath so it can be inserted behind the wall. Tied to a strip of wood across the wall exterior, the lath will be held in place until the new plaster has set.

The repair is done in two stages. Start with a plaster mixture containing one-third sand. Apply the batter with trowel or putty knife so it squeezes into the perforations of the lath, and spreads along the sides to grip the undercut edges of the opening. Do not fill the area completely: leave a depth

excess amount to harden on the surface. You may find it useful to work the wet plaster with a sponge until it is smooth and flush. A bit of practice will show you how much to apply and how to level it off so the wall is smooth as new.

Plaster also makes a quick, perfect, and permanent repair of damaged moldings, separated miter joints, and wood dents. An open space between

Lath is placed behind the wall, held in place by stick or dowel at the front of wall, to which it is tied with string.

Plaster is pressed into honeycomb of the lath, and against sides of the hole. When plaster has set, cut thread holding retainer stick.

of ¼ inch or so for final finishing with plaster or Spackle after the initial patch material has hardened. For this final step, if the area is quite large, use a long trowel, or a straight board that bridges the area, so the new plaster is smoothed perfectly flat. After the first plaster application hardens, cut away the retaining string. The lath should now be fully secured in place.

Plaster is an amazing substance—it is soft enough to scratch with a fingernail, but does not have the slightest "give," and is terribly difficult to sand or cut. So be watchful—don't leave an

the wall and base shoe molding is packed with plaster simply by running a fingertip along the wall joint. Plaster may be tinted, if desired, by mixing dry color pigment with white lead, then stirring into the plaster batter. Never paint directly over a new plastic patch. Allow thorough drying, then apply a coat of primer or shellac. Large repairs should be allowed to dry out for 4 to 6 weeks.

Scarred Walls. What about a badly scarred wall or ceiling that shows the uneven remnants of old paint jobs and poorly patched cracks? This condition, quite common in older homes, may require radical measures for successful redecorating.

An effective solution is to apply an underlayment lining that forms a new, smooth base for paint or wallpaper. Canvas or burlap may be pasted to the old wall to smooth out the imperfections, then painted after receiving a coat of primer. Also suitable is a heavier material like Sanitas, a vinyl-coated fabric available in special weights, that provides a smooth base for painting. The Sanitas actually reinforces the wall to retard further cracking.

A badly crumbled plaster wall can be resurfaced with gypsum wallboard panels, cemented directly over the old wall, the panel joints covered with tape and spackled for a smooth, continuous surface. A similar solution may be applied to plasterboard panels that have "popped" through their nails, each panel showing separately. Nail down the old panels tightly and securely, then cover with new gypsum board panels placed in the opposite direction (horizontal, if the original ones are vertical), using contact cement for the adhesive.

Ceilings that are badly scarred may be finished attractively with acoustical ceiling tiles, cemented directly to the old ceiling or stapled to furring strips that are nailed to the ceiling. An alternative may be the suspended ceiling system developed by Armstrong, in which translucent plastic panels are supported on special framing members.

Exterior conditions, such as cracked or softened window sills and fascia boards, may be patched with a waterproof fiberglass membrane, such as Tuff-Kote, cemented into place and carefully caulked at the edges. A more effective method is to encase damaged exterior trim with enameled aluminum siding accessories, eliminating need for further maintenance except for annual caulking of the joints.

ROLLER PAINTING

Rollers are easier to use than a brush and cover larger areas more quickly. As mentioned before, an extension pole attached to the roller handle permits you to work comfortably from the floor while reaching the ceiling or high on the walls. This will greatly reduce the need for shifting a ladder around, although the stepladder still will be needed for painting the edge strips.

Start by painting a strip several inches wide at the ceiling line, using a narrow brush or pad applicator. The roller cannot properly reach into the wall corners, but the prepainted strips will be neatly overlapped by the roller. The vertical wall corners (both sides of the corner) and the edge along the baseboard also must be stripped in.

Paint rollers cannot reach fully into corners, so edges are painted first with a brush, along the ceiling line if only ceiling is to be done, at the wall corners and along door and window frames if wall is to be painted.

Using the Roller. Pour paint to about half the depth of the tray reservoir section. Clip the tray securely onto the stepladder platform, or place it on the floor out of the way if you're using an extension pole. Run the roller into the paint reservoir, then roll it back and forth on the incline to remove excess paint that would drip. Reload the roller frequently rather than trying to cover as much surface as possible each time. Roll the wall surface from two directions, the second stroke crisscrossing the first. No need to press hard on the roller—easy does it, if the roller is kept well loaded with paint. Nor need you be concerned about variations in paint density—latex paint will have a uniform appearance when dry if sufficient paint has been applied, and any uneven spots can be touched up as needed.

Some hints for roller usage: keep the roller turning, don't drag or twist it across the surface, as that will cause variations in the texture. Raise the loaded roller to wall or ceiling with a smooth action; avoid jerky motions that cause splattering. Also, when using the roller pole, keep the paint tray on the floor in a safe position where you are not likely to kick it or knock it over. The latter applies also to the paint can—as soon as paint is

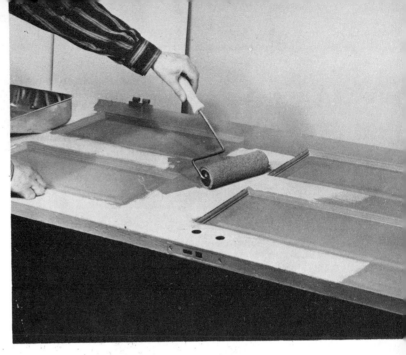

Door panels can be painted with a roller, too, but narrow roller is needed to fit into the panel sections.

Keep the roller always loaded with paint, rather than trying to eke out last bit of paint coverage with each dipping.

Paint pan should be of right size for roller, so it doesn't bind at the sides. Pour enough paint to fill the deeper well section of the pan.

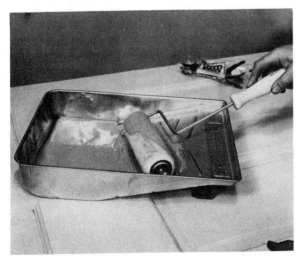

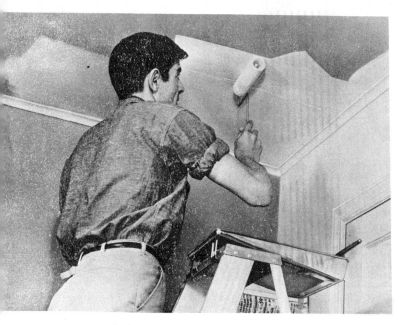

Ceiling may be painted close up by standing on the ladder, but that means constant shifting. A long pole on the roller handle makes it possible to do the painting from the floor. Be careful about placing the pan with paint so it won't spill.

Using a pole simplifies painting a ceiling with a roller.

poured, cover the can and place it safely in a corner. Tipping over a paint can would cause an awful mess. When the roller becomes sticky and difficult to use, it is likely that paint has begun to harden inside the handle core. Rinsing the roller and handle in water will give you a fresh start.

BRUSH PAINTING

The secret of brush painting is how the paint is carried to the wall. Dip the brush only a third of its length into the paint, stroke the end of the brush against the rim of the pail to wipe off excess paint, then quickly bring the brush up and place a dab of paint onto the wall. The object is to carry a good quantity of paint each time without splattering. You will find it helpful to keep the paint pail close by, and to develop the smooth swing that carries the loaded brush across, bristle

Load the brush by dipping the lower third of the bristle length into the paint, wipe off excess against the side of the can, then quickly dab the tip of the brush onto the wall. Keep the can as close as possible to avoid splatters.

end upmost. It is not necessary to wipe the brush so firmly that little paint remains; on the contrary, the brush should be quite well loaded, the wiping action removing only excess that cannot be held by the bristles. With latex paint, particularly, the well-loaded brush is easier to handle, provides greater coverage with each stroke. You'll do best by first brushing out the paint for a thin coat, then with a loaded brush flow the paint more heavily for a uniformly finished surface.

Latex paint offers the very great advantage that it can be blended. Thus, you can go back and touch up any spots that are not uniformly coated, even after the original paint has dried, without leaving a tell-tale mark.

The quickest and neatest way to paint is with a Speed Brush consisting of a foam pad with hundreds of tiny nylon bristles. The flat "brush" can be used on any type of surface.

Masking tape speeds painting of door and sash mullions. Remove tape after paint has dried, but not hardened. When applying tape, press hard along the edges so paint won't seep underneath.

WASHUP OF ROLLERS AND BRUSHES

Latex paint washes off with water, but it's not enough just to run the water a while over the roller and brushes. Remove the roller cover from its core, squeeze and work the nap and brush bristles in the water, then wash thoroughly with sudsy soap or detergent. If this latter stage is neglected, the roller nap will mat down, the brush bristles become hardened at the ferrule. Do a good job of cleaning up, including the paint pan, roller handle, and all other materials that have been used, even the drop cloths and any streaks left on the ladder. It will be more pleasant to use the

Wash roller under the faucet with warm water, use soap or detergent for total removal of paint. Don't count on just soaking in pan of water, as some paint will remain and harden.

equipment next time if it isn't streaked with paint.

MASONRY PAINTING

A coat of colorful paint on the drab foundation walls instantly converts your basement into a bright and pleasant living space for a family recreation room and other purposes. Paint the floor also (unless you plan to install a vinyl tile surface) to eliminate the annoying concrete dust, retard condensation, and make the surface smoother and easier to keep clean.

The exposed portion of an exterior foundation wall, when painted, has a neater appearance and

greater resistance to moisture penetration, spalling, and mildew. A coat of dark gray paint will magically improve a depressingly drab concrete retaining wall. Patios are cleaner, smoother, less likely to crack when kept well painted. And it's quite easy to perk up a brick wall with an attractive color, of which light green and pale yel-

Special rollers with longer nap speed painting of brick walls and other masonry surfaces, reaching into the rough and irregular areas for a uniform finish.

low are current favorites, as a welcome alternative to an unbroken line of red brick houses. In many countries of northern Europe, the masonry walls of all buildings are kept painted for both coloring and as a preservative against the weather.

But if you've ever noticed a house whose painted brick walls had become splotched with scaling paint, or a basement floor scarred with unevenly abraded and peeling paint, you will appreciate the two essentials for satisfactory masonry painting: good adhesion through adequate surface preparation, and the use of the right paint for the job.

Good adhesion may require nothing more than a clean surface, if the floor or wall is presently painted and the existing paint is sound and well-bonded. A proper scrubbing to remove wax and dirt usually will suffice before repainting. There are, however, several additional details that may require attention.

First, check whether any sections of the original paint are still glossy because they were sheltered from weathering or out of traffic range. These areas should be sanded to cut the gloss, or treated wtih a chemical deglosser like Wil-Bond, PPG Surface Conditioner—or just washing with TSP detergent may be sufficient in some cases. Any mildew, which would soon cause the new paint to break down, must be removed by scrubbing with household bleach and detergent. Do this immediately before repainting to prevent regrowth of the mildew spores.

Another difficulty may be encountered with a wall that is coated with cement paint, which isn't really a paint but rather finely ground portland cement with color pigments. This does not provide a sufficient base to hold a new coat of paint, and therefore must be completely removed. Fortunately, the cement paint is extremely brittle and can be removed by vigorous scraping with a wire brush. Be sure to clean off every trace of the paint, down to the raw concrete.

Mild chalking generally can be brushed down sufficiently so that the paint can adhere to a sound substrate. Moderate to heavy chalking, however, will require a surface conditioner or a primer coat of thinned finish paint.

Cleaning Streaked Walls. Efflorescence, the whitish streaks often seen on brick and other masonry walls, is caused by mineral salts leeching through the masonry. It would be a mistake to paint over the streaks, as the salty powder does not provide an adequate bond for the paint, and peeling will result. If the efflorescence cannot be completely removed with a wire brush, wash with muriatic acid, which will serve also to etch the surface slightly.

Unpainted concrete should be acid-etched to assure better adhesion of the paint and help neutralize the destructive action of the alkali in the concrete. Acid etching is particularly recommended for basement floors, decks, patios, steps, stoops, walks, and garage floors, which are subject to underfoot abrasion.

Acid Etching. Use a solution of 1 part muriatic acid to 3 parts of water. Always pour the acid into the water to prevent dangerous splattering. The gallon of solution will be sufficient for an area of 100 square feet—a floor 20 by 20 feet will take 4 gallons. The solution can best be prepared in a glass gallon jug, using a plastic funnel. Pour 3 quarts of water into the jug, then add the acid slowly. Handle carefully, wear rubber gloves and boots, heavy old clothing, and eye goggles. If any acid is spilled on the skin, rinse immediately with plenty of clear water. Spread the solution on the floor, allow to stand until it stops bubbling, then flush thoroughly with water. This may create a problem in a basement if there is no floor drain. The only way then is to mop up the water or use a suction pump. When the floor has dried, proceed with painting.

Masonry Sealers and Undercoaters. Transparent liquid sealers are used primarily as a moisture barrier on unpainted masonry walls. But they contribute another value—without the sealer, the brick or concrete would literally sop up the paint, and instead of getting 400 square feet of coverage per gallon, you would have to use double the amount of paint. Transparent liquid sealers like PPG Cementhide Masonry Sealer and Varathane Plastic Sealer provide a sound base for finish coats. Apply with a brush or spray, not with a roller, in sufficient quantity to assure full penetration and binding of any chalky layer; allow at least overnight for complete drying before putting on the finish coat.

Previously painted surfaces in sound condition may be primed with a thinned coat of the same paint that will be used for the finish coat. Generally, it is advisable to use an undercoater that is designated by the same manufacturer for compatibility with the finish coat.

Masonry Floors. Latex floor paints are a good choice for exterior masonry floors that are weather-protected, as in covered breezeways, roofed patios and decks. Where moisture conditions may be more extreme, on open patios, concrete steps, and walks, use a solvent-thinned rubber-base floor enamel like PPG Florhide No. 3. Apply in two coats, the first one thinned with one pint of solvent to a gallon of enamel; follow with the full-strength finish coat after allowing about 8 hours to dry. Exterior oil point also has good abrasion qualities but will not stand up as well to alkaline and moisture conditions.

Concrete Walls, Brick and Stucco. Regular latex house paint is suitable for both exterior and interior masonry walls, and can easily be applied with a roller. It is durable and won't blister even when the wall is damp. Solvent-thinned rubber-base paints (not latex) are also suitable, but must be applied over only dry walls.

Unpainted walls, or those on which the paint is badly worn or excessively chalky, should be given a sealer coat, such as PPG Cementhide No. 37-40, or other bonding primer, to provide a sound base for the finish coat.

Asbestos-Cement Shingles. Sometimes called mineral wool, these shingles are made of compressed portland cement and asbestos fibers, surfaced with a vinyl acrylic enamel and a water-repelling glaze. The factory-applied coating can provide satisfactory service for a decade and even much longer, but eventually these shingles will need repainting. Incorrect paint will result in messy scaling and mildewing.

The chief problem with painting the shingles is the alkali content, but there are additional characteristics that will determine the correct approach for refinishing. After the surface coating has weathered, the shingles tend to absorb and retain moisture, which favors the growth of mildew. The oil paints formerly used on the shingles broke down and caused unsightly scaling. Now latex paints overcome the problem.

Asbestos cement shingles should not be re-painted until they have weathered at least six months to roughen the glaze. Remove dirt and grease with a detergent. With a wire brush, remove any chalked, scaling, or peeling paint. Eliminate mildew stains completely. Apply a coat of latex bonding primer; finish with latex house paint.

Painting the shingles may be done with a brush or roller, but spraying is most effective. Painting should be done at temperatures above 50 degrees.

WALLCOVERINGS

The new wallcoverings are very much a part of today's scene, brightening the home with splashes of lively colors in bold, traditional, even exotic patterns that are more decorative and interesting than the old-time wallpapers. Imaginative use of the floral, geometric, symbolic, and other designs will create the sparkingly beautiful rooms you've always wanted.

Although considerably more expensive than wallpaper, the vinyl materials are tougher, longer lasting, smoother, more soil-resistant, and fully washable. The vinyl coating produces cleaner colors and brighter patterns than we have known in wallpapers. There also are very attractive designs in flocks, metallic foils, tissue-thin natural cork, sand-textures, and other types that lend themselves to innovative wall treatment. The colors retain their fresh appearance for years.

Methods Changed. Patience and adequate preparation are, as with painting, the chief requirements for successful wallpapering. The technique for hanging the new wallcoverings varies somewhat from that for the old wallpaper, one main difference being the type of paste used, and even here, the pre-pasted types eliminate the pasting step. Most homeowners and apartment residents have, at one time or another, done some wallpapering, and they can tackle the vinyls with full assurance. The proof is that fully 60 percent of all wallcoverings are sold directly to the user for do-it-yourself installations.

The most widely used wallcoverings are the

WHAT YOU NEED FOR PAPERHANGING

Tools and supplies needed for every paperhanging job are: a long table, preferably a portable paperhanger's table that can be rented for the day, a stepladder, plumb line and chalk, straightedge ruler, recommended paste, paste brush and bucket, cleanup sponge in bowl of water, smoothing brush, seam roller, razor blades, screwdriver for removing switch and outlet plates, and a sufficient rollage of the wallcovering. Kraft paper or a batch of old newspapers for covering the table after each strip is pasted will help keep the work clean.

"unsupported" vinyls, which have a non-woven paper backing (in contrast to wallpaper with a thin vinyl coating). The pre-pasted wallcoverings are in this group. Vinyls backed with woven textiles are heavier and somewhat more difficult to apply, but offer advantages in reinforcing plaster walls and providing a more durable surface. The foils, flocks, and "grass cloths" are more delicate, requiring special handling.

SCHEDULE FOR WALLPAPERING APPLICATION

The stages in wallcovering application are: cutting wall-length strips, each matched to the pattern; dropping a plumb bob to guide alignment of the first strip on each wall; applying the paste; hanging and butting the strips; cutting clearance for electric outlets; smoothing and sponging the surface, and finally trimming the ends.

An important detail is the method of turning corners. Strips are never folded around corners; they would soon buckle. Instead, the turn is made with only ½ inch width, the next strip on the side wall overlaps that narrow foldover, whether an inside or outside corner. Use the plumb bob to align the first strip on each wall; otherwise the paper may end up somewhat tilted.

Allow ample time, especially if this is your first wallcovering job. Unless the room is in almost new condition, you will want to repaint the ceiling, moldings, doors, and closet interiors before wallpapering. For a room that is in very good shape, with walls that require no preparation, the papering can be done in a single day, including the necessary cleanup time. Experience will, of course, enable you to speed up the work so that other rooms may be done in shorter time.

The wallpapering stages should proceed in the following order:

1. Remove old wallpaper and clear the room.
2. Patch damaged walls.
3. Paint ceiling and woodwork.
4. Measure for quantity of wallpaper.
5. Assemble tools and supplies.

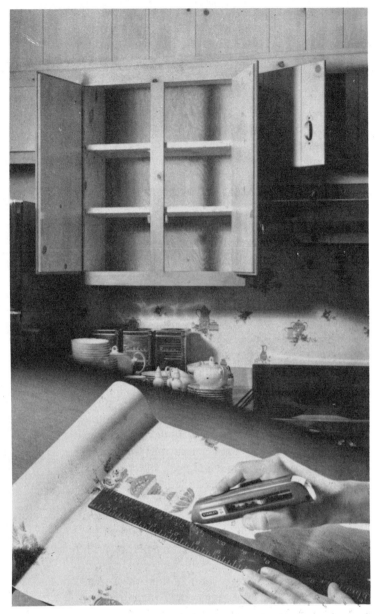

When a strip must be sliced to fit space at the end of a wall, use a straightedge and sharp blade, or fold it over on measured line and use scissors.

6. Drop plumb line for first strip.
7. Cut strips and apply paste.
8. Hang first strip.
9. Trim ends; roll the seams.

10. Continue with the other strips, butting the edges and matching the pattern.
11. Cutouts and fitting at doors and windows.
12. Cut bubbles, wash off excess paste, smooth.
13. Clean the tools.

WALLPAPERING TOOLS

Paste applicator (pad or brush) and pail
Scissors, double-edge razor blades
Water bucket and clean, soft rags
Plumb bob and line
Smoothing brush
Seam roller
6-foot folding rule or steel tape
Pasting table (at least 8 feet long, 2 feet wide)

REMOVING OLD WALLPAPER

In a presently wallpapered room, your best assurance of a satisfactory redecoration is to start at the beginning—that is, strip off all old wallpaper for a perfectly smooth base. You may, of course, apply the new wallcovering over the old, but do this only if there are no more than two layers, all tightly pasted down, without blisters or peeling, the seams neatly butted rather than overlapped. But there are several good reasons for removing all old paper even though it meets the above requirements. The new wallcovering is a good bit heavier than most old papers and may drag the old paper off the wall; the special pastes used on vinyl wallpaper may not be compatible with the previous paper, therefore preventing a strong bond. And any mildew on the old paper will eventually attack the new wallcovering. Stripping the wall down to the raw plaster and patching where necessary will make possible the most attractive result.

The quickest way to remove the old paper is with an electric steamer, which can be rented from any hardware store for a few dollars a day—enough time to do a couple of rooms. It's portable—small enough to fit into the trunk of a car. The alternative of soaking with water is a slow, tedious

Wallpaper steamer is heated by house electricity. Start with boiling water in the tank to reduce heatup time.

job, and dripping water may cause extensive damage to a wood floor.

Textile-backed and vinyl-coated papers are easier to remove. Just release a corner of each strip, preferably at the top, and pull the strip gently off the wall, all in one piece. Some vinyl-backed papers are different; only the plastic surface skins off, leaving a fine paper backing which can serve as a suitable base for the new paper; however, if this paper backing is roughened or uneven so that it does not provide a completely uniform base, it should be removed by soaking and scraping.

A coat of glue sizing is recommended by most wallcovering manufacturers, particularly over enamel paint, plasterboard, and vinyl-coated walls. The sizing, in powdered form that is mixed with water, is very quickly applied with a wide brush or a roller.

The electric wallpaper steamer removes layers of old paper quickly, is simple enough to operate and has a safety relief valve. Just make sure there is enough water in the tank at all times. When starting, fill with boiling water to save heating up time. A large metal plate, linked by a hose, delivers the steam—just hold the plate flat against the wall, squeeze the trigger for a moment to release a shot of steam, then move to the next spot. The old paper will loosen and curl off the wall, so it can be removed in strips with a putty knife. Be sure to cover the floor with lots of newspapers to catch paper flakes which otherwise will stick stubbornly when dry.

When the job is finished, go over the wall with a putty knife to scrape away any paper particles that remain. If there were many old layers piled

Trigger on plate releases steam into area confined by the plate, rapidly softens the wallpaper paste. Large area is completed quickly.

onto the wall, steaming may take longer but will remove all layers. Some coated papers must be scratched slightly with a vegetable grater or similar tool to let the steam moisture penetrate.

Broad knife scrapes paper specks as large strips curl off the wall. Keep carton handy for disposing of the scraps.

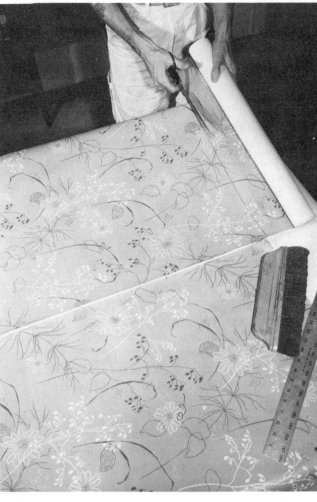

Allow an excess of several inches top and bottom of each strip for adjustment and trimming. Match the pattern of each strip exactly before cutting.

HOW MUCH PAPER?

The standard single roll covers approximately 30 square feet; this is true whatever the width of the paper, which may range from 18 to 24 inches. Some rolls are 15 feet long, others 18, 21, or 24, depending on width of the paper. A single roll of 15 linear feet provides for only one full-length strip, as the wall is at least 8 feet high, and a few extra inches must be allowed, top and bottom, for trimming. A considerable waste thus is avoided if you use double or triple rolls, giving you the flexibility of greater length. Remember that pattern matching will cause a certain amount of waste in any case, especially when the pattern figures are large. It is important to note the repeat of the pattern when cutting your strips to match.

Most manufacturers trim off the "selvage" edge on each side, eliminating a troublesome task and permitting the strips to be butted edge to edge. If the wallcovering comes wtih its selvage, your dealer most likely has an automatic trimmer and possibly will do the cutting without extra charge.

You can't estimate exactly the amount of paper necessary, so it is better to order an extra roll or two. Most dealers will accept return of unopened rolls, making a charge of 10 percent or so for handling. Check to see that all the rolls have the same lot number, so there is no variance in the colors.

Single rolls of wallpaper contain material to cover 30 square feet of area, double rolls contain twice that amount of material in a continuous length, thus reducing waste. Triple lengths also are available and may permit considerable savings particularly when doing high stairwell walls.

Estimated Rollage

Ceiling Height	8 Feet	9 Feet	10 Feet	Single Rolls Needed for Ceiling
Size of Room	SINGLE ROLLS			
8 x 10	9	10	11	3
10 x 10	10	11	13	4
10 x 12	11	12	14	4
10 x 14	12	14	15	5
12 x 12	12	14	15	5
12 x 14	13	15	16	6
12 x 16	14	16	17	6
12 x 18	15	17	19	7
12 x 20	16	18	20	8
14 x 14	14	16	17	7
14 x 16	15	17	19	7
14 x 18	16	18	20	8
14 x 20	17	19	21	9
14 x 22	18	20	22	10
16 x 16	16	18	20	8
16 x 18	17	19	21	9
16 x 20	18	20	22	10
16 x 22	19	21	23	11
16 x 24	20	22	25	12
18 x 18	18	20	22	11
18 x 20	19	21	23	12
18 x 22	20	22	25	12
18 x 24	21	23	26	14

Single rolls of wallpaper contain material to cover 30 square feet of area, double rolls contain twice that amount of material in a continuous length, thus reducing waste. Triple lengths also are available and may permit considerable savings particularly when doing high stairwell walls.

WALLCOVERING PASTES

Special Paste Needed. The economical old-time wheat pastes are still used, but the newer vinyls, flocks, foils, and the heavier textile-backed wallcoverings require extra-strength adhesives, otherwise the strips might peel off. Special pastes are available, including cellulose powders that are mixed with cold water. Heavy pre-mixed paste, sold in quart and gallon cans, is quite expensive. On the other hand, the Wallclad No. 7 paste, which is recommended for Sanitas and Wallclad and similar materials, costs very little, a 1-pound package being enough for five double rolls.

Other pastes include Rex, product of Patent

The thicker pastes used with modern wallcoverings are difficult to spread with the old-time bristle brush. New pad brush speeds the pasting, produces better coverage.

Cereals Company, Glutoline 77 powdered adhesive (in which lumps in the mixture disappear after a 15-minute wait), GT-12 and GT-22 by General Tire Company, and Jellitac, Defiance, and Red Stave brands.

The thick, creamy prepared mixes are difficult to spread with the standard brush. An improved applicator is the 7-inch-wide, pad type paste brush, by Product Development and Manufacturing Company, which spreads the paste more easily and permits better control, especially at the edges.

It's a good idea to add a small amount of Lysol to the paste as a mildew inhibitor.

Applying the Paste. Cover the worktable with kraft paper (newspaper can be used us you're not concerned about soiling the wallcovering with newsprint). Place the strip pattern side down. Apply paste generously, making sure the entire surface is uniformly covered, particularly the edges, then fold over the top quarter of the strip length onto the pasted side, preventing premature drying of the paste. Do the same with the lower end, but be careful not to crease the paper at the folds. Allow the paste to soak into the backing for about 5 minutes. Turn over the kraft paper or cover the table with fresh paper for each strip, so that the previous paste will not smear the face of the wallcovering.

PLUMB ALIGNMENT

Before starting the first strip, measure a distance on the wall from a corner about ½ inch shorter than the width of the paper, drive a small nail or tack at that point near the ceiling from which to drop the plumb line. Mark the position of the plumb line along the wall—this will be easier if you chalk the string and snap the line, but be sure that the line remains perfectly plumb by holding the bob in correct position firmly against the wall.

Carry the strip up the ladder. With the right hand free the top quarter of the strip and place it carefully on the wall so that the edge follows the plumb line, or butts uniformly against the

preceding strip. Smooth the paper lightly so it clings, then lower the next quarter length and smooth it out. Now open and ease down the remainder. If the paper is not in proper position start the adjustment at the lower section, then lift the top part off the wall sufficiently to shift it into line. The narrow edge that turns the corner is smoothed into place. When two strips are joined, the pattern must be matched exactly, and

Each wall is plumbed so the strips hang correctly. Plumb line may be chalked and snapped, or its positions marked with pencil to guide the strips.

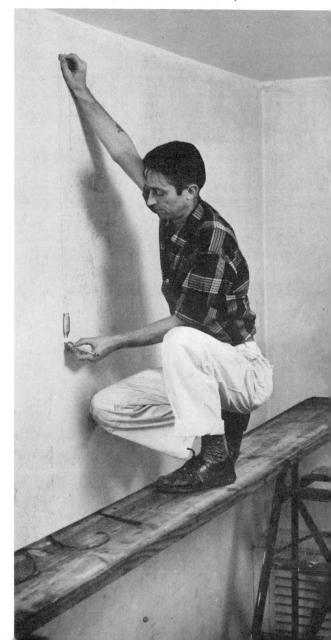

squeezed-out paste with a damp sponge before it dries.

Overlapping of the strip edges is easier, but of course will result in bulges and will not be as pleasing, also the pattern figures will not coincide properly.

TRIMMING

Long sharp scissors and a batch of new double-edge razor blades are needed for trimming at the ceiling line, baseboard, and around doors and windows. This is a critical part of the work, and preferences as to method vary; some get better results using only the blades; others find the scissors more accurate. Most likely you'll find the razor blade best for thin wallpaper, while heavier wallcoverings, such as Sanitas, are trimmed more precisely with scissors.

The following method is recommended: run

Pasted strip is unfolded, edges aligned with the plumb markings, then brushed out to eliminate wrinkles and air pockets.

Trimming is done by running tip of scissors blade along the ceiling or base molding to indent the paper, then cutting with the scissors along the crease. Another way is to run razor blade carefully along the molding edge.

the edges butted neatly the entire length—it won't do to stretch the vinyl paper to meet, as it will shrink back again.

When the material is in proper position, use the smoothing brush to work out any air pockets, but don't worry about small bubbles. Use the seam roller on the butted joint; wipe off all

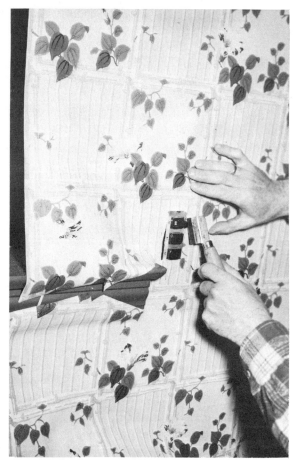

Paste the paper completely over electric switches and receptacles, then slice with razor blade. Opening will be covered by the switch plate.

(Right) High wall at stairwell requires setting up of a trestle, which can consist of a stout plank. One end rests on ladder step, the other end is placed in the stair landing or railing, as needed.

Ceiling application requires two persons. Paste is applied directly to the ceiling, the paper smoothed with a brush as it is unrolled so it clings to the ceiling.

the point of the scissors along the ceiling corner or baseboard edge, lightly creasing the paper. Pull the paper away from the wall and with the scissors, cut along the creased line—but a bit toward the outside of the crease rather than exactly on it. When the paper is brushed back, it should fit neatly, but any visible excess can be trimmed neatly with a sharp blade, pressed firmly into the paper.

Here's a hint for neat trimming at openings such as electrical fittings or switches. Paste the paper right over the openings. Make the cutouts later by crisscrossing to form an X, then trim to size but keep the cutaway area smaller than the

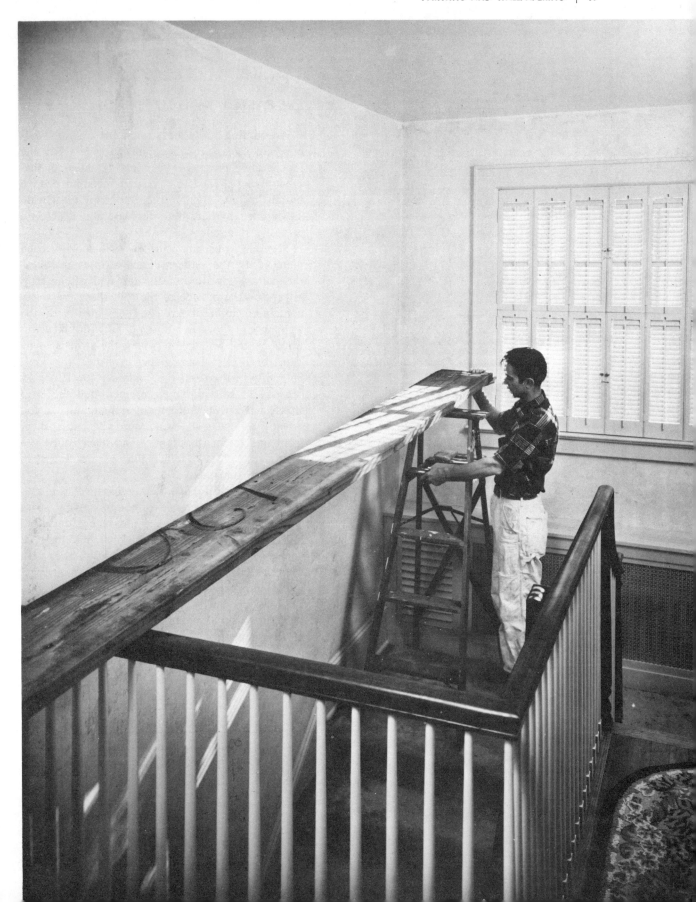

Strips must be supported to prevent slipping off the ceiling while the ends are being trimmed. A broom covered with a towel is used here.

sufficient section to clear the fixture. The two lower segments of the strip then are butted together and will fit neatly.

PRE-PASTED WALLCOVERINGS

Accounting for almost one-fourth of all wall-covering sales, pre-pasted materials simplify the redecorating process by eliminating one step, that of applying the paste. You still need to drop a plumb line for aligning the first strips on a wall, as outlined earlier, but otherwise the procedure is vastly different.

Several strips are cut to wall length, each matched to the pattern. Each strip is re-rolled, the pattern inward but the top end of the strip always on the outside of the roll. Place the water container (a cardboard box obtained with the wallpaper), about two-thirds filled with lukewarm water, at the wall below where the strip is to be hung, on a pile of newspaper to protect the floor. Submerge one roll in the container for 10 to 15 seconds to soften the paste, then pull the strip slowly upward its full length, and smooth the top directly on the wall. Make sure the entire strip, front and back, is wet; if it had been rolled too tightly, there's the chance that part of the strip may have remained dry.

Butt the strip edge neatly along the plumb line or against the edge of the preceding strip. You have 15 minutes to do this before the paste dries. Smooth out any air pockets, but don't be concerned about tiny air bubbles, as they will dry out. Press the seams down with a wet sponge, but do not use a seam roller. Trim the ends.

Move the water container along the wall as you continue with each strip, together with the pad of newspaper to protect the floor from dripping water. Check back on previous strips as you progress to see that they are fully attached before the paste dries.

covering switchplate. At wall fixture boxes, hang the strip all the way down, then slice the strip up from the floor to the fixture; cut away a

(Right) Neat and trim! Freshly redecorated with wall-covering in sparkling daisy motif, room is as bright as the great outdoors, but with a homey feeling. Pattern is Flamboyant, by Sanitas.

5. ELECTRICAL PROBLEMS

In addition to your lights, electricity powers or controls your heating plant, refrigerator, freezer, air conditioner, washing machine and dryer—in fact all your appliances, and in many homes, the cook stove and even the water supply. Any interruption of service causes extensive disruption. Little can be done when the power is cut off temporarily by a storm or generator breakdown, unless you have a stand-by emergency power plant, but most other electrical difficulties can be avoided by the homeowner who is knowledgeable about the proper use and maintenance of the equipment.

Electricity enters the home through large service wires which go through the meter into a metal panel called the circuit box. There the power is divided into branch circuits of smaller (thinner) wires which have lower current capacity. These circuits are distributed to various parts of the house, or connected directly to certain items of equipment like the furnace, which require individual lines.

Each circuit has its own protective fuse or circuit breaker, selected to match the capacity of that particular wiring. Circuits with 15-ampere fuses have a capacity of 1,800 watts, are intended only for lighting and small plug-in appliances. A 20-ampere circuit for plug-in appliances, or the refrigerator and freezer, has heavier no. 12 wiring to supply 2,400 watts on a 2-wire circuit,

Typical panel boxes with fuses or breakers for branch circuits, and the main cutoff switch. The 30-ampere service, now archaic, was intended only for lighting and small appliances like a fan; a 60-ampere service permits more convenience receptacles and appliance circuits of heavier wiring, but may become overloaded by high-wattage air conditioners and other equipment. A 100-ampere service is usually adequate for present-day requirements.

ELECTRIC SERVICE PANELS

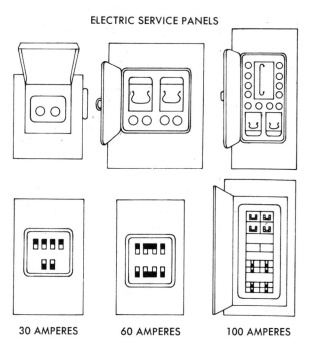

30 AMPERES   60 AMPERES   100 AMPERES

or 4,800 watts on a 3-wire circuit (the latter is really two 20-ampere circuits having a common ground or neutral wire). Still heavier wires on circuits with 30-ampere fuses are for electric ranges and dryers, have a special receptacle so that smaller appliances cannot be plugged into it.

FUSES

Why Fuses Blow. A short circuit, or an overload that occurs when too much current is being drawn by an excess of appliances, heats up the wires all the way to the circuit box and almost instantly melts the thermal strip in the fuse or trips the circuit breaker to shut off the current. If there were no fuse, the wire insulation would burn off and sparking could start a fire inside the walls.

For example, when a toaster and hand iron are being used at the same time and a broiler or casserole is plugged into the same circuit, the current drawn by this combination exceeds the circuit's capacity, and the fuse blows. However, if there were outlets of an additional appliance

circuit in that room, thoughtful distribution of the electrical load would prevent such an occurrence. Sometimes the outlets of a second circuit are overlooked because they are not conveniently located, but it is not too difficult to relocate these outlets to accessible positions. This is a project that should be tackled only by persons who have acquired some skill in electrical wiring and who live in areas where local codes permit homeowner installations. In all electrical work, the requirements of the National Electrical Code must be observed to avoid fire hazards.

Receptacles can be relocated for greater convenience, and to provide additional plug-in facilities. Special heavy cable and quick-connect devices are part of General Electric's surface equipment that helps solve a widely existing problem.

The "octopus" wall outlet is a source of trouble, often results in overloads and blown fuses. Additional circuits with more outlets are needed. Lamp cords are of lightweight wire, should be used only in short lengths.

Shifting of receptacle positions, or adding receptacles to a circuit so that appliances can remain plugged in, is done most easily with surface cable wiring, which was introduced by General Electric. The heavy plastic cable connects to the various devices by spring tension, eliminating terminal screws.

If blown fuses occur frequently on various circuits you obviously need additional circuit wiring from the fuse panel—but that raises the question whether your house service can provide

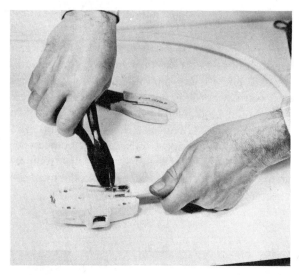

Plastic junction connector has spring contactors; wires are stripped to length designated on case, then simply pushed into the feed openings. Surface devices include switches, lamp sockets, receptacles, and plug-in connectors.

for extra circuits. The typical 60-ampere service in older homes is not large enough to supply current for today's appliances. The best solution is to have the utility company increase the service wiring to 100 or 150 amperes.

Delayed Action Fuses. Some tools and appliances cause fuses to blow because their motors draw a heavy surge of current momentarily when they start, as when an air conditioner compressor is switched on. Delayed action fuses allowing for this momentary high current drain should be used on circuits for bench saws with powerful motors, washing machines for the start of the spin cycle, air conditioners, and refrigerators. In fact, some local regulations require that all fuses be of the delayed trip type. Never switch the size of a fuse, however, to accomplish the purpose of a "slow-blow" fuse.

Circuit Chart. Having a permanent chart, numbered to match all outlets and lights with their fuse positions, will be very helpful when you have to

locate a fuse for replacement, or to disconnect a circuit temporarily for a repair.

It's quite easy to trace the circuit links when all switches and outlets are in working order. Draw a chart on cardboard with as many boxes as there are fuses. With someone watching the lights, start at any room, tripping or loosening the fuses one by one until a shout lets you know that you've located the correct one. Check each receptacle in the same way by plugging in a drop light or lamp. List the locations on the chart, continuing until you have identified the fuse for each receptacle and light. Keep in mind that every room is served by at least two circuits as required by the National Code, so check each outlet individually. Identify also the fuses for the heating plant and air conditioner, which have their own circuits on direct hookups. Tack up the fuse chart near the circuit box so it will be handy for reference.

Finding a Short. Suppose a fuse blows and you replace it, but the fuse blows again and again. Obviously there's a short somewhere, and you will have to find its source to correct the condition in order to use any part of that circuit again. First, unplug all appliances and lamps from that circuit (if you've made the fuse chart you will know all the outlets and switches on that circuit; otherwise you will have to unplug every possible appliance). It won't be necessary to turn off any lights as obviously they're not on the unfused circuit.

Remove the blown fuse and turn a 100-watt frosted bulb into that fuse socket. If the bulb lights, the short is in the circuit wiring itself; most likely within some switch or outlet box where frayed insulation or a loosened splice allows the hot wire to touch the metal box.

If the bulb does not glow, the fault is with one of the disconnected appliances, since the bulb lights up only when current is flowing through the shorted circuit. Have someone watch the bulb in the fuse box, while you flip the switch for each ceiling or wall lamp, one by one. If there's still no result, remove the bulb and replace with a fuse of the correct original size, since the culprit is most likely one of the appliances that had been plugged into the circuit. These should not be tested with the light bulb as the current drain may be rather high and cause excessive overheating of the wires. Instead, check the appliances for shorts with an ohmmeter or Amprobe, if you have one. Lacking this instrument, use up another fuse by plugging in the appliances one by one—the one that shorts out should be immediately disconnected and not used until it has been repaired.

TESTERS

A simple device you can use for testing electrical continuity is a lamp socket with two 6-inch wires, the tips of which are stripped of insulation to form probes, and a 15-watt bulb. For safety and resistance to damage when dropped, the socket should be of rubber, such as the ones used for exterior lighting. The tester is used by touching the exposed wire probes to the electrical terminals of an appliance, for example; if the lamp glows, there definitely is current. You can also find which is the hot side of a receptacle by inserting one tester probe into either slot, and touching the other wire to the outlet plate—if the lamp does not light, it is the ground side; if the lamp lights with the probe in the opposite slot, that is the hot side, linked to the brass "positive" terminal of the receptacle. The tester also can be used to check whether the right fuse has been pulled before working on a circuit device.

A neon tester is similar, but smaller, safer, and more dependable, as the neon lamp and its resister are encased in plastic. Both testers will work only on 120-volt lines, however, so cannot be used to check low-voltage installations such as a doorbell.

A more complex tester is the combination ohmmeter, voltmeter, and ammeter called Amprobe. This device is invaluable for tracing shorts and grounds, testing for variances in voltage, and locating excess current that can destroy wiring and start fires. The instrument has its own battery to supply current; appliances thus can be checked for shorts when the circuit is disconnected.

CURRENT CONSUMPTION

The electrical current drain, which is the "quantity" of electrical current required for operation, varies with each type of equipment. The current (wattage) rating is always clearly indicated, usually on a metal plate attached to the equipment or appliance. Everyone is familiar with the wattage of electric bulbs, which in household use ranges from 15 to 150 watts. Many small appliances consume similar low rates of current, for examples, 100 watts for a small radio, 125 for the average vacuum cleaner, a little higher wattage drain for food blender, electric drill, and fan. But current consumption is much higher for any appliance that involves heating, such as the percolator and electric iron, 1000 watts; broiler and toaster, average 2500 watts; and up to 16,000 watts for the electric range and oven (if several burners are used simultaneously).

The importance of these wattage figures is that electrical circuits in the home are designed for limited wattage capacity. As explained in this chapter, a proper division of the appliance connections between various circuits will help prevent blown fuses. The wattage figures also may be useful data in efforts to conserve energy and help keep utility bills at reasonable levels. The knowledgeable consumer can benefit when purchasing appliances by making comparisons of both wattage consumption and output—in the case of air conditioners, for example, you may find that one machine exceeds the cool air output with a lower current consumption than its competitors. The list supplied here, compiled from government figures and reports, shows average wattage ratings, but you can modify them by substituting the actual wattage figures listed on your own electrical equipment.

Wattage of Typical Appliances

Electric water heater	2000-4500
Window air conditioner	750-3500
Automatic washing machine	700
Clothes dryer	4500-9000
Range	8000-16,000

Built-in oven	4000
Dishwasher-waste disposer (combined)	1500
Water pump	700
Freezer	350
Hand iron	1000
Percolator	1000
Food blender	250
Portable heater	1000
Radio	100
Television	300
Vacuum cleaner	125
Toaster	1250
Hair dryer	235
Broiler-rotisserie (average)	2500

GUARDING AGAINST SHOCK HAZARDS

The Anatomy of Electric Shocks. Every attention has been given to assure that your home electric system, your appliances and tools, are safe and convenient to use. Even a child can safely turn on lights and the TV. But electricity nonetheless is a powerful force. Overloaded or improper electrical wiring has caused many home fires when the insulation burned off, exposing superheated wires and causing sparks inside the walls. Also, under certain circumstances there is the potential of an electric shock, which can indeed be serious and sometimes lethal. It is important to know how electric shock comes about, and why its effect on a person varies under different conditions.

Electric current flows on two wires to an appliance—the "hot" wire and the neutral or ground wire. If you were to put a finger inside an open lamp socket and touch both terminals there, you would feel a mild shock at the finger. But if you touched the "hot" terminal with one finger, while holding onto a water pipe with the other hand, the current would flow across your chest to the hand on the pipe. Electricity seeks the nearest ground—in one case contact was limited to just one finger, in the other it went across the body, paralyzing the major nerve centers.

Water is a conductor of electricity, and the human body, largely composed of water, is a very good conductor. An important point to remember is that although the shock was mild when current passed through just one finger, it could be very serious when it crosses the vital organs in the chest.

How Are Shocks Caused? Every electric appliance has the "hot" wire and the neutral ground wire connected inside to terminal screws. The case, or housing, of the appliance is insulated in some manner from these connections. If the insulation on the cord becomes frayed and exposes a wire, or a small part inside the device falls off and touches the terminal or wire, the appliance housing itself can become "alive" with electricity. There's no way you can know this visually, unless you use a test lamp, and even that may not be conclusive as the contact may just occur momentarily when the electric tool or appliance is held in a certain position. But when it is "hot" and you touch a sink faucet or similar ground, or stand on a wet floor and a continuous ground is established, shock results.

Grounding Plug. One of the best protective measures against electric shock is the 3-wire cord and 3-prong plug, for use in new-type grounded receptacles. The third wire is attached to the shell of the tool; in the event that the shell becomes electrified, the current flows through the grounding wire and shorts out, protecting the user. Instructions on converting your present receptacles to the newer grounded type are given further on in this chapter. The newer double-insulated tool is another major defense against the shock hazard, as its housing and some internal parts are of non-conductive plastic.

Other Shock Hazards. The grounding plug does not cover all situations. One of the most hazardous is a radio near a bathtub. A person bathing is particularly vulnerable because of the presence of both water and metal piping at the tub. There have been instances of a radio falling into the tub and electrocuting the occupant. (Battery-powered transistor radios, however, are safe.) Also in the bathroom, care should be taken when

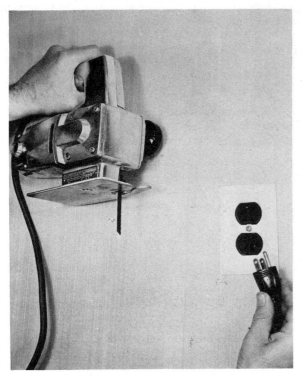

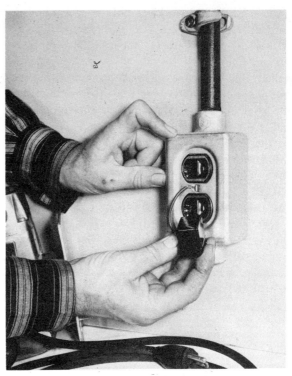

Many appliances and tools now have 3-prong safety plug, intended to be used in a grounded receptacle. The third plug is **U**-shaped, connected to the shell of the appliance so that any short in the appliance housing will be diverted through the ground of this third plug.

Adapter is required when the wall receptacle is old-fashioned type without grounding connection. The green "pigtail" wire must be attached to the cover screw of the receptacle box.

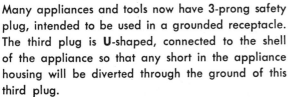

using hair dryers or other appliances while standing on a wet floor or when barefoot—only the insulated knobs may be touched. Electric shavers have plastic cases, so are quite safe, unless they drop into a sink full of water—the thing to do then is to disconnect the shaver cord. Have the thoroughly dried shaver tested for electrical integrity before using it again.

Outdoors, use only safely grounded extension

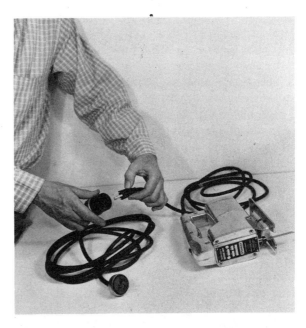

Electrical grounding is continued through the extension cord only when the cord has 3 wires, including the extra ground wire that will be linked to the **U** prong of the appliance cord.

cords, and forego working with electric tools in rainy or damp weather. At swimming pools, make certain all underwater lights are U.L. *(Underwriters Laboratory)* approved and properly installed; that there are no overhead lamps or wires that might fall into the water; that the pump cables are rated as waterproof, and all outside receptacles and switches are grounded and have insulated weatherproof covers.

Particularly hazardous is a hand-held emergency pump powered by an electric drill which is advertised to remove water from flooded basements. The conditions under which this device would be operated create the possibility of electrocution. Only a regular sump pump, specially wired and grounded for submerged operating conditions, and controlled by either an automatic float or a remote control switch, should be used for this purpose.

ELECTRICAL REPAIRS

You are allowed to make certain electrical repairs in your home—replace switches and receptacles, change wall and ceiling lamps, and similar "surface" work. Installing or extending a circuit, however, is restricted by ordinances in many localities. If you do make such basic installations or changes, it is wise to get the work certified by the Fire Underwriters, or other local inspection service, to make sure that it conforms with safety requirements.

The basic tools and supplies needed are a screwdriver, needlenose pliers with side cutters, a penknife, roll of electrical tape (cloth or plastic), and plastic "wire nuts" of the correct sizes, for splicing wires. An inexpensive insulation stripper is a very useful tool, as are an instantaneous soldering gun and linesman's pliers. Snaking cable will be helpful if you're going to do concealed wiring or install a burglar alarm system.

Changing Receptacles. Convenience outlets deteriorate in time—their contactor springs lose tension and fail to hold the plug prongs firmly. This results in arcing and burning inside the receptacle box. The receptacles are easy to change,

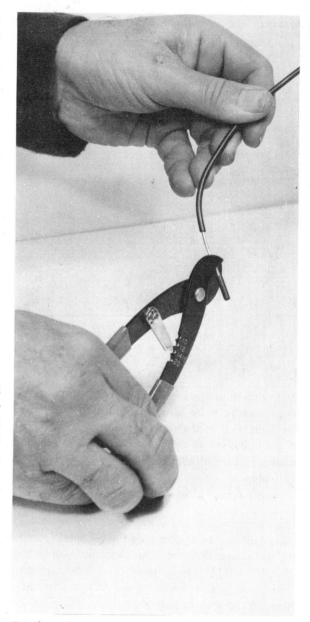

Simple and practical, this small wire stripper is quickly adjusted by shifting a lever to the wire size position indicated.

but when you do this, put in the safety grounding type; some models cost less than a dollar.

The grounding receptacles have, in addition to the two regular plug slots, another opening for

Multi-purpose electrical pliers by Stanley have insulated handles, cut wire, strip insulation, shear bolts and screws to size, and will properly crimp terminal connectors. Price about $3.75.

arrangement in the new receptacle, breaking out the center lug if necessary.

When making the wire connections, turn the terminal screws out as far as they will go without forcing them out of the housing, to obtain sufficient clearance for the wire. Shape the wire end with needlenose pliers into a loop around the terminal screws, in the direction that the screws will turn, then with the pliers compress the wire ends more closely around the screw. Turn down the screw as tightly as you can, holding the wire so it won't twist out of position.

You may encounter a receptacle in which the wires are not attached to terminal screws, but are inserted at the back and held by spring pressure. To release the wires, push a narrow blade screwdriver into the adjacent slot and pull out

the round grounding plug of the appliance cord that is connected to the appliance shell. This receptacle has at the back a green-color screw for attaching a grounding wire, if needed. Installation usually is no different from that of an ordinary receptacle, other than to make sure a good ground is established.

First disconnect the current by removing the fuse or flipping the circuit breaker. Do not depend on the wall switch to disconnect current, as the switch may control only one side of the duplex receptacle, the other outlet being directly connected into the circuit. Use the bulb or neon tester to confirm that the current is indeed disconnected.

Remove the wall plate and two screws holding the receptacle. Pull it out as far as the wires permit, loosen the terminal screws, and remove the wires. Transfer the wires to the replacement receptacle, but watch the polarity—connect the black ("hot") wire to the brass screw, the white wire to the silver-colored screw. If there are two black wires on the terminals, and the metal lug between those terminals is intact, then the second black wire leads to another receptacle on the same line, but if the connecting lug is broken out or cut, then one part of the duplex receptacle is controlled by a wall switch. Duplicate this

Changing receptacles. First, remove the screw at center holding the cover plate. Pull fuse on that circuit, test to make sure current is off.

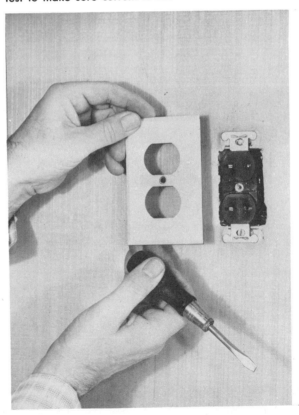

(Above left) Loosen the receptacle by turning out the two retainer screws as shown. The receptacle can now be pulled out of the box on its wires.

(Above) Wires removed from old receptable terminals. A grounding connection wire is attached to a screw inside the receptacle box. This wire is not necessary if the box itself is grounded, as proved by test.

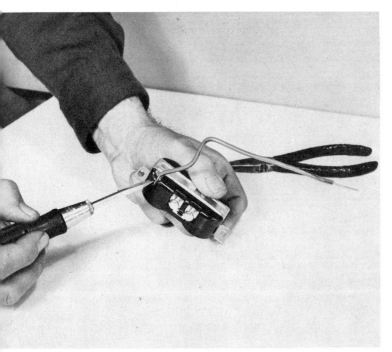

(Left) Grounding wire is attached to the green grounding screw at top of the receptacle. The connections are now made, black 'hot' wire to the brass terminal screw, white wire to the silver colored screw. The receptacle is then folded back into the box and cover plate attached. Turn on circuit current, test for ground.

the wire. These spring pressure receptacles have gauge strips showing the correct length of uninsulated wire for the spring-held connection, and the terminal holes are clearly marked for the white and black wires. Just push the wires into the cup-shaped holes and they will be gripped securely, but see that there is no bare wire extending beyond the openings.

Grounding the Receptable. A good ground connection is automatic if the feed wires are in an armored cable or steel conduit, and connected to a metal box. In the receptacle, the grounding lug is linked to the attachment bracket—thus, attaching the receptacle to the metal box with screws provides grounded continuity.

All splices of wires must be made inside an approved type of box, called a junction box or splice box. Most non-metallic cables, such as Romex, contain a third grounding wire. If the splice box is of metal, this ground wire is clipped to the box rim, establishing a ground for the receptacle. In a non-metallic plastic box, the ground wire should be attached directly to the green-colored grounding screw of the receptacle. Where there is no ground wire in a non-metallic cable, the ground must be established by clamping a wire from the green terminal to water tubing, drain pipe, or the copper line of a hot water heating system.

After the wires are connected, fold them back into the box to obtain clearance for replacing the receptacle without crowding. Replace the two receptacle retainer screws, but leave them just loose enough so that the receptacle can be shifted sufficiently to permit lining up the wall plate when that is attached. Some receptacles have a metal extension on each end, with two holes in each, known as "ears," intended for certain installations such as surface boxes. If they are in the way, break them off by bending back and forth.

After the receptacle is installed, replace the circuit fuse and check the ground with a bulb or neon tester, placing the exposed end of one wire into each side of the receptacle in turn, the other probe into the grounding outlet of the new receptacle. The bulb will light if the ground is adequate.

How to Splice Wires. Knowledge of this basic technique is important for safely installing new lighting fixtures on ceilings, walls, and the house exterior, or making any alterations of your electrical circuits, such as adding or relocating an outlet, and putting up outdoor floodlighting or a lawn lampost.

Wires may be solid or stranded, the latter consisting of a cluster of fine wires. The plastic insulation is stripped off either type by notching the coating with a knife and ripping off the plastic, or using an insulation stripper which resembles pliers with an opening that can be adjusted to the gauge (thickness) of the wire. When handling stranded wire, avoid cutting away any of the strands, as this reduces the size and therefore the carrying capacity of the wire. The bared end of solid wire should be scraped with the edge of a knife blade until the metal shines clean and bright, for good contact. Stranded wire is used where flexibility is needed, as in lamp cords.

The essential objectives of the splice are to obtain good electrical contact and to be certain that the wires do not come apart. Always see that wires of the same color insulation are continuous, to maintain polarity; that is, black to black wire, white to white (except when connecting switches). An approved splice is made with wire nuts, which are plastic caps that screw tightly onto the twisted wires, then covered with electrical tape to prevent loosening.

Twist the wires tightly together using a flat pliers. Clip off the end so it is square and neat, leaving about ½-inch length and providing a good start for the plastic nut. Now screw the wire nut on as tightly as you can. It should completely cover the uninsulated part of the wire. If there is an exposed bare section, unscrew the nut and clip off as much of the wire as necessary, and replace the nut. Some wire strippers are marked with gauges showing the correct length of exposed wire for splicing.

The wires of ceiling and wall fixtures usually are the stranded type, which are difficult to twist properly over a solid wire. Soldering the strands lightly will keep them in place, make the wire more easily handled for splicing. Lamp cords, stranded bell wire, and burglar alarm wire also should be soldered to keep the strands intact and assure good splicing or terminal contact. An instantaneous electric soldering gun makes this a quick, simple job.

Hooking Up Wall Switches. Replace switches that cause arcing when operated, or if the toggle springs have weakened. Disconnect the circuit, remove the wall plate and switch retainer screws. The switch is replaced in the same manner as a receptacle, except that there are usually only brass screws on the switch. The switch leg wires are connected to the two terminals, the only problem being which is the lead wire so that the "on" side should be retained as before. Usually the black wire (in a black-white cable) will be the "hot" line and goes to the "on" side. It isn't always so, but you have better than a fifty-fifty chance of guessing correctly.

Attach the two wires and turn on the current to see which side of the switch controls the lights. If you're wrong, just reverse the wires to opposite terminals so that the switch toggle is uppermost when the light goes on.

Rewiring a Lamp. Lamp cords with frayed or dried-out insulation should be replaced. It's poor thrift to salvage the old cord by cutting away a damaged section and splicing the rest together; the splice is unsightly and likely to part under strain, leaving live wires dangling. New wire costs very little, is easily hooked into the lamp socket assembly. Use no. 18 plastic-insulated stranded wire of sufficient length to reach the lamp's receptacle.

Replacing the Lamp Wire. Unplug the cord. Remove the lampshade by turning out the top ferrule and the bulb. Separate the bulb socket cap and shell (in some makes, this is done by pressing up where the shell is marked "press"); in other types, use a screwdriver to push up the shell.

The socket interior can now be unscrewed. Pull it up while feeding some wire from the base of the lamp for clearance. Unscrew the wires from the terminals, withdraw the old wire.

Push the new wire through the opening in the lamp base. With a wire stripper, remove about ¾-inch of insulation from both wires. Twist the

wire strands tightly, attach to the socket terminals—polarity need not be followed—making sure that the wires are completely around the terminal screws and the screws are turned very tight. Clip off any excess exposed wire and loose strands, reassemble the socket by screwing on the cap and snapping the shell into position.

The other end of the wire is threaded into the original attachment plug. Separate the two wires, tie an "underwriter's knot," as illustrated. Start

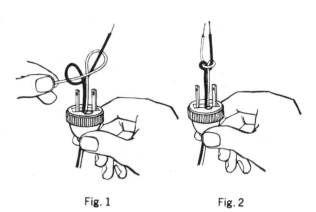

Fig. 1   Fig. 2

The Underwriter's knot is designed to relieve strain on the terminals in lamp sockets and extension cord connectors. In Fig. 1, both wires are formed into loops, and each wire is turned into the loop of the other. When pulled tight (Fig. 2) the knot is small and flat. The knot prevents live wires being loosened from their terminals and becoming exposed to contact.

the knot with loops of both wires, then bring each wire through the loop of the other wire. Pull the wire ends to form a tight knot, push it down into the plug. The wire ends are stripped, then tightly attached to the plug terminals. Replace the protective fiber disk. Use a new plug if the prongs on the original one have become loosened.

TWO-SWITCH LIGHT CONTROL

A "3-way" switching system permits control of

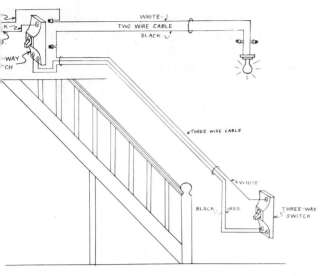

Circuit diagram shows wiring of 3-way switch to control a ceiling lamp from two points. White wire from the power feed goes directly to the fixture, the black goes on one switch terminal, and two "traveler wires" join the bottom terminals of both switches. A black wire leads from the single terminal on the other switch to connect with the lamp fixture.

a lamp from two (and even more) separate switches, at the top and bottom of a stairway, for example, or at widely separated entrances to a room. The system is useful also to turn garage and lawn lighting on or off from either outdoors or inside the house, and is adaptable to numerous convenience arrangements for electrical appliances.

The installation is based on special switches, identified as 3-way type, to control lights from either of two points. These switches have three wire terminals; two are independent terminals which are linked to the same terminals on the second switch with black wires, called "traveler wires," and one is a shunt connection. The independent terminal connections serve to bypass the toggle control, providing current to both switches.

The lead wires of the circuit are distributed so that the white neutral wire is spliced directly to the lamp fixture, the hot wire going to one of the shunt terminals of either switch; a black wire from the opposite switch shunt terminal brings the hot line to the lamp. Thus, either toggle can make or break connection to the lamp because of the current bypass independent of the shunt.

Typical 3-way switches for residential installations are the Hubbel No. 9643 and Circle F No. 1630.

LOW-VOLTAGE SWITCHING

Control of lights and electrical appliances from any number of locations, however widely sepa-

A relay switch controls each light fixture or appliance. An impulse from low-voltage switches actuates the relay to turn the light on and off. Any number of low-voltage switches can be linked to each relay, as shown in this photograph. The relays are encased in standard metal boxes, but the low-voltage wire splices can be made outside the box.

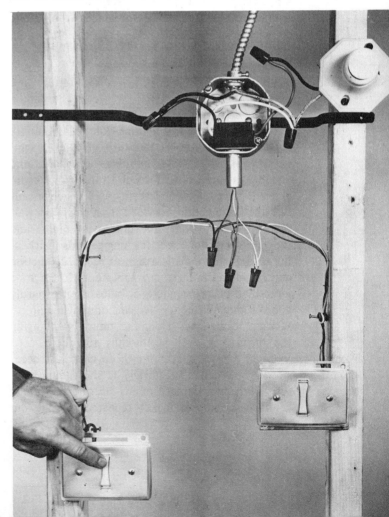

rated, is the result of a modern concept in which the switch connections are made with low-voltage wiring, similar to bell wire. Each light has its own relay which serves as the full-voltage switch. Low-voltage wires lead to the relay, full-voltage wires from relay to the lamp. Low-voltage current thus operates the relay on or off, and it in turn puts the light on or off.

With this system, a gang of switches in a bedroom can turn on or off any lamps in the house or all at once by a master switch, start the electric percolator, floodlight the lawn, shut off a record player, or activate whatever controls are in the low-voltage system. The power to the relays is supplied through a 16-volt chimes transformer connected into the house current.

Because no. 22 bell wire is used, the installation eliminates costly heavy cables; wires can be safely snaked through closets, along floor moldings, or other convenient pathways. The switch relays are made by General Electric, Square D Company, and Remcon Division of Pyramid Instrument Corp., Lynbrook, N.Y. Additional installation details can be obtained from those sources.

FLUORESCENT LAMPS

These lamps have become widely used in residences, primarily for lighting kitchens, laundry rooms, and playrooms, because of their brightness, true white color, absence of glare, and economical operation. They are three times more efficient than the incandescent type, which means that the illumination provided by a single 40-watt tube is equal to that of two 60-watt bulbs, and they perform trouble free for long periods. Darkening of the lamp ends is a sign of reduced function and beginning failure. The tubes cost just a little more than plain incandescent bulbs, so it is hardly good economy to try for maximum length of service. Rather, set a definite time for changing the tubes, say every 6 months for those used frequently, once a year for those used just occasionally. A defective starter, a short aluminum tube with two contact points at one end, may cause the lamps to flicker repeatedly. Take out the lamps for access, remove the old starter by twisting it a quarter turn, install the new one the same way.

Instant-start fluorescent lamps do not require starters, which formerly were the prime cause of lamp failure. The starters are a sort of condenser switch that deliver a surge of current to heat up the mercury in the lamp tube and turn it into gas. Instead, the necessary starting voltage is delivered by a higher-rated ballast. This is an autotransformer that has the purpose of balancing or limiting the current drawn by the lamps.

Ballast Replacement. Every fluorescent fixture contains a ballast, which may, after a long period of use, begin to fail and leak its asphaltum packing, creating a mess and ruining the fixture. If this deterioration occurs, change the ballast, a black rectangular metal case inside the fixture housing, which can be purchased at any electrical supply store. Disconnect the circuit current or the wall switch, remove the lamps and the inside metal cover for access to the ballast, which is held by two screws. The wires are color-coded and easy to follow. Install the replacement, attaching the wires as before, splicing with wire nuts.

Replacement of fluorescent lamps may be tricky for the inexperienced. The tubular lamp has two pins at each end. These fit into plastic lampholders at the sides of the fixture. Stand at the center of the fixture, hold the lamp so the pins are vertical. Slip the pins of one end into the lampholder slot, then without turning the lamp, do the same at the other end. When you are sure that the pins at both ends are fully in their slots, rotate the lamp a quarter turn, until you feel a definite snap that indicates the lamp pins have been gripped by the spring clips inside the holder. Do not let go of the lamp until you're sure that it is secure. Try the switch—the lamps will not light unless properly seated.

Keep extra lamps in their corrugated wrapper; store them where there is no possibility they will be shattered.

DOORBELLS

Nine times out of ten, when the doorbell stops ringing, the failure is caused by poor contact at the outside button. The bell operates off batteries or a low-voltage transformer, so the wires are safe to handle. Before going into any extensive wire tracing, remove the door button and disconnect the two wires. (Some buttons are not held with screws but are press-fitted into the frame and can be pried out.) With a knife, scrape the wires so they are copper bright, then rub the wires together to see if the bell rings. In some cases, the contacts in the button itself may have become dirty or corroded, and can be cleaned by rubbing with fine sandpaper. If the bell rings, simply reconnect and replace the button (or install a fresh one) and it should function properly again.

If there is no response to the door button test, further investigation will be necessary. Do your bells work on a battery? If it has been in service longer than 6 months, the battery may be weak and need replacement. Most bells operate on a transformer of 6, 16, or 24 volts. Transformers rarely fail unless tied into a circuit that has a blown fuse. You can check the transformer with an extra bell, attaching short lengths of bell wires with bare ends and touching them to the transformer terminals. Just "jumping" the low-voltage terminals with a bare wire will produce a spark, showing the transformer is functioning, but be sure not to touch the heavy lead wires on the other side of the transformer, as these carry the full 110-volt house current.

The next step is to check the bell or chimes, looking also for a broken wire or loose connection. The bell armature may be at fault, its contacts spread too far, or corroded so they fail to close. A low-voltage tester, contacting the bell terminals while someone is holding down the door button, will show whether current is coming through. Replacement of the bell may be necessary. In the chimes, the solenoid plungers may be operating but not striking the brass tubes that make the sound. Adjustment of the plunger rods located underneath the cover overcomes this difficulty.

When the push button, power source, and the bell or buzzer prove in working condition, then the cause of trouble most likely is a broken wire.

Doorbell failure is nearly always caused by corrosion of the bell button contacts. Recessed type of button is pried out with knife blade. Remove wires and run fine sandpaper across the contacts, scrape wire until bright metal shows.

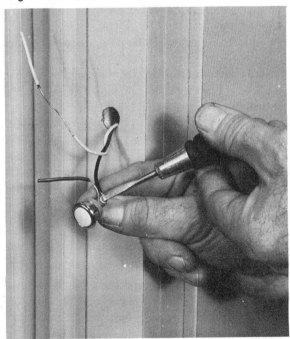

Doorbell or chimes hookup shown in diagram, with two buttons at remote doors. One wire from transformer is attached to the metal case of the bell or buzzer, rather than to the terminal.

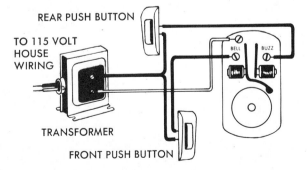

REAR PUSH BUTTON

TO 115 VOLT HOUSE WIRING

BELL   BUZZ

TRANSFORMER

FRONT PUSH BUTTON

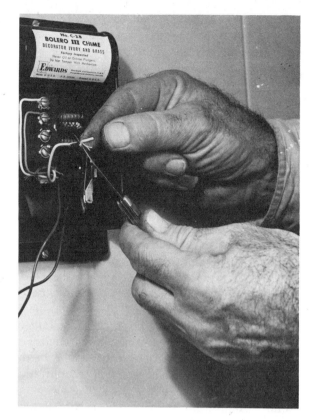

Plungers of chimes, which are actuated by a solenoid cell, may become stuck and can be released by resetting the wood dowel that serves as the striking hammer. Never grease or oil the plungers.

Locating the point of break is usually very difficult unless it is in an exposed location, strung along the joists in the basement. If the break cannot be located, installing new wires may be the easiest remedy. The new wire, 18 or 22 gauge, is snaked down inside the door frame, through the floor, into the basement, then brought up to the location of the chimes or bell, usually adjacent to a closet. This concealed wiring is done with the aid of a thin wire tape, sometimes called a "snake," about 25 feet long. The flexible wire is worked inside the door frame or walls until it finds an opening to pass through, then the bell wire is attached and pulled through by the snake.

Switching to a Transformer. Batteries last only 6 to 12 months, are expensive, and are undependable. If your bell system now works on batteries, change over to a transformer, which costs only 3 or 4 dollars for a 6- or 16-volt unit that rings up to two bells or buzzers simultaneously, and will last indefinitely. The price is somewhat higher for a 24-volt type, which is required for some chimes.

The easiest installation of the transformer is to plug its 110-volt leads into any convenient wall receptacle. The transformer also can be connected to the power line inside any junction box, using a short pipe nipple to cover the wire leads into the box. A more dependable, but difficult, installation is directly at the fuse panel, the transformer attached to the panel box with a connector fitting through a knockout opening so that the wires are not exposed.

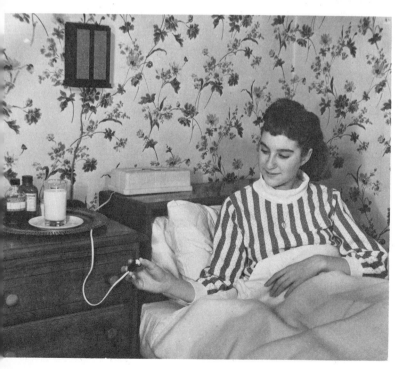

Extend the doorbell system to serve as annunciator, phone call signal, and sick bed call. The wires are merely extended from the present doorbell terminals, or directly from the transformer.

6. PLUMBING REPAIRS

THE PLUMBING SYSTEM

The plumbing system, the most expensive installation in the average home, normally functions without attention, safely and quietly. It all seems so simple—open a faucet and hot or cold water flows at comfortable pressure; release the drain plug and the waste water disappears. Yet, when the slightest difficulty develops, the plumbing becomes awesomely complex to the uninitiated. A little familiarity with the elements of the system, and the specific details supplied in this chapter, however, should enable the homeowner to make nearly all repairs himself, from changing a washer to replacing whole sections of frozen or corroded pipe, usually at nominal cost.

Briefly, the system consists of two main parts: the water lines, which bring cold and hot water to the individual fixtures, and the drainage system, which disposes of the waste water. The drainage system includes water-filled, U-shaped traps to block sewer gas, and every fixture is vented by a pipe leading through the roof to provide air for free flow of the waste. Vacuum breakers and air gaps at fixtures prevent health-threatening siphonage of waste water into the potable water lines.

No routine care of the plumbing system is needed, but malfunctions do occur on occasion in every home and should be corrected promptly. The most frequent are dripping faucets, but even these happen less often now, following development of washerless faucets. Drain stoppages, also commonplace, usually yield to the action of a plunger or flexible sink auger. Other troublesome defects are malfunction of the toilet tank valves, hammering noises in the pipes and chattering faucets, clogging of water pipes by lime buildup so that the flow dwindles to a trickle, frozen and leaking pipes, blockage of an air vent at the roof, and perhaps worst of all, overload of cesspool or septic tank. All but the latter condition can be handled satisfactorily by the homeowner with a modest collection of tools. Pipe, tubing, fittings, and other necessary supplies are readily available at local hardware stores, plumbing supply firms, and from mail-order houses.

Copper tubing is easily joined by sweat soldering (see Chapter 2); brass or iron pipe must be threaded to fit the fittings, while cement is used for CPVC plastic pipe.

STOP THAT DRIP!

Good housekeeping requires that all faucets function efficiently—that is, they shut off the water quietly, without undue tightening of the handle, and they never drip or chatter. Until quite recently, all faucets were of the compression type, and repairs usually meant just changing the washer—a quick and easy chore. The newer washerless faucets are more attractive in appearance, perform trouble-free year after year, but these also eventually need adjustment or repair. The single-handle, push-pull, and other types of faucets, some with rinsing diverters, temperature tuners, and other refinements, are more complex and require special replacement parts when they go out of order.

The vast majority of homes still have the standard faucets in which a spiral-geared stem compresses a resilient washer against a polished metal seat. This washer deteriorates in time and dripping occurs. Sometimes there's more to faucet repair than just replacing the washer. Damaged washer seats and worn stems may be the source of trouble. Leaking swing spouts, malfunction of the diverter valve, and a sand-clogged aerator also are part of faucet maintenance.

Washers. Keep a supply of washers on hand— they cost just pennies apiece and will save running out to the store, which will be closed each time you need one. Washer assortments are likely to contain only a couple of the size you need. However, if you're in a new home and do not yet know the correct sizes, the assortment will give you a start, but then standardize on specific sizes. Keep all washers together in a jar with a supply of bibb screws for seating washers, valve packing, and similar materials related to faucet repairs.

Washers come in an array of colors. Many people assume incorrectly that the red washer is for the hot water line, white or black for the cold. Actually, any color washer can be used for either faucet. The only distinction is that certain off-beat colors may designate particular materials of which the washers are made, including hard rubber, Neoprene, nylon, and various plastics.

The synthetic rubber washer *TPS* (tripolysil) by Kirkhill, identified by its sky blue color, provides featherweight faucet control and more constant temperature because of its limited expansion when heated.

In washerless faucets, water flow is controlled by contact of metal-to-metal or polished ceramic disks. The action of Moen faucets, however, is

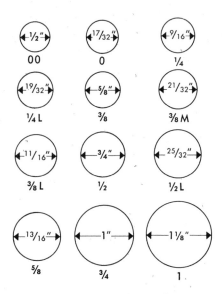

Faucet Washer Sizes. Dimension inside circle is actual diameter; dimension outside circle is trade designation.

based on a sliding, self-adjusting cartridge rather than pressure.

In addition to faucet washers, you may need at one time or another various washers for flush tank assemblies, sink trap plugs, slip-joint connections, garden hose, and other fixtures. It would be difficult to anticipate those requirements, so each replacement is obtained as needed, and duplicates accumulated.

Preparation for Faucet Repairs. (1) Shut off water supply to the fixture; (2) assemble the necessary tools; (3) protect chrome and porcelain surfaces. When shutting off the water, avoid if possible using the main house valve, which is of the gate type and subject to breakage. Most plumbing fixtures have individual shut-off cocks, called angle stops, usually located directly under the sink or lavatory, and have a round or oval-shaped handle. In some installations, the water stops are located through the adjacent wall, accessible under a removable panel. In toilet flush tanks, the stop valve may be found directly below the tank, while toilet flushometers, which are detailed later, have the supply stop as part of the intake valve itself.

If it is necessary to use the main valve, open all faucets above the one on which you will be working to drain the lines; otherwise water retained by vacuum in the pipes may be released suddenly and flood down at the open fixture. When you turn on the valve again, do this slowly to avoid a pressure surge that could damage some pipe joints. Then open each faucet in the house for a moment to release trapped air.

The correct tools make washer changing quick and easy, and help avoid damaging faucet and fixture finishes. A screwdriver, adjustable wrench with smooth jaws, and slip-joint pliers usually are sufficient. Socket or open-end wrenches of the correct sizes may be needed for some faucets to provide a sure grip that can save skinned knuckles and avoid rounding the corners of hex nuts. A basin wrench is necessary for reaching pipe connections back of the sink or lavatory bowl.

Protect the Finish. Cover chromed surfaces with masking tape or cloth to protect the finish; place

Basin wrench reaches deep under kitchen or lavatory sink, exerts powerful torque to loosen pipe nuts. Wrench head is reversed on its pin to alter direction, clockwise or counterclockwise.

Wrench head is wrapped around nut, shaft turned with T handle at bottom. The wrench may be used on other locations where great force and control are required.

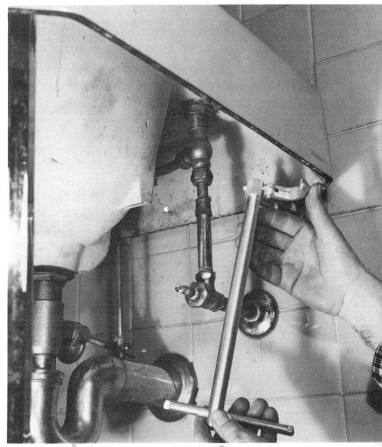

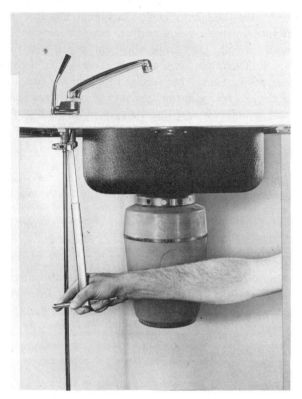

Variation of the basin wrench by Rigid tools, leading manufacturer of plumbing tools.

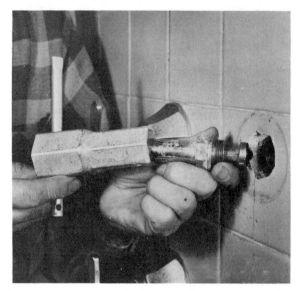

Deep socket wrench, the kind made for auto spark-plugs, is needed for certain faucets deeply set into the wall, such as those in shower stalls and at bath-tubs.

a towel inside the sink bowl or tub to protect the porcelain if a tool is dropped. Provide a pad of newspapers on the floor for laying out the tools, and a small bowl or other container to hold all parts that are removed so none will be lost.

Disassembling the Faucet. The washer is recessed into a cup at the end of the "stem," a shaft with spiral gear cuttings that compresses the washer against its seat. The stem is held in place by a large cap or bonnet nut. In the old-fashioned types (still used on laundry tubs and garden hose faucets) this nut is external and easily accessible. In the more modern and elaborate designs, the retainer nut is covered by a decorative plate or otherwise concealed.

Removing the Handle. First step is to remove the handle. It may be held by an exposed screw at the center of the handle, but more likely the screw is hidden by a decorative disk threaded or pressed into the handle. Removal of the covering disk may present a problem, since it usually is almost flush with the handle surface and you want to avoid marring the chrome. Cover the disk with tape (the plastic electrical type, not paper) and try to turn it with the thumb, counterclockwise. In some cases, a rubber eraser pressed tightly on the disk will grip sufficiently to do the trick. A last alternative is with pliers, using the front edge of the jaws, to turn the disk. Once started, the disk can be turned out with thumb pressure. Underneath there's the screw that retains the handle. In a few faucets, the handle is locked in place with an Allen setscrew at the side. Disks that are press-fitted can be pried up with the edge of a knife blade.

Because the stem shaft is tapered slightly, the handle may stubbornly resist removal. It can be loosened by tapping gently from underneath. Do not try to free the handle by twisting it, as that spreads the interior splines and may prevent proper seating later.

The large bonnet nut holding the faucet stem may be covered with a round plate, held in place by a small setscrew on its flange, or may be threaded onto the faucet housing. The best way to loosen the plate is with a book strap wrapped around the plate edge and pulled tight with pliers.

In some fixtures, particularly the bathtub and stall shower, the faucet housing may be deeply recessed into the wall. It can be reached easily with a deep socket wrench, the kind used for automobile sparkplugs.

After the bonnet nut is removed, replace the handle temporarily to turn the stem completely out of the housing. Note the condition of the washer—extensive wear is to be expected, but shredding may indicate a corroded or chipped washer seat, which will require a further step in the repair. But if this is the first time the faucet has begun to drip, or a long time since a washer has been replaced, just put in a new one. If it does the job, all's well.

Replacing the Washer. Turn out the brass screw at the tip of the stem and pry out the old washer. If the screw is corroded or its head broken off so you can't use a screwdriver, chip out the old washer with the point of an awl, then the remaining part of the screw can be turned with pliers. Clean the washer cup of any old shreds.

The new washer should fit snugly into the cup, without forcing. Washer sizes vary by $\frac{1}{32}$ inch, and correct size is crucial. Install a new bibb screw of the same thread and length each time—these should be part of your household stock at hand. Make sure that this screw is turned in tightly; a loose screw can cause annoying faucet chatter, and there's even the possibility that the screw may fall out and settle in the water lines, where it can damage an appliance valve.

Fixing a Damaged Washer Seat. When a faucet requires frequent washer replacement or continues to drip right after a new washer has been put in, the fault is nearly always a damaged washer seat. This tiny brass collar, threaded deep inside the faucet body, can become corroded, roughened, or chipped by sand in the water supply. In the better quality plumbing fixtures, these seats are replace-

Photograph shows bibb screw being tightened against new washer which is snugly fitted into cup at bottom of faucet stem. Bonnet nut is shown at bottom.

Cross-section of old-type faucet, still widely used on laundry tubs and garden hose installations, shows internal threads for stem and washer seat. Persistent washer failure usually is due to a chipped washer seat. Use a hex wrench to turn out the seat.

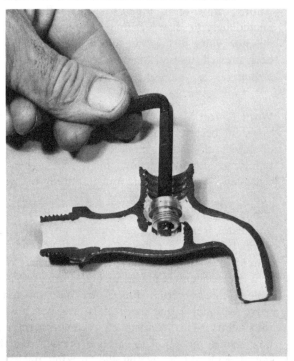

able and can be purchased at hardware and plumbing supply dealers. The cost is nominal, but there are many shapes and sizes, so take along the original to match an exact duplicate.

Using a Seat-Dressing Tool. Sometimes it is possible to resurface the faucet seat without removing it, using a low-cost dressing tool. This is useful when you can't find a replacement for the original seat or with faucets that do not have a replaceable seat. Resurfacing is successful only if the damage to the original seat is a slight nick or scratch, not a large chip.

The dressing tool is a steel shank threaded along most of its length, on which there is a knurled nut at the top. The cutting edge at the bottom has a number of sharp splines. The top end is drilled for a T handle.

Remove the faucet stem, insert the dressing tool so the cutting end touches the seat. Run the knurled nut down to engage the bonnet thread lightly, insert the T handle and rotate clockwise several turns while gradually tightening the adjustment nut to maintain pressure, then reassemble the faucet. Note: as brass dust is formed by the cutting, draw off a little water at full pressure immediately to clear the line. Do this by opening the stop valve just for a moment. If the seat has been dressed smooth, the washer will now function properly.

Worn Faucet Stems. When the spiral threads on the stem become worn, usually after some years of service, the faucet handles must be turned very tightly to stop water flow. Stem replacement is indicated. Although there are hundreds of types and sizes, hardware dealers carry large assortments and it is usually possible to obtain an exact duplicate. Remember that on some faucets, the spiral turnings are different for the cold and hot water sides, so make sure to get the right one. If a replacement is not available, it may be possible to renew certain faucets by inserting a re-valve assembly, but the results are not always satisfactory. This consists of a valve barrel and new stem to match. The barrel is pressed into the faucet body by tightening the packing nut. The

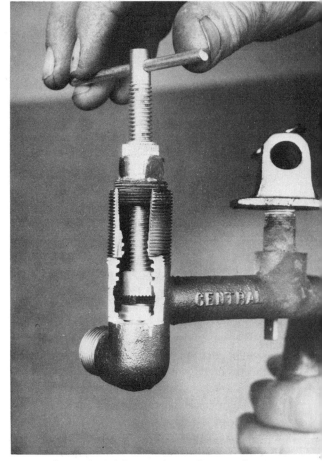

Faucet dressing tool has cutting splines on bottom to resurface damaged washer seat. Gradual tightening of the bonnet nut applies pressure. Make only two or three complete turns of the cutter, be sure to flush out the brass shavings.

internal surface is precut to receive the matching stem.

Single-Lever Faucets. Technical advances in recent years have vastly improved faucet performance and, thankfully, replaced their stereotyped appearance with more varied and attractive designs. The new faucets turn on and off more smoothly, are quieter, and maintain water flow at a more uniform temperature because there is no intermittent swelling of a resilient washer. The single-lever and push-pull types quickly gained wide acceptance and have been thoroughly proved in performance. The new generation faucets are also less troublesome, performing for years without attention, and any malfunction that ultimately may develop can be quickly and easily corrected with special replacement kits that restore the faucet to new condition.

One interesting development is the washerless faucet, utilizing various devices for the valve action in place of the compressible washer. These devices include, as in the Sears, Roebuck models, polished ceramic disks which slide together in a scissors action to shear off water flow, or spring-tensioned valve seats, manipulated by a ball assembly. Moen faucets use a cartridge-type valve which is illustrated in the exploded sketch of the parts assembly. One particular advantage of the Moen cartridge system is that any malfunction of the water flow control is corrected by replacement of the cartridge, restoring the faucet to original condition. The same cartridge fits all Moen models. Installation is quick and fairly easy, following this procedure:

Close the cutoff valves for both water lines. Disassemble the faucet by prying off the handle cover (if that model has one) and turning out the center screw to release the lever handle or knob. Lift out the retainer ring and grooved sleeve, then the spout, pull the cartridge clip, and lift the cartridge out of the faucet body.

Install the replacement cartridge with the stem extended upward, ears perpendicular, and the red, flat section of the stem facing squarely toward the front. Push down the cartridge stem, insert the clip, the spout, the sleeve, and the retainer nut in sequence. Attach the handle with its ring hooked into the grooved sleeve. The stopcocks can now be opened. If there is excessive chattering of the lever when it is turned to either the hot or cold side, the cause is unequal water pressure; open or close one of the cutoff valves under the sink to equalize the pressure of both water lines.

Some Moen faucets are equipped with a balancing piston to maintain a preset water temperature despite momentary drops in either the cold or hot water supply. The piston accomplishes this by shifting instantly from side to side to widen or narrow the hot or cold water entry, thus com-

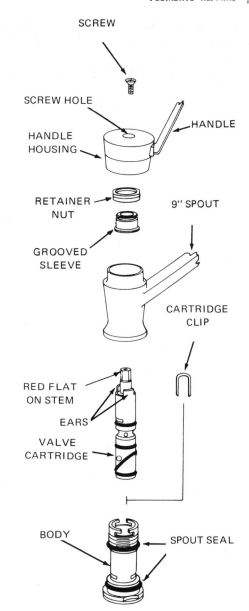

Self-adjusting cartridge controls both the water volume and temperature in Moen single-knob and single-lever faucets. Servicing is rarely needed, but any malfunction is quickly corrected by installing a new cartridge, which fits all models.

pensating for any sudden drop in supply from either side.

This piston may become stuck when affected

by materials in the water. Water flow will decrease to a trickle, or just one side will open, delivering only hot or cold water. To correct this condition, remove the handle and decorative plate. With a wide-blade screwdriver, turn out the spool that is above the cartridge. The inner piston of this spool should slide back and forth freely; if not, jar it to loosen any sediment, then replace and reassemble.

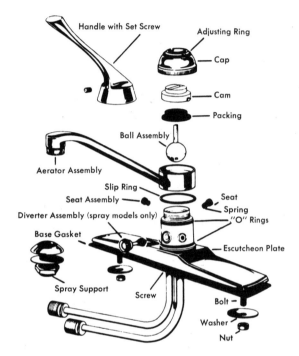

Three different parts kits are available for easy do-it-yourself repair of Peerless washer faucets, including the single-lever model shown in this exploded view. One kit has a new ball stem; another contains replacement valve seats and springs, the third includes valve seats, packing, two rubber "O" rings, and special wrench.

Rinser Spray Repairs. Most sprayer trouble is caused by sediment inside the nozzle, the aerator screen, or the diverter valve. Flushing out the foreign matter usually solves the problem. Hose replacement may be necessary when the old one has become frayed or loses its resilience and

seems to be "water-logged." Replacement hoses come in 30- and 48-inch lengths, for ledge- and deck-mounted types. They have standard fittings for the spray head, and a coupling at the connection end that will permit hooking into any one of the three types of fittings on the diverter valves. A 2-inch pipe nipple extension installed underneath deck-mounted faucets provides greater clearance for easier spray hose installation.

The spray hose is linked to a diverter valve containing a piston that rests against a valve seat. When the faucet is turned on, water pressure lifts the piston away from the seat and water flows to the faucet spout. Triggering the spray cuts the water pressure, and the piston drops to seal off water flow to the spout, diverting full flow to the spray. For hose replacement, detach the plastic spray head by unscrewing the coupling and prying off the wire snap ring that will be found in a groove on a brass fitting.

Repair parts and assembly procedures vary for other makes and models of washerless faucets. If a cross-section diagram or other instructions for repairs are not supplied with the fixture, you can obtain this literature by writing to the manufacturer. It may be well to do this at once, even though the faucets may be in perfect working order, so that you will have the necessary instructions on hand should they be needed.

TOILET FLUSH TANKS

The toilet flush tank is a complex, fully automatic mechanism. When its valves do not function properly, insufficient water is retained in the tank, or water continually enters, dripping past the flush ball or through the overflow valve, causing considerable waste of water that is accompanied by hissing, squeaking, and other noises. An understanding of this mechanism will be helpful in maintaining the tank in perfect working order.

The tank holds some 6 to 8 gallons of water, kept at the designated level by a hollow "float ball." A separate heavy rubber "flush ball" covering a tube leading into the closet bowl is held down by the weight of the tank water. Tripping the tank handle tilts this flush ball so that water starts to flow into the bowl, and the rubber ball rises on its lift rod. When the tank is emptied, the flush ball drops down, guided by its lift rod, to seal the outlet tube gain. Meanwhile the float ball has opened the inlet valve, and the rising water presses on the flush ball to seal the outlet tightly, and fills the tank. A certain amount of water also is directed into the overflow tube to refill the bowl trap. When the float has risen to its maximum level, pressure on its brass rod closes the inlet valve and the action ceases.

Continuous Tank Filling. The fault may be (1) sticking trip handle; (2) roughened flush seat, deteriorated flush ball, or misaligned lift stem guide; (3) the float waterlogged or set too high; and (4) worn intake valve washer or corroded valve lever screws. The correction for each of these conditions is given below, keyed to the numbers.

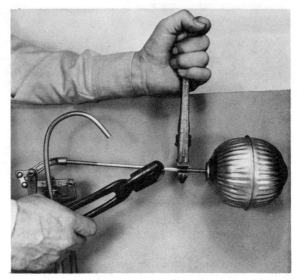

Adjustment of water level is made by bending the float arm with two pliers. Water in tank should rise to about 1 inch from overflow opening.

Water inlet valve assembly in flush tank has a washer at the bottom of the stem. Washer can be removed after taking out the two pins at the side.

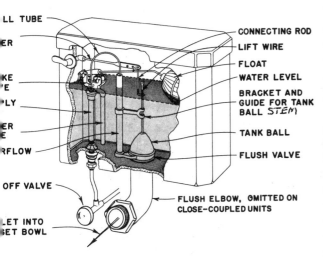

LL TUBE
ER
KE
E
LY
ER
E
RFLOW
OFF VALVE
LET INTO
ET BOWL

CONNECTING ROD
LIFT WIRE
FLOAT
WATER LEVEL
BRACKET AND GUIDE FOR TANK BALL *STEM*
TANK BALL
FLUSH VALVE
FLUSH ELBOW, OMITTED ON CLOSE-COUPLED UNITS

Toilet flush tank is an ingenious mechanism. Float arm keeps water at preset level. A rubber flush ball, seals the outlet tube. When trip lever lifts the flush ball, water pours into the bowl, the lowered float opens the intake valve to refill the tank. Meanwhile, the flush ball, guided by its brass stem, has dropped back to close the outlet tube. At the end of the flush cycle, the tank has been refilled to its normal level, but additional water pours into the overflow tube to replace siphoned water in the toilet trap.

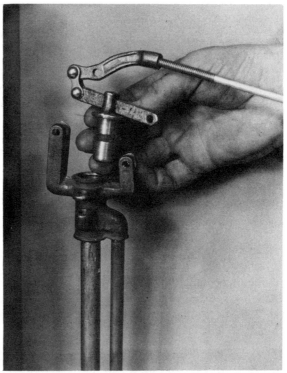

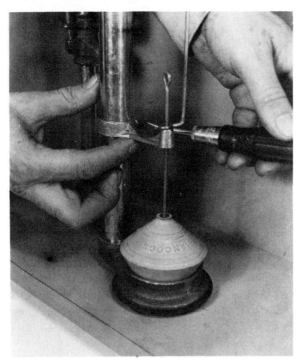

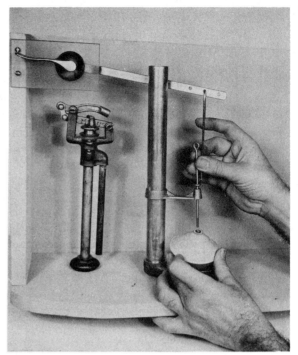

Replace flush ball if waterlogged or out of round, smooth the flush tube seat with steel wool.

Ballcock stem must be in perfect alignment with the outlet valve. Adjust the stem guide after loosening the retainer screw, so the rubber ball drops uniformly on the valve seat.

1. Make sure the trip handle and lever arm move freely. A drop of oil every few months will help prevent binding.

2. Flush valve: Check the flush ball lift stem to see that it is perfectly straight and is accurately aligned with its guide loop to drop exactly into the outlet valve. Replace the rubber ball if it is worn, bloated, or out of round. To check the flush ball and the valve seat, close the water line and flush the tank (if there's no stop cock, tie up the float rod with a cord to close the inlet valve). If the .valve seat is rough with scale, use fine steel wool or Brillo pads to smooth it.

3. The float ball should close the intake valve when the water level is about 1 inch below the overflow tube opening. Water level adjustment is made by bending the brass float rod. If the hollow float fails to rise sufficiently for positive water shutoff, the ball may be waterlogged as a result of pinholes. This can be checked by unscrewing the ball from its rod and shaking it to see if any water has entered. Before removing the ball, be sure to shut off the water line. The float ball formerly was either of copper or hard rubber, but now most are plastic.

4. The inlet washer, located at the end of a stem, is similar to that of a faucet except that the pressure is applied by the leverage of the float. If the thumbscrews holding the float rod lever are missing or corroded, replace them.

Improved Flush Valve. Modern technology's contribution to the toilet flush tank appears likely to end water trickling, whistling noises, and other shortcomings of the float ball that have plagued homeowners for generations. The Fluidmaster, which operates by direct hydraulic pressure, completely replaces the float ball valve assembly. Its prime advantage is that water intake is at full flow until the tank is full, when the valve is shut by positive action, rather than the gradual closing as the float rises, thus eliminating annoying noise. Another feature is that if for any reason the intake valve fails to close (because of grit at the flush valve, for instance), the tank would flush repeatedly to signal the condition for attention. With the standard float ball, malfunction could instead result in wasteful trickling of water for a long period unnoticed. The Fluidmaster costs about 5 dollars.

The new unit, approved in most local plumbing codes, permits easy adjustment of the tank water level, and includes a cup to catch sand and grit. Made of plastic and stainless steel, it can be expected to provide years of troublefree service.

Installation, using only an adjustable wrench, is shown in the photographs. After shutting the water source and flushing the tank (water remaining in the bottom of the tank should be sponged out), the old float and valve assembly is completely removed by unscrewing a coupling nut on the underside. A new coupling nut and washers

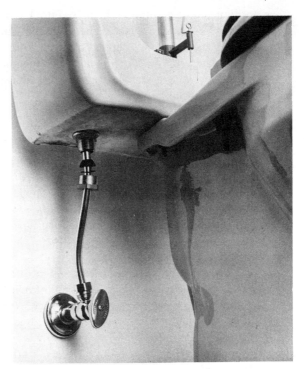

Simple connection to water entry tube is major part of the changeover installation. Special slip nut and washer are provided with the new unit.

New Fluidmaster flush tank assembly replaces old-time float valve to eliminate constant running and dripping of water, and whistling noises from slow shutoff of entry valve.

Installation is completed by adjusting the float level and attaching water tube to overflow pipe.

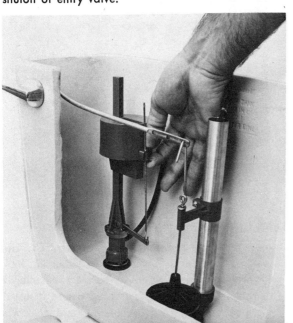

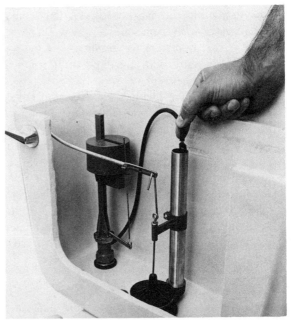

are positioned on the supply tube before the Fluid-master unit is set into place. The coupling nut is tightened, the refill hose clipped to the overflow pipe, and water supply turned on. Adjusting the water level by sliding the float cup up or down completes the installation.

Flushometers. Many homes and apartments are equipped with flush valves, or "flushometers," such as those in office buildings and department stores. These valves are installed where there is sufficient water pressure, at least 50 p.s.i. (pounds per square inch), and the internal water lines are large enough in diameter—at least ¾-inch pipe—to deliver the required volume of water. These devices flush at full pressure and shut off in approximately 6 seconds, in contrast to the 1 to 2 minutes of a standard toilet tank, take up far less wall space, operate with minimum noise, and can be flushed repeatedly without waiting for the tank to refill.

The controlling device of the unit is a leather diaphragm, with a tiny bypass screen. Water filtering through this screen during the flush fills an upper chamber and closes the intake valve. Continual flushing, then, indicates that the screen is clogged, while decreased length of flush would result from a leak in the leather diaphragm, even as small as a pinhole. Repairs are made quickly and easily with an inexpensive kit that contains three washers in addition to a new diaphragm. Here is the procedure for servicing a Coyne and Delany Flushboy unit, the type most frequently installed in homes.

The flush valve includes its own stopcock, located at the front of the inlet line; turning the handle clockwise shuts off the water. The valve can now be disassembled, but protect the chrome surface with windings of elastic tape. With a wrench adjusted to fit, unscrew the dome-shaped cap at the top. Lift out the operating assembly, which includes the diaphragm and a valve stem. Assemble the new diaphragm and set it in place, pushing it down beyond the housing's threads so that it rests perfectly flat on the seat. Replace the stem.

While you're at it, install the other washers that are in the kit. Turn out the handle unit on the

side, slip on the new packing and coupling washers. Reassemble the handle and cover, and the flushometer is ready for use.

Leaky Stop Valves. Two types of stop valves are

Stop valve located on water line under lavatory. Water tube into the valve is a slip joint, has compression ring.

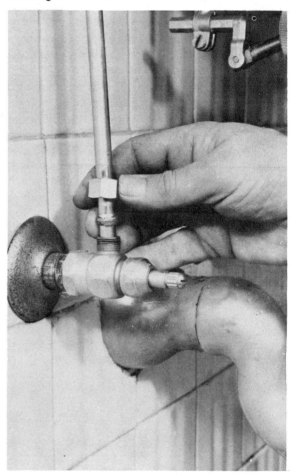

in general use for residential purposes. The Globe valve resembles a faucet in its mechanism, having a threaded stem that compresses a washer against a brass seat. This valve is used where it must be opened and closed occasionally, and also where complete shutoff of the water is required. This valve is found in washing machine connections, angle stops under kitchen and lavatory sinks, in the boiler filler line, steam radiators, and outside hydrants.

Installation of lavatory valve includes sealing of pipe joint with cotton strands and plumbing compound.

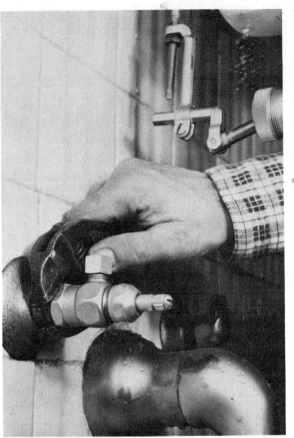

Stop valve is angle type. Flexible tubing is bent to fit between valve and faucet.

times around the stem under the nut, then turning the nut back on to compress the packing. The valve packing is a standard item at hardware stores, costs 25 cents.

HOUSE WATER MAIN

The gate valve, usually used at the main water entrance to the house, functions by lowering a metal disk across the flow passage. When open, it allows full flow of the water with practically no resistance. But the gate closure wears rapidly and can even break if disturbed. Also the valve does not shut off the water completely. Individual shut-off cocks at the various fixtures and on branch

Valve leaks, mostly occurring at the stem, are easily repaired by turning out the nut on the faucet stem that is threaded onto the faucet body, the retainer nut, wrapping a strand of graphite-impregnated valve packing cord one and a half water lines at the boiler and water heater will reduce use of the main valve when making repairs.

PLUMBING NOISES

The sound of running water is acceptable (for short periods), but the noise of water hammer each time a faucet is closed, chattering and rumbling when water is turned on, gurgling drains, and constant dripping are annoying to most people, and the sounds sometimes indicate faults in the system.

Water Hammer. If you're not an hydraulic engineer, you may not know that water, fluid as it is, is absolutely incompressible. When you shut the faucet, the onrushing stream of water slams against bends in the pipes, causing the hammer noise. The cure is to put a "cushion" into the line, consisting of air chambers. These are short lengths of pipe or coils of copper tubing, empty except for the air that takes up the shock of water momentum like a cushion. Water hammer develops when water seeps into the air chambers, nullifying their effectiveness.

The solution would be to uncouple and drain the air chambers. But in many homes, these air tubes are located behind walls, so any effort to reach them would be messy and very costly. It's much easier to abandon them and simply put in new ones at more accessible locations, perhaps at the water heater or some other part of the water line in the basement. The coil type of air chamber, made of copper tubing, is available as a standard item at plumbing supply dealers and can be installed with adapters at any place where a line now ends with a cap, or a T fitting can be cut into the line. An air chamber can be made from a 12-inch length of ¾-inch pipe nipple, which is a piece of pipe threaded at both ends, capping one end and turning on an adapter coupling at the other end for attaching into a T fitting in your system line. Thread a drain cock near the bottom of the nipple so any water that seeps in can be drained.

Chattering sounds at the faucet when the water is turned on can be blamed on a loose washer

Water hammer can be completely eliminated by placing air chambers into the water lines. This one, of ¾-inch pipe, has drain cocks to clear water that has seeped in.

screw or worn stem. Disassemble the faucet as described previously, tighten the washer screw or replace the stem as necessary.

Gurgling Drains. Insufficient air entry at the vents causes gurgling noises when waste water flows into the drains. An individual vent line may be clogged, or the top of the main soil stack, which is open above the roof, can be blocked by matted leaves, a wasp hive or bird nest, or overhanging tree limb. Probing with a wire snake will sometimes clear the vent, or an inspection can be made on the roof to see that the vent stack is unencumbered.

Groaning Pipes. Vibration or groaning of water pipes (as distinct from whistling and chattering) is caused by inadequate or improper support of the plumbing lines. Provide additional supports for the pipes, using steel strapping nailed to the ceiling joists. But because the pipes expand and contract, place matting or gasket material between pipe and straps to prevent rubbing of metal on metal. Risers running to the first or second floor should be supported by wood blocks underneath in the basement to take the weight, rather than letting the pipes hang from their branch lines above.

CLOGGED DRAINS

It's reasonable to expect that when you pull the stopper, the waste water will quietly run down the drain. But sometimes this doesn't happen, or the water seeps down in an exasperating trickle. What's wrong? Most often, the trouble is right at the sink, or rather in the trap just below it. Incidentally, the "trap" is not there primarily for

Groaning of pipes can be reduced by providing sufficient support straps on the wall or ceiling joists. Place rubber sheeting or gasket material under straps to absorb the creaking from expansion and contraction.

Plug in sink trap gives access for clearing drain line with auger. Washer on plug must be in sound condition to avoid leaks.

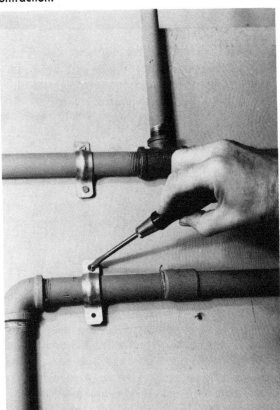

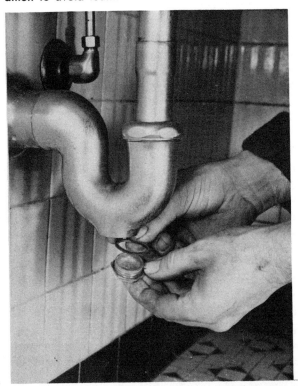

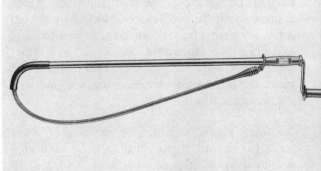

Standard drain auger with handle for turning and a knobbed end. The springy auger rod can make turns in the waste line to reach clogged section.

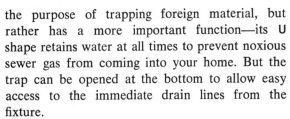

For clearing lavatory outlet, loosen and remove screw at plunger so pop-up drain stopper can be lifted.

Drain auger rotated by an electric drill can manipulate bends in pipe to reach distant section of drain pipe.

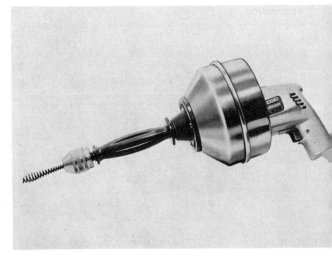

the purpose of trapping foreign material, but rather has a more important function—its **U** shape retains water at all times to prevent noxious sewer gas from coming into your home. But the trap can be opened at the bottom to allow easy access to the immediate drain lines from the fixture.

Tools needed for drain cleanout are a force cup (sometimes called a "plumber's helper"), which is a large rubber or plastic cup attached to a wood handle; a drain auger, which is a springy, coiled steel wire about 3 feet long having a knob at one end and a rotating handle at the other, and the usual Stillson and open-end wrenches.

Commonsense household practices can help prevent or reduce the occurrence of clogged drains. At the kitchen sink, grease and coffee grinds should be discarded separately in cans and not poured down the sink. The grease congeals as it comes to the cooler pipes. Washing of plants always results in a considerable amount of sand that will settle somewhere in the drainage lines and slow the flow of waste water sufficiently

to cause buildup of debris. Regular cleaning of the strainers in bathtubs, lavatories, and stall showers will help prevent drain stoppages.

Toilets are frequently blocked by small items that fall into the open bowl, such as soap, brush, a toy, or medication jar. If small enough to be flushed past the trap, they cause a blockage at a hard-to-reach bend in the soil lines. These in-

Professional type of drain snake. Coiled steel wire will extend along waste lines far enough to reach the debris. The wire comes in lengths up to 100 feet.

preferably the type with the extra flap around that is efficient also in clearing toilet bowls. This flap folds back when the cup is used in sink drains. When working on a sink, run in enough water to completely cover the cup. Set the cone directly over the drain and start a series of strokes. The water that is pushed out will flow back between the strokes. But then you suddenly alter this pattern with a master stroke—pushing down hard on the returning water. This offsets the water that has been sent up into the vent pipes, concentrates the entire force against the blockage. One or two efforts like that can produce the desired result, if it is possible to clear the drain by force cup alone.

Toilet clearance is hampered because the force of the water from the plumber's helper moves up into the flush tank rather than into the drain passage to budge the clogging matter. You can overcome this by sealing the tank flush valve opening, holding a rubber pad over it, or better still, placing a smaller force cup over the opening. This will require removal first of the rubber flush ball, by turning it free of its stem wire, but don't forget to tie down the float ball or close the stop valve to prevent flow of fresh water into the tank during this process.

cidents can be avoided if the bowl covers are kept closed.

Exaggerated claims are made for various chemical drain cleaners, and the average housewife is apt to use these remedies haphazardly in the hope of immediate results. They seldom do the trick, and most contain caustic substances that dissolve the strands of lampwick cotton that seal the pipe threads, resulting in leaks that are difficult to correct. More important, the chemicals can cause serious burns and eye injuries. These chemicals are effective mostly on congealed grease, and are best used routinely to prevent buildup in the drain lines, but once a blockage occurs, they cannot reach the clogging material to clear the lines.

The Force Cup. The first line of attack against drain stoppage is the "plumber's friend," the force cup. It pays to get the largest size, and

Sink and Lavatory Drains. Check the stopper or strainer in the bowl for matted hair or other accumulations. If all seems clear at the top, open the U trap cleanout under the sink by removing the plug with an adjustable wrench (there's water in the trap, so place a pan or pail underneath before loosening the plug). Accumulated sand and grit will wash down with the water, but use a bent length of stiff wire from a clothing hanger as a hook to pull out any accumulated debris. When replacing the plug, make sure that the washer is in perfect condition; otherwise replace it with a new one to avoid leaking.

Some sink traps do not have a drain plug, and instead have to be disassembled for cleaning. If the sink is full, bail out as much water as you can. Place a pail underneath the trap. The trap consists of a U section attached to a tube leading from the sink outlet with a large chromed hexagon nut, called a slip joint, and at the other end to the drain line, with a similar hex nut called a union joint. Open the union nut first. These nuts are of chromed brass, quite thin and hollow, and should be handled carefully to avoid distorting them or the trap sections.

The nuts are usually quite easy to start turning, but if you find one frozen, don't apply any force until you've supported the bent U section so that it won't twist out of position. Hold a narrow board across the U, pulling on it in opposite direction to the torque on the nut wrench. Once the nut has started, it can be turned out by hand, as there are only a few threads. After loosening the slip-joint nut, pull the U section downward to clear the top tubing, removing the entire trap unit. The opening into the drain line will now be visible, and can be attacked with a drain auger or wire snake. You may find that this opening into the drain line is clogged tightly with sand, grit, and grease. Use a spoon or some such tool to remove that material, rather than push it further into the soil line.

If you have to work the auger snake inside the drainage pipe, you may find it difficult to force the auger beyond the pipe nipple, which is fitted at right angles to the connecting drain. This nipple is quite short and can be turned out to obtain better clearance. Use a large Stillson wrench and if there is sufficient space, place a piece of pipe on the wrench handle for more leverage, or tap the wrench sharply with a hammer. This treatment will very likely distort the nipple out of round, but it may be rusted at the threads and should be replaced in any event. A new section can be obtained at any plumbing supply dealer.

If the blockage has not been broken up, it may be some distance in the line from the sink trap and cannot be reached with an auger, or because of bends in the drain connections, even with a long wire snake. The solution is provided by cleanout plugs in the main soil stack of the house, the large vertical pipe through which all its sewage passes, allowing entry of the wire snake from another direction. The plugs have caps of heavy steel lined with lead for easier removal. Use a large adjustable wrench on the square nut, at the same time tapping the face of the plug sharply with a hammer, but be careful not to

crack the soil pipe itself. The auger or wire snake should now reach the drain blockage, but be wary about releasing a flood of sewer water at the cleanout plug once the drain is unclogged—keep a couple of pails handy or be prepared to slap the plug cap back on immediately.

If there is no cleanout plug within range of the clogged line, the problem can be solved by drilling and tapping a ½-inch-diameter hole in the drain pipe at any accessible point before it enters the soil stack. This permits a wire snake to go in both directions to locate and break up the blockage. The hole then is tapped and sealed with a standard ½-inch plug.

Before reassembling the U trap under the sink, check the rubber washers, one on the slip tube, the other inside the union nut. Replace if they are worn or brittle. The trap parts must be lined up perfectly in order to start the hex nuts correctly on their threads. If the nut threads are out of shape or damaged, they will most likely leak, so it is better to get new ones.

Bathtub Drains. The exasperatingly slow water drainage from bathtubs results from an accumulation of soap sludge and hair at the drain stopper. Bathtubs with a "pop-up" type stopper are easily cleaned. Other types usually can be cleared using a force cup, but the overflow opening must be sealed with a wet rubber or plastic sheet so that the full punch will be directed into the drain. The strainer plate inside the tub is held by a single screw. Removing this plate and probing with an auger or bent wire may be effective in clearing the blockage, as the bathtub trap is under the floor and not easily accessible for cleaning.

Clogged Toilet Bowl. The force cup is the preferred approach to clearing a blockage, and it is worth while persisting for some time to obtain results. The drain auger also can be effective, but be careful not to crack the porcelain bowl, which may result if the auger knob becomes caught and requires excessive tugging to get it free. If the force cup does not do the job, the likelihood is that something has been dropped inside, a cake of soap or a toy. Try to retrieve

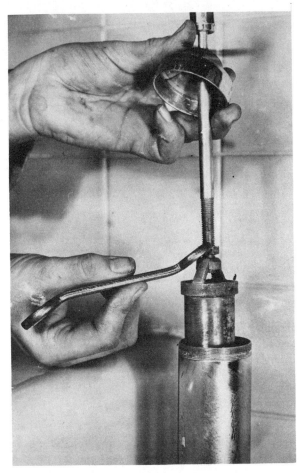

Bathtub standpipe drain is cleared by removing the slotted cap and withdrawing the weighted stopper. Threaded stem permits adjusting for positive drain closure.

it, reaching by hand if necessary; otherwise the toilet will have to be lifted off its base.

Removing Toilet Bowl. Shut the intake valve of the flush tank, bail out the water from the tank and also from the toilet bowl, as much as possible. Disconnect the water line, remove the tank from its hangers, and carefully set it aside to avoid cracking the porcelain.

Loosen the toilet bowl retainer bolts. The bowl is set into a waterproof wax seal and bed of caulking compound, and will have to be rocked or jarred to break the seal. Provide a stack of newspaper or folded blanket on which to turn the bowl upside down. The obstruction can now be dislodged and removed.

Replacement starts with a new wax seal, or gasket, sold at hardware and plumbing supply sources. Also caulk the outer rim of the bowl to assure a watertight joint. Set the bowl back in position, watching to see that the bolts slip into place. Draw up the bolts snugly, making sure that the bowl is level. If the floor is sloped, the base will need shims. Be careful not to overdraw the bolts. Remount the water tank and connect the pipes. Check for leaks at the bowl base and water connections.

Sewer Trap Cleanout. A blockage that cannot be reached from the drain lines or floor trap usually indicates that the house sewer line is clogged. This requires opening the main sewer trap; if you don't know where it is, just follow the large soil pipe in the basement to where it extends out through the foundation wall. An S-trap will be at that spot, possibly in a pit below floor level, with a 4-inch-diameter cleanout plug. If there are two such plugs, remove the one on the far side—that is, toward the exterior wall, but be careful because if the blockage is backed up all the way to the house fixtures, you may encounter a flooding release when the plug is loosened. Nearly always there is some slight seepage even in a clogged line, however, so if you allow some time to elapse after the blockage, a couple of hours at least, sufficient effluage will drain away to relieve the pressure. Also, make sure that no faucet is opened or tank flushed during that time. If necessary, shut off the water main.

You will surely have difficulty removing the trap plugs, particularly if they've been on a long time. If the screw plug is of lead-coated cast iron with a square knob on top, the only way to remove it is to rap the plug smartly with a hammer, while turning with a wrench on the knob. A brass cleanout plug has a hexagonal knob; if this plug is "frozen," it will probably be necessary to destroy it to get it out. Punch a hole with a pointed chisel, or drill a series of holes around the outside, then bend up the top and break it off completely.

The sides of the plug now can be bent inward with a chisel to clear the threads of the cleanout, and thus the remainder can be lifted out. Be sure to have a replacement plug of the right size on hand.

When the trap is opened, insert a wire snake, 25 or 50 feet long, into the exterior sewer line. The snake should be flat steel, ⅜-inch or ½-inch wide, coiled around a special holder; handle the wire carefully as it is of spring steel and can snap out with great force. Feed the wire from the center of the coil. When the blockage is encountered, jam the snake back and forth until it penetrates. You'll know this has happened when the excess water in the trap suddenly flows away. Keep at it until the blockage has been fully broken up. Most snakes have a sliding gripper handle to assist in moving the steel tape back and forth, but make sure that the entire snake doesn't slip away and land far into the sewer line, where it just can't be retrieved short of breaking open the entire line—a very costly job.

Sewer blockages often result from tree roots making their way between the pipe joints. A routine chemical treatment, such as Hercules Root Destroyer, usually will correct this condition. The crystals should be used about twice a year, flushed down a toilet bowl.

When the sewer line is cleared, and while you have the trap open, use a spoon with a curved handle to remove any debris that has collected at the bottom of the trap and in the soil pipe leading into it.

Failure to reach or break through the blockage will require the services of a plumber, who has heavier equipment, including long rotary augers that cut up root accumulations. In extreme cases, excavation and replacement of the sewer line will be necessary.

LEAKING PIPE

Emergency mending of pinhole leaks can be made as follows: for steel pipe, use epoxy glue or iron cement. Wrap with a strip of heavy canvas clamped tightly with perforated steel strapping and a bolt. For brass pipe, the best tem-

Emergency repair of leak with screw-type clamp. Place soft gasket material under clamp for adequate pressure on the leaking spot.

porary repair is a saddle clamp, in half sections shaped to fit snugly over gasket material wrapped around the pipe, and tightened with bolts. If you can't get a saddle clamp immediately, use a piece of rubber sheeting (a piece from an old tire tube will do) over the leak, and tighten a C clamp directly over the leaking spot.

Copper tubing is more easily and permanently repaired by replacing the damaged segment. You will need a union fitting, a coupling and a length of the same size tubing. The instructions for sweat soldering in Chapter 2 include information on measuring and inserting the new section. A temporary repair, if you don't have these materials at hand, might be possible with a short piece of rubber hose of the right inside diameter, and a couple of hose clamps. (Auto radiator hose comes in various sizes.) Cut out the leaking section with a tubing cutter, slip on the hose clamps and force the tubing ends into the hose. Tightening the clamps should stop the flow of water at that point temporarily, but the rubber will bulge under pressure. A coat of shellac on the tubing ends is also helpful.

Replacing Defective Pipe. Water lines deteriorate in time and need replacement. Galvanized steel, particularly, is apt to develop pinholes or become constricted internally by deposits of lime and other materials that the water flow slows to a trickle. Horizontal pipes, usually the first to go, are located in the basement and are easily reached.

Vertical pipe risers and branch lines leading directly to the plumbing fixtures are less accessible, and replacement normally would involve ripping out floors and walls.

Copper tubing fortunately can be used for replacement at low cost and with much less mess. Copper tubing, used with adapter fittings, can be integrated into a plumbing system that presently is of steel or brass pipe. The tubing can be snaked up behind walls from the basement, through holes

Union joint reassembles cut pipe. Half of the union is threaded on one side of opening, the second half unites the two sections in a leakproof joint. Union is used when tapping into a line, or when section of a line is cut away.

When turning pipe, always use two wrenches, one of which holds the remaining pipe in place to prevent loosening of the threads and protect rest of pipes from distortion.

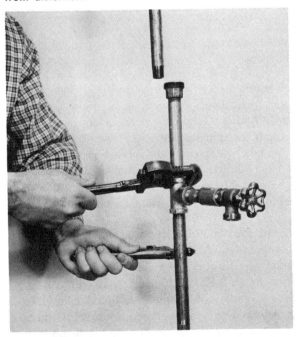

drilled into the joists, in a continuous length, bent as required to overcome obstructions, easily cut and joined to its fittings by sweat soldering right at the site. Only a few small wall openings may be needed. The original pipe can be left where it is, the openings sealed with standard caps.

As previously mentioned, when using plumbing compound to seal threads of rigid pipe, always apply the compound to the outside pipe threads, never to the internal threads of a fitting; otherwise the compound may get into the pipe and taint the water. This problem does not exist with "tape dope," a thin Teflon plastic that serves the same purpose of sealing the pipe threads.

Plastic Pipe. Least expensive water line replacement is the rigid plastic pipe—not just any kind of plastic, it must be the CPVC type (chlorinated polyvinyl chloride), rated to carry water at 180 degrees under 100 pounds pressure. Until quite recently, plastic pipe was listed for only 140 degrees, which was inadequate. But first check with your building department to learn whether installation of the plastic pipe conforms to its sanitary code. The CPVC pipe has certain advantages over metal pipe: it won't rust, corrode, or clog, is not affected by alkalinity of the water, and its fittings are so smooth that water flow is not impeded. It is not, however, as resistant as **is** brass or iron pipe to penetration by nails **or** damage from pounding or movement.

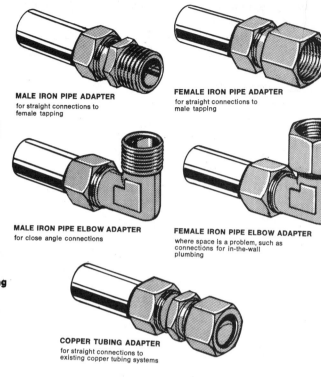

MALE IRON PIPE ADAPTER
for straight connections to female tapping

FEMALE IRON PIPE ADAPTER
for straight connections to male tapping

MALE IRON PIPE ELBOW ADAPTER
for close angle connections

FEMALE IRON PIPE ELBOW ADAPTER
where space is a problem, such as connections for in-the-wall plumbing

COPPER TUBING ADAPTER
for straight connections to existing copper tubing systems

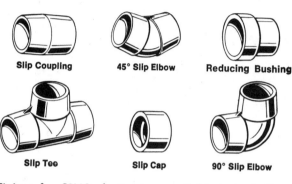

Slip Coupling   45° Slip Elbow   Reducing Bushing

Slip Tee   Slip Cap   90° Slip Elbow

Fittings for CPVC plastic pipe, available in both ½- and ¾-inch sizes, meet every condition encountered in domestic water line assembly.

Adapters permit installing a run of CPVC pipe in existing systems, whether pipe or copper tubing, without cutting threads or soldering. The plastic pipe is cemented into the adapter fitting.

A 10-foot length of ½-inch rigid CPVC costs less than half as much as rigid copper tubing and is one-third as heavy. Fittings, however, cost a bit more for the plastic type. The great saving is in the time and effort required for installation; the plastic is cut easily with an ordinary hacksaw, the sections are simply cemented into the fitting. The cement sets in an hour, ready for use.

With the water shut off, to substitute for sections of accessible metal pipe, make two cuts in the pipe near a fitting, using a pipe cutter or hacksaw to remove a section a few inches wide. With a Stillson wrench, turn out the two pieces of pipe from their fittings, using a second wrench to support the remaining pipe so it does not become twisted and start leaks elsewhere.

Adapter fittings are used to install plastic pipe as a replacement for sections of metal pipe or copper tubing. Obtain a "male" adapter coupling if it is to be threaded into an existing pipe fitting, a "female" adapter if the plastic pipe is to be attached directly onto the threaded end of a metal pipe. Various fittings, including tees, elbows, bushings, and caps, are shown in the illustration.

Joining Plastic Pipe. Cut the pipe with a fine-tooth hacksaw. Make the cuts square across and all the way through the pipe; do not try to break off at the end. Remove inside burrs with a round file. Clean the end of the pipe and the inside of the fitting thoroughly with emery cloth. Cementing is the critical step. Apply cement to both the pipe and fitting, using the correct cement for CPVC pipe. Cover the joining areas fully, but avoid piling on an excess—there should be just enough so a little cement squeezes out at the shoulder of the fitting. Insert the pipe into the fitting immediately, rotating it a bit so it is fully seated. Wipe off the squeezed-out cement with a rag, leaving a neat, continuous bead visible around the fitting shoulder. Check back on all joints; apply more cement at the fitting shoulder wherever there is an uneven bead.

While the cement begins to set up in less than a minute, it does not reach full strength for an hour at normal room temperature. Wait that long before turning on the water, opening all faucets for a moment to release the trapped air. The new pipe connections then will be under full pressure. Check each joint to see that it is watertight.

Leaks will show up at any joint that has not been correctly cemented. The joint will have to be cut out and replaced, using additional couplings and short pipe inserts to fill the lost space. Support plastic pipe adequately *every 32 inches,* with metal straps nailed to the ceiling joists, or with wood supports across the bottom of the joists.

For a free booklet on typical installation of CPVC piping, including tapping water lines for laundry tubs, washing machine, shower, and garden faucets, write to Sears, Roebuck, Philadelphia, Pa. 19132, requesting booklet 39K 7473.

CONDENSATION ON PIPES

High humidity during the summer months causes condensation on cold water pipes, particularly in basements. The dripping may damage wood floors, furniture, even the house framing. Covering the pipes with insulating tubes, which come split lengthwise for easy installation and are fastened with metal straps, can stop condensation. Another satisfactory method is to wrap a plastic self-adhering insulation tape around the pipes. Coating with special plastic paint containing ground cork will stop dripping and rusting of iron pipes. The No-Drip coating by Mortell Company is effective also in preventing condensation on concrete walls, water tanks, and air ducts.

FREEZE-UP PROTECTION

Numerous families returning home after a short winter vacation have been confronted with a messy, almost devastating situation. The heating plant failed during a severe cold spell, and as a result pipes froze, toilet bowls cracked, fixture traps burst. New leaks continued to show up months after plumbing repairs had been made.

Some water lines are subject to freezing, even in well-heated homes, during extreme cold weather. Bathroom or kitchen fixtures over crawl spaces, laundry tubs in colder areas of the basement, water lines in the garage, and all pipes near windows, are vulnerable. Dependable protection, except in the far north area, can be obtained by insulating the pipes with layers of asphalt-saturated wool felt, completely covering the pipes and all fittings to leave no air gaps. Better still, box in the piping and traps with boards, and pack the space inside with mineral wool or other insulating material such as ground cork or sawdust.

Families with vacation homes that are occupied on occasion the year round should establish a routine program of freeze protection, completely draining the water lines each time when leaving the home. Leave all faucets open, pour antifreeze solution (the less expensive automobile grade) into the toilet bowls, sinks, and bathtubs to protect the drain traps. Water heating tanks are usually safe if the heater is kept on, the aquastats turned down low.

Dependable, automatic protection against freezing of water pipes, waste lines, and drain traps—even those that run through exposed places—is obtained with the use of electric heat tapes and cables, wrapped around the pipe in a continuous spiral, with an insulating cover such as fiberglass to conserve heat. The closer the winding, the greater the freeze protection—provided, of course, that there is no electrical blackout. The installation may be manually controlled or operated by thermostat.

The heat tape is available in various lengths from 6 to 100 feet. The 7-watt-per-foot wire provides protection to minus 13 degrees Fahrenheit for pipe of 1-inch diameter when installed straight along the pipe and insulated with a suitable outer wrapping. For temperatures down to minus 40 degrees, spiral wrapping 3 turns per foot would be necessary. Larger pipe, exposed drain traps, and water tanks may require cable of higher wattage rating and 2-inch mineral wool insulation cover. Special kits are available also for roofs, gutters, and downspouts to prevent damaging ice dams. Care must be taken to avoid overheating—space the wire strands at least an inch apart, taped securely in place. A booklet with additional details can be obtained by writing to Chromalox Division, Emerson Electric Co., 8100 Florissant Avenue, St. Louis, Mo. 63136.

Hose Faucets. To prevent freezing of garden hose faucets, remove the hose and drain the water. Shut off the valve inside the house, leaving the outside faucet fully open. If your valve is the drain cock type with a removable plug on the faucet side, you can easily drain the pipe leading to the outside faucet. Replace the plug but leave the valve closed.

A more convenient arrangement for hose faucets is the Mansfield hydrant in which a long-stemmed handle outside operates the valve inside the house. When it is installed at a downward pitch toward the outside, there is no water in the line at any time, hence no chance of freeze-up.

Thawing Pipes. The easiest way to thaw pipes is to place an electric space heater near the pipe, or tie a length of Chromalox heating wire along the pipe. But be careful of electric shock. Also, stand ready to close the water main quickly if thawing reveals that the pipe is cracked.

A propane or gasoline torch will give quicker results, but must be used properly as steam formed by the heat may be blocked by the ice and crack the pipe. Start always at the faucet end, slowly working toward the supply side, and leave the faucet open so the thawed water can start flowing.

When using the blowtorch near wall framing or other flammable substances, place a fireproof barrier between the torch and wood (a piece of asbestos shingle can serve for this) and keep a pail of water or an attached water hose with trigger spout handy. Also check out the area when you're through to make sure there are no burning embers.

LEAKING HEATER TANK

A puncture in a hot water tank may be temporarily repaired with a self-threading screw, drawn up tightly against a piece of gasket material or thick rubber sheeting under the screwhead. The hole must be drilled first to enlarge it to correct size so the screw can be started. Punch a hole in the gasket material smaller than the screw shank, then turn the screw in very tightly so the gasket will seal the leak. A special utility plug is available that is used in a similar manner.

Where the tank has corroded so that there are numerous pinholes, or the metal has cracked, no such temporary measures would be effective. Replacement of the tank is the only answer.

HOW TO THREAD PIPE

You can have pipe threaded by any plumbing supply dealer and at most hardware stores for a modest charge. If you expect to do an extensive pipe installation, it may pay to own your own threader, which ranges in price from 25 to 75 dollars, depending on the number of cutting dies, of which there are six common threads. The dies also can be rented by the day at low cost.

Sizes of steel pipe for home plumbing purposes range from ½ inch to 2 inches in ¼-inch variations. You will probably use only two sizes, one for the water lines, ½ or ¾ inch, the other for drain pipes, 2 inches.

In addition to the threading dies, you will need a pipe vise, a rotary cutter, and a reamer. A solidly mounted bench vise will serve for the pipe cutting if fitted with pipe jaws, or you can use a low-cost chain vise mounted on a solid surface.

Pipe must be cut square across the end. A rotary cutter makes clean, square cuts; when cutting with a hacksaw, take pains to hold the blade at right angles to the work for a square end.

For threading, the pipe is securely locked into

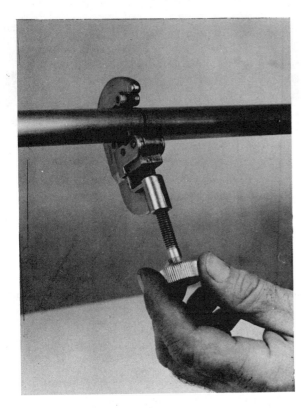

(Left) Tubing is cut square across with a wheeled cutter. Reamer at side of cutter removes burrs.

(Left below) Another cutter for copper tubing and plastic pipe. The knurled wheel at side is tightened gradually to bring cutter closer to the tube.

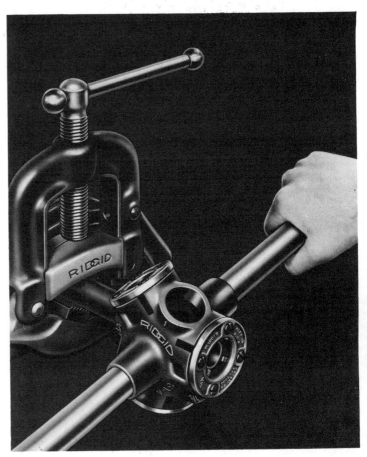

Threading a pipe with a Rigid bench yoke vise and 3-way pipe threader.

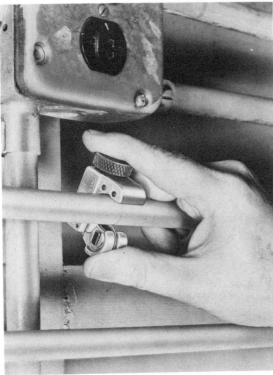

the vise, the die fitted into a long ratchet handle for leverage. A free-turning flange helps hold the die straight. Cutting starts with the fine threads of the die. The handle is turned clockwise, only half a turn at a time, then backed off a bit to eject the metal chips.

Two things are essential when threading: one is to keep the die lubricated with cutting oil, the other is to avoid cutting too far along the pipe. The threads should stop just short of the thickness of the die itself, as the inner threads (the ones away from the pipe end) are not as deep as the forward ones, forming a taper that produces a tighter joint.

After threading, use the cone-shaped reamer to remove any inside burrs, then stand the pipe upright and tap it to remove loose metal chips inside. Also tap the die handle to dislodge any clinging chips.

Copper tubing is bent neatly with springlike tubes. Set of springs includes assortment of sizes.

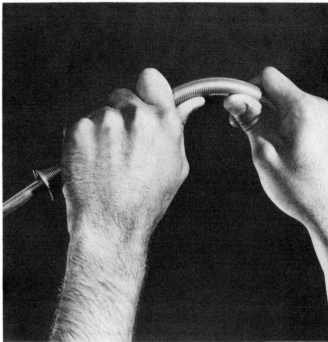

Slide spring over the tubing to place where it is to be bent; apply force equally to both sides.

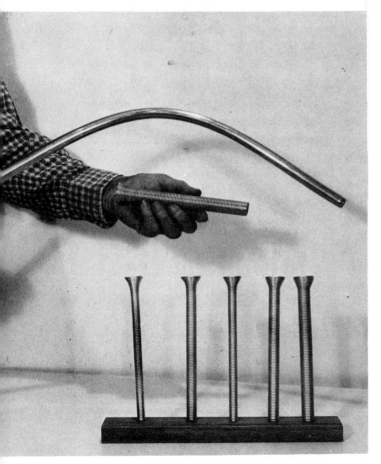

Metal-to-metal pipe threads do not pull up sufficiently in a fitting to be watertight, so a sealer is needed. The standard way is to wrap strands of lampwick cotton over the threads, then coat with plumber's dope compound, which hardens to form a seal and also prevents freezing of the joint so that it can be "broken" again when necessary. More convenient are Locktite Sealant, which is simply brushed on the threads, and Hercules Tape Dope, a Teflon film that is wrapped one and a half times around the threads. Both these materials are as effective as the original "dope" method.

LAWN SPRINKLER A MENACE?

Sanitary engineers sounded the alarm some years ago when thousands of homeowners began installing underground sprinkler systems. Not that they had any objections to the new plastic tubing

Flange tool shapes tubing ends for joining with compression fittings.

or the sprinkler heads. Their concern was that do-it-yourself installations often omitted a vital detail—the vacuum breaker. Many communities since that time have tightened their regulations to make sure the sprinklers are properly safeguarded.

Why all this fuss about the vacuum breakers? These devices, known also as anti-siphon valves, are present (or should be) in every home, but they are not visible and many people do not know their purpose.

The particular menace of the underground sprinklers is that the "pop up" sprinkler heads are normally at ground level and during even a momentary drop in water pressure at the house, subsoil water could be siphoned into the fresh water lines, threatening serious pollution. Directly connected domestic fixtures and appliances such as the toilet flush tanks, dishwashers, and washing machines have built-in preventive devices. But the subsoil water contains masses of harmful bacteria that could cause an epidemic if the lack of anti-siphon breakers permits such pollution to enter the potable water lines.

The menace from plumbing fixtures within the home has been eliminated by the requirement for a sufficient air gap between water inlet and sink bowl overflow level—otherwise, if the faucet were immersed in the water-filled bowl at a moment when the pressure dropped, some waste water would be sucked back into the line.

Water pressure may drop at any time the sprinkler is on—you have a visual demonstration of this every time you use the garden hose for washing the car and the water flow dips suddenly, then surges again. In the anti-siphon valve, a rubber or plastic seal allows water to flow in one direction only, closes simultaneously with the drop in pressure. One type designed for a sprinkler system is a plastic tube, just a few inches long, fitted onto the line just before the faucet. Most such devices range in price from 3 to 10 dollars, are available from plumbing supply firms.

Standard sprinklers on a raised base, and the pulsating type mounted on a post like Rainjet, need not have a vacuum breaker on the line because there is a considerable gap between sprinkler outlet and the lawn.

7. HEATING AND COOLING

THE HEATING SYSTEM

We expect our heating system to keep the home comfortably warm, operate quietly and cleanly at reasonable cost. While some systems are inherently more efficient than others, proper maintenance and adjustment can greatly improve the performance of any heating system.

Heating comfort depends also on other factors: insulation, weatherstripping, storm doors and windows, the limit range of the thermostat, underfloor exposure. Humidity rarely receives the attention it deserves as a factor—keeping the vapor content of the house at optimum level, which is 50 percent relative humidity, assures greater comfort, enhances health, and prevents the ungluing or shrinking of furniture joints that occurs in an overdry atmosphere.

Better heating starts at the furnace or boiler. Accumulated soot in the firebox, smoke pipe, and flue affects heating plant efficiency, so the cost of annual furnace and chimney cleaning is well spent. Do-it-yourself furnace cleaning is not an unpleasant task, though obviously to be followed by an immediate shower. Use a vacuum cleaner, preferably the large-capacity workshop type, with a long pipe extension on the hose, and a long-handled stiff bristle brush.

You will need also a pound or so of asbestos cement for sealing the smoke pipe leading into the chimney opening. Cleaning is best scheduled right after the heating season, eliminating soot that otherwise retains moisture and causes rusting. Take off the firebox doors, brush down the boiler tubes and inside walls, vacuum thoroughly to pick up the soot and ash accumulations.

Separate the smoke pipe from the chimney so it can be vacuumed and to provide access to the ashpit under the flue for cleaning. Extend the brush upward as far as it will reach into the flue to dislodge soot from the walls. The flue also can be cleaned by lowering a small sand-loaded cloth sack down the chimney on a rope; this, of course, may require climbing a long ladder. Work the sack up and down a number of times, then vacuum the soot accumulation in the ash pit. When replacing the smoke pipe, seal any small holes with rivets or bolts, but replace the section if it appears rusted or porous. Make sure the pipe sections are properly assembled and securely fitted into the chimney opening. Seal the chimney joint with asbestos powder mixed with water into a cement-like paste.

Watch Your Boiler Water. The glass tube located at the front or side of the boiler shows the interior water level, which must be maintained at about the midpoint position during the heating season. Check this gauge weekly unless the boiler is equipped with an automatic filler device. Add water by opening the filler valve while you keep an eye on the gauge. Never walk away leaving the valve open—if you get sidetracked and forget it, the water will rise through the pipes and flood the rooms, causing incalculable damage throughout.

The boiler filler pipe is, or should be, part of the hot water supply line. Start the flow slowly, opening and closing the valve a couple of times until hot water starts to flow, to avoid cracking the boiler casting.

Cleaning the Water Gauge. Sometimes the gauge glass becomes so discolored with sludge that the water level is no longer visible. The tube can be removed for cleaning, even while the boiler is in operation. Close the side petcocks at the top and bottom of the tube by turning their wing knobs to horizontal position. Open the bottom petcock to drain the glass.

Loosen the two large nuts at top and bottom of the glass with a wrench. Slide the nuts onto the glass—do this gently as the rubber washers inside the nuts grip the glass tightly. The tube then will clear its sockets and can be lifted out.

Caution: Do not open the petcocks while the glass is removed, as steam and very hot water will gush out.

Clean the tube with a ball of cotton wadding or a thin round brush, then wash the glass in soapy water. Before replacing the tube, check the condition of the washers, install new ones (a standard hardware item) if needed. Make certain the tube is properly seated before tightening the nuts.

When you reopen the petcocks, if water does not flow into the glass it may be because the boiler water is too low and needs filling. When the glass is partly filled, drain it once or twice to eliminate any sediment. The drain cock itself probably will become clogged, but it can be cleared easily by inserting a thin wire.

In the event a gauge cracks, simply close the inflow petcocks until a replacement is obtained at a hardware store, where the glass tubing is cut to length with a special tool. It's worth while to buy a couple at that time so that an extra replacement can be kept on hand.

BOILER TREATMENT

Chemical cleaners remove sludge, rust, and scale from boilers of both steam and hot water systems. The chemical, in liquid or powder form, is poured directly into the boiler, using a funnel, through the opening obtained by turning out the relief valve. Make certain there is no steam in the system before removing this relief valve. Use the quantity of conditioner compound recommended by the manufacturer for your size plant.

Replace the relief valve, fill the boiler to the halfway mark, and fire it up for an hour or so until steam pressure rises. Shut off the burner, drain the boiler completely through the bottom faucet, in bucketfuls or through a heavy rubber garden hose (not the plastic type) leading into a floor drain. After cooling, remove the relief valve again to pour in a rust inhibitor, refill with water to put the boiler back into normal operation.

Give It Air. One little-recognized cause of poor boiler or furnace performance is lack of sufficient oxygen. Tightly insulated homes provide little intake of fresh air, especially in wintertime, and the heating plant may be starved for oxygen. If the furnace is in an enclosed space, install one or two ventilating grilles of perforated sheet steel or aluminum, at least 4 square feet, through the partition wall. A small air duct leading to the outside is recommended by many heating engineers. The improved furnace efficiency will more than make up for the introduction of fresh air which, in itself, can have a salutary effect on family comfort.

HOT WATER HEATING

In a circulating hot water system, heated water is pumped through copper tubing to all parts of the house; the cooler water flows to the boiler. The main tubing does not run directly into and through the radiators; rather, branch lines lead off to individual radiators. Thus any radiator may be shut off without blocking heat to other radiators in the system.

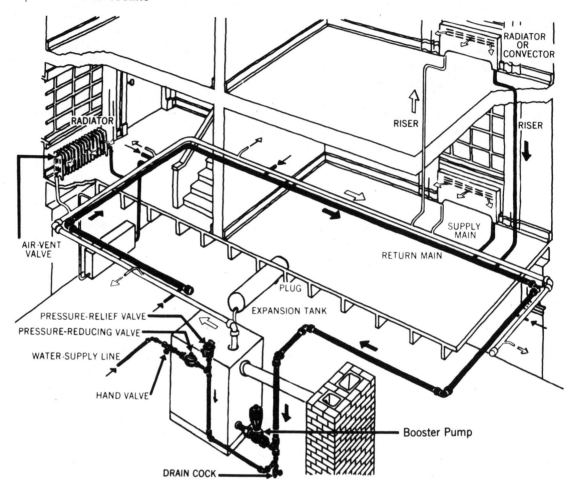

Two-pipe hot-water heating system, showing the supply line to room radiators, and return pipes bringing the cooled water back to the boiler.

In a gravity system, water rising as it is heated replaces the cooler water; thus an upward pitch of the tubing is essential. Sagging of any branch line (from warping of floor boards, which could be caused by a leaking tube) would prevent the heated water from reaching the radiator. The return lines are sloped back toward the boiler, and here, too, any distortion of the tubing will affect the flow of water, preventing uniform heating.

Hot water heating is a closed system—that is, it is completely filled with water (except for the expansion tank, explained later). There must be no air in the radiators. Persistent failure of radiators on upper floors to heat up may be due to

air pockets. This occurs even though the system has been fully vented at the start of the season, because a quantity of air from tiny bubbles in the fresh water that is put into the boiler has accumulated in the higher radiators. Open the air vent of the radiator, add water to the boiler until it starts to flow through the open radiator vent, expelling the air. Place a pail under the vent so the floor won't become flooded.

Expansion Tank. A copper or monel tank, usually mounted at the ceiling above the boiler and supported by straps across the joists, requires "bleeding" to drain excess water that has seeped in. The purpose of this tank is not always understood and the necessary maintenance often overlooked. Water expands when heated, but is not compressible. Air occupying half the tank provides the cushion for this expansion; otherwise the pressure would damage the tubing. Periodic "bleeding" of the tank, by opening the drain, draws off excess water, restoring the quantity of air to at least half the area of the tank.

STEAM HEATING

The boiler heats water to produce low-pressure steam which is carried through large pipes to individual radiators. When these radiators cool, the steam condenses and the water flows back through return pipes to refill the boiler. The process is simple enough. There are, however, a number of complaints, the most common of which are that some radiators "never heat up," rising steam causes pounding noises, and radiator vent valves tend to leak.

Unequal Heating. Air in the radiators blocks entry of the steam. Each radiator has a vent valve whose purpose is to release air as the steam moves up, but prevent escape of steam into the room. One reason for a "cold" radiator is that the vent valve is damaged or clogged with sand or rust so it fails to open.

Air valves vary in their venting action. A radiator with a quick-venting valve will heat up sooner than one with a slower vent. This makes possible control of the system so that selected rooms will receive steam sooner and for a longer period.

A balanced system, in which all radiators are served in the desired rotation, is accomplished by locating valves of selected venting action, or with adjustable valves that can be set as required by turning the cap to a numbered position. Quick-venting valves would be located in bathrooms or rooms farthest from the heating plant, for example, while slower valves would be in locations closest to the heating plant. A period of trial and error, shifting valves or settings as necessary, will produce the most desirable arrangement. This balanced system also results in more frequent but shorter firing of the boiler, which is more economical because steam pressure is kept low. Insulation of steam pipes in the basement or other areas that need not be heated can improve performance.

Noisy System. Loud pounding noises result when some of the condensed water does not flow back to the boiler, but remains trapped in a radiator. Check the radiator to see that it is pitched slightly toward the supply end. If necessary, tilt the radiator by placing shims under the vent end. Keep the supply valve always fully open or fully closed; otherwise water will collect there and cause pounding of the steam. Check also the return lines for proper pitch, adjusting their support blocks on the basement floor, using an auto jack for lifting, if necessary.

Creaking of steam pipes when they become heated is difficult or impossible to eliminate, since the pipes are mostly behind walls. The creaking results when the heated pipes expand and move along their supports.

Cleaning Air Valves. Steam venting valves are inexpensive, last for many years, need no attention other than to see that they are not damaged while moving furniture. A valve that has been dropped may become inoperative and should not be installed.

Heating systems using higher steam pressures in very cold weather ($1\frac{1}{2}$ pounds or more) may be subject to leakage at these valves. The Dole no. 3 valve is specifically designed to overcome this condition.

Corrosion or rust in the valve can cause it to sputter or leak, discharging mist or steam into the room. Replacement is advisable, but a valve usually can be restored by immersing it in vinegar, the valve nipple uppermost, for about 24 hours. Vinegar is a light acid and will dissolve any lime or calcium. Rinse, then wash with a cleaning fluid to remove any grease. *Caution: It is extremely dangerous to leave a radiator without its valve, even if you intend to replace it promptly. When a valve is removed, for any purpose, put in a temporary spare, or seal the opening with a metal plug. Do not depend on merely closing the supply valve.*

Fuel Oil Tank Leak. Water in the fuel oil tank settles in the bottom and eventually will corrode the steel container, causing holes or making the metal porous. A small hole can be repaired with a special self-threading plug, backed up by a rubber washer.

Replacement of a porous tank is extremely difficult if the tank is in a basement that does not have an outside stairway. The alternative is to weld a curved steel plate around the lower part of the tank. This work can be done right in the basement by a local welder at moderate cost, and the repaired tank should serve as long as a new one.

Underground Oil Tank. Homeowners with underground oil tanks should take sharp notice when fuel consumption soars precipitously. Some owners find that a tank that had been fully filled during the summer is almost empty at the start of the heating time. The oil did not evaporate—it seeped into the ground after the tank metal became porous. What is to be done? Costly rebuilding of the excavated tank, or abandoning it to sink a new one, are the only options short of switching to another fuel. But here's a tip: If you have a service contract, read it carefully to see if it includes the oil tank. Some do, most don't. If it covers, you're in luck.

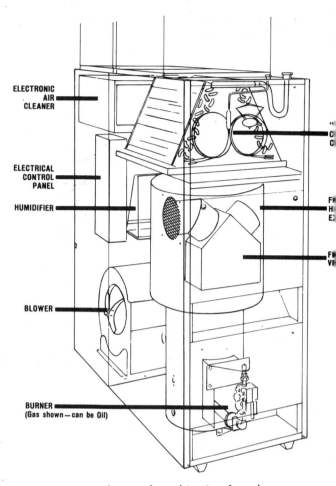

ELECTRONIC
AIR
CLEANER

ELECTRICAL
CONTROL
PANEL

HUMIDIFIER

BLOWER

BURNER
(Gas shown—can be Oil)

Main parts are shown of combination forced warm-air furnace with cooling coils, electronic air cleaner, and humidifier.

HOT AIR SYSTEMS

The most common complaint about forced air heating—poor heating in parts of the house—often has a simple answer: the supply registers are blocked by drapes or furniture. The system is designed for free movement of the warm air, and any obstruction of the supply registers or the recirculating grilles retards efficiency.

Improved heating can be obtained by partially closing registers that are closest to the furnace, thus assuring better delivery of the forced air to rooms farther away. Additional registers cut into the ducts for the more remote rooms also help to balance the distribution, as will following a practice of closing registers in certain rooms when they are not being used—the basement playroom, for example.

One of the benefits of forced air heating is that it filters the air in the home, but this is not accomplished if the filters at the furnace are clogged with dirt. Regular monthly or even more frequent replacement of the filters will be helpful; do this year round if you have air conditioning also. Check the belt on the fan motor periodically to see that it has not become frayed and is at the proper tension.

Dust-clogged filters make your warm air furnace work overtime, retard air movement. Change the filter at least three times during heating season.

mental heat where needed to overcome deficiencies; independent heaters also can be a useful installation in house additions to avoid overburdening the existing heating plant's capacity.

A prime rule for electric heating efficiency is to keep the thermostat setting constant. Avoid erratic switching back and forth from excessively high to extremely low settings. Actually the automatic controls use current only intermittently. Raising the thermostat won't increase the temperature faster; instead it ultimately becomes too high, so the setting has to be lowered again.

Good weatherproofing is essential. Presumably, the insulation has been found adequate before the heater installation, but further attention may locate sources of drafts, at a door or exhaust fan, for examples. The flue dampers on fireplaces must be kept closed, the hearth faced with well-fitted glass doors to avoid heated air going up the chimney. Closed windows, quicker shutting of exterior doors, less frequent use of exhaust fans, are all part of the requirements for reasonably economical electric heating. Most effective of all will be an efficient humidifier during the winter, a dehumidifier for summer months.

The performance of gravity warm air systems is affected by both the number of registers in a duct and the distance of the registers from the furnace. Closing or covering the nearer registers will help bring the heat more quickly to upper rooms, such as the bedrooms, but this may not be a fully satisfactory solution. Additional direct ducts to the higher registers can be installed using the methods and devices that have been developed for installation of central air conditioning systems in existing houses—bringing the ducts through closets and other inside wall spaces, thus increasing the number of registers.

RADIANT HEATING

Electric heat is cleanest, easiest to control, maintenance-free, and by far the most expensive. Adequate weatherproofing of the house and proper setting of the controls can help reduce the cost. In some homes, electrical panels supply supple-

AIR CONDITIONERS

Your air conditioner is doing its job when it maintains indoor temperature at about 76 degrees, and a relative humidity of 50 percent. If it falls short of these objectives, the fault may lie with insufficient or excess condenser capacity for the space it serves, excessive house traffic, incorrect location of the machine, direct sunlight in the room, or malfunctioning of the appliance controls.

Cooling capacity, or "size," is stated in BTUs (British Thermal Units). Formerly, the capacity was rated in "tons," a ton being 12,000 BTUs, the amount of cooling provided by a ton of ice in a 24-hour period. A window unit rated at 6,000 BTUs thus would be equal to a half-ton model. Certification of both the capacity rating and electrical efficiency are worth close attention when you buy a machine; don't be impressed merely by a cluster of initials and a symbol unless you can identify them as representing a creditable institute such as A.G.A. (American Gas Association) and C.S.A. (Canadian Standards Association) The symbols and initials found on some products are merely merchandising gimmicks.

The capacity requirement for a room air conditioner is computed by an area-space formula, modified for the type of location—the kitchen, for example, where cooking and dishwashing add both heat and moisture, differs in its requirements from a small bedroom. Seasonal heat ranges in your geographical area also are a factor to be taken into account.

How Many BTUs? Any knowledgeable dealer will recommend the correct size you need in either an individual room cooler or central air conditioning —just let him know the area dimension. For a quick, rough estimate of air conditioner requirement, measure the floor (length times width) to get the number of square feet, then multiply that total by 25. For example, a room 14 by 20 feet will be 280 square feet of floor area, multiplied by 25 results in 7,000 BTUs. An undercapacity conditioner will not provide sufficent cooling, but its frequent cycling will maintain humidity level quite well; an oversize unit, cycling less frequently, will cool very well but will do a poor job in maintaining favorable humidity. But keep in mind the variables for different locations, as mentioned previously.

Humidity Control. Humidity—too much or too little—has an important part in both heating and cooling comfort, in addition to its effect on personal well-being, condensation damage of the house framing, and furniture deterioration. In the winter, a relatively high humidity makes us feel more comfortable; in the summer, a relatively low humidity (dry air) keeps us cool. The optimum level is the same for both seasons—50 percent relative humidity.

Humidity is simply the evaporated water in the air—or vapor, which is always present in varying amounts. Relative humidity is the proportion of actual vapor to the maximum that the air can hold at a specific temperature—warm air holds more, cold air less. Thus the air in an average home, for example, may contain 2 gallons of water at 70 degrees but less than a quart at zero. The humidity changes relative to temperature— 30 percent at 70 degrees becomes 20 percent at 82. In the winter, humidity in the house may drop lower than that of the Sahara desert, which is about 20 percent; a humidifier on a forced air furnace, or pans of water kept on radiators, help maintain vapor levels. When the humidity is too low, the body feels chilly, nasal and throat passages are irritated, furniture and woodwork dry out and shrink, glued joints separate. But if the humidity becomes excessive, over 50 percent, moisture condenses on windows, walls, and water pipes, then drips to cause damp odors, mildew, rotting of the house framing, and blistering of exterior paint.

Proper Use of Air Conditioner. Comfort and economy are best achieved when the air conditioner thermostat is left at a constant setting, as with heater controls. Set it at the start of the season and leave it alone, even during mild weather and cool evenings to maintain a uniform temperature level. The machine has to work much harder and longer to restore the comfort level after periodic shutdowns.

When entertaining, close the registers in unused rooms to divert more cool air to the living room, rather than adjust the thermostat. Use the kitchen ventilator when cooking to reduce vapor accumulation; open a window slightly to replace the exhausted air. The laundry dryer is a source of considerable vapor—it should be properly vented to the outside. A roof ventilator or small attic fan, thermostatically controlled, will assist the air conditioner. Dirt-clogged filters in the machine put a strain on the conditioner fan, often causing inadequate performance. Wash or replace the filters at regular intervals, as experience has indicated.

The thermostat in central air conditioners runs on low voltage current from a transformer. Erratic operation of the machine may be due to lint or dust preventing good contact in the thermostat's on-off switch. Remove the instrument's dust cover. Wipe the switch contacts with a cleaner made by Honeywell, or use a hard-surfaced paper—a bristol business card is best—between the mov-

AIR CONDITIONER MAINTENANCE

Air conditioner louver housing is removed by lifting slightly to clear the retainer hangers on the appliance casing.

Better performance will be obtained if the compressor vanes are kept clear of lint and other debris. Occasional vacuuming will assure this.

Make sure that the electric cord is in good condition, the terminal tightly connected, and the cable not compressed by the louver housing.

Air conditioners and other appliances that operate on double circuits—or 220-volt systems—have special receptacle plug in which the blades are horizontal rather than vertical.

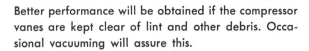

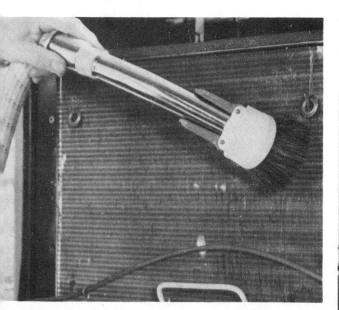

able contactors of the switch. Press the contactors lightly together, slide the paper back and forth a few times. Never use a file or any type of sandpaper, or a fibrous paper that can shred and stick to the contact points.

If the thermostat calibration seems incorrect, it can be checked and corrected as follows: Determine the room temperature with an accurate thermometer. Remove the thermostat cover, raise the pointer setting to turn off the cooler. Wait about ten minutes, then slowly move the pointer toward room temperature position on the dial. If the switch contacts close at approximate room temperature as shown by the thermometer, the thermostat is correct. Recalibration, if necessary, is done by turning the adjustment screw until the switch breaks contact; then bring it back slowly until contact is made again, and tighten the scale atop screw.

These are the practical limits for air conditioner servicing. Other procedures, particularly repairs of the compressor and fan motor, should be left to trained equipment servicemen.

BLOCKING MILDEW

Mold spores, the cause of mildew, flourish in damp, dark, warm places where the air is stagnant. Humid basements, unventilated crawl spaces, shower stalls, closets with cold exterior walls that induce condensation dampness, all are vulnerable to the fungus that causes a musty odor and often the destruction of clothing, books, wall coverings, and furniture.

The first step in preventing mildew is to eliminate dampness. Foundation leaks, condensation on water pipes, cold floors and walls, excessive humidity in the house, wet clothing collected in the laundry hamper, are typical sources of moisture that can be corrected.

Air circulation is important—a small fan will be helpful for non-vented areas. Air conditioners and exhaust fans are valuable for removing moisture-laden air. An electric dehumidifier, or containers of chemicals such as copper sulphate, or silica gel, may be necessary in basement or closets that are subject to high humidity. The chemicals can be reused after drying them in an oven at 300 degrees for several hours, but the vapor from the oven should be exhausted outdoors. Small closets can be kept sufficiently dry by the heat of a small light bulb. Doors on stall showers and enclosed tubs should be left open at least part of the day for adequate airing.

Periodic spraying with fungicide may be necessary if mildew is a recurrent problem. Moth crystals such as paradichlorobenzene help prevent mold growth in tightly sealed closets. When putting up wallpaper, as mentioned earlier, a small amount of disinfectant like Lysol included in the wallpaper paste can prevent development of mildew.

Removing Mildew. Prompt action to counteract mildew can prevent development of musty odors. Air the room or area, applying heat if necessary to get it dry. Scrub floor and walls with chlorine laundry bleach diluted 1 cup to 1 gallon of water, or a mild alkali like trisodium phosphate (TSP); follow by spraying with a fungicide.

Bathroom tiles in which the grouting has deteriorated allow moisture to collect behind the walls. Regrouting (see Chapter 2) can cure the condition. Wood paneling that is badly infected and does not respond to treatment should be discarded and replaced.

Restore upholstered articles, rugs, and carpets by careful brushing and vacuuming, then dry thoroughly by exposing to sunlight in the open air or with an electric heater. Sponging with carpet shampoo followed by a fungicide spray will help prevent recurrence of the mildew.

Leather goods may be salvaged by wiping with denatured alcohol and scrubbing with saddle soap or a soap containing a germicide. Contaminated shoes are restored by application of a formaldehyde solution, after which they should be aired thoroughly and the insides sprayed or powdered with a fungicide.

8. THE USEFUL BASEMENT

A dry and well-lighted basement is a boon to any family. Properly utilized, it provides excellent social and recreational facilities, including a family playroom perhaps larger than any other room in the house, an efficient laundry, a workshop, and possibly a gymnasium, home office, darkroom, pottery room, or provision for other hobbies, in addition to storage space and a wardrobe for out-of-season clothes.

These extra facilities can be obtained, attractively fitted up and brightly lighted with fluorescents, at much lower cost and far quicker than other home space. The walls, floors, and ceiling are already there—only the finishing and fittings are needed. The project includes wall paneling, partitions, floor and ceiling tiles, and electrical lighting, plus plumbing in the case of a laundry, darkroom, or extra lavatory. Because this is interior work with no structural changes, there are no plans to file, no approvals to obtain (except for the plumbing and electrical work), and you can use any materials that suit your taste and budget. The homeowner can do the project almost completely by himself, piecemeal, in spare hours or a vacation period, at considerable saving in cost. The information supplied here, together with instruction booklets available from materials manufacturers (listed at the back of this book), provides the guidance needed to do a creditable basement finishing project.

CURE DAMPNESS FIRST

A basement that is damp and clammy is not suitable for such a project until the condition has been corrected. Not only is such an atmosphere unpleasant because of the dampness odors, it also signals a serious threat to the house structure itself, as the excess moisture and the resultant condensation encourage termite infestation, "dry" wood rot, and mildew fungi. The insidious damage, continuing unseen and unheeded, becomes alarmingly apparent in certain ways.

The first indication of decay that you observe may be new squeaks in the upstairs floors, sagging floor boards, or strange wall cracks. These conditions sometimes result normally from settling of house sills and joists. However, ragged peeling of paint at door frames, window sills, and siding may signal termite infestation. Mildew does not itself threaten the structure, but it can cause extensive staining of wall paneling and stored articles, while creating a musty odor that makes the basement untenable for family purposes.

Cause of Dry Rot. Certain fungi, which are microscopic plants, attack and destroy wood fibers. The fungi grow only in the presence of moisture, thus it is not "dry" rot, even though the decayed wood is found to be very dry. Actually, wood is one of the most durable building products, as attested by

(Above) This well-designed family room in the basement includes a handsome soda fountain and sprightly refreshment tables, all in the lightest and brightest colors, for happy entertaining. Floor is Excelon vinyl asbestos.

(Below) Another enormous recreation room, this one decorated to exemplify winter sports. Note floodlights over the pool table.

(Above) *From This:* Many a spacious basement is wasted as a cluttered refuge for cast-off furniture, when the space could be converted into an attractive recreation room for all the family.

(Below) *To This:* With a little planning, minimal expense, and a few handy remedies for concealing architectural shortcomings, poorly used basement space is converted to a quiet zone for enjoyment of music or games. Acoustical Cushiontone ceiling and "Oracle" Perky Print carpeting are featured. From Armstrong Cork Company.

wood structures that have survived for centuries in dry climates, such as parts of Egypt, or when preserved with protective coatings. Wood framing members are subject to decay when the moisture content is more than 20 percent. In a new home, dry rot can take place in green wood used for construction, or wood that is in contact with the ground, or in structural members of a poorly vented crawl space.

Sources of Moisture. Tracking down the source of excessive moisture is sometimes most frustrating. The dampness may result from water entry through cracks in the foundation wall or concrete floor, dripping water pipes, inadequate outside drainage allowing water to seep through window walls and detached mortar joints, rainwater dripping inside the walls from a clogged roof gutter or defective chimney flashings, an unvented clothes dryer, or simply high relative humidity in a tightly insulated home. One other common source is environmental, as in areas subject to exceptionally high atmospheric humidity along lakes and seashore.

Correcting Foundation Leaks. The preferred treatment depends on the type of foundation and the cause of the seepage. A test for porosity may be done in humid weather by taping a small mirror or piece of shiny metal face against the wall, and allowing it to remain overnight. Drops of moisture on the mirror indicate water penetration.

Corrective treatment starts outside, to eliminate accumulation of water at the walls. The ground must be sloped away from the foundation walls on all sides—if this is not possible because of the land grade, then terra cotta drain pipes must be laid in a trench alongside the foundation footing, leading to a sump deep enough to collect the water. Excavating a trench along the foundation, applying stucco cement over a waterproofing coat of asphalt, is the most effective seepage barrier.

See that splash pans carry away the water runoff from roof gutters, so it won't collect in puddles against the house walls. Connecting the roof downspouts directly into the sewer line is usually the best arrangement.

Coatings of waterproof sealer paint on the in-

Most effective waterproofing treatment involves excavating a trench along the outside wall, which is given a coat of asphaltum sealer.

side foundation wall sometimes will do the trick, if water pressure against the wall is slight and the mortar is in good condition. The paint is applied with a roller in the density specified by the manufacturer. In recent years, interior waterproofing paints have been considerably improved in effectiveness by the development of epoxy sealants.

A wall that has already received a waterproofing treatment cannot be given a second chance with new paint unless the previous coating has been completely removed by wire brushing.

Cement stucco protects the asphalt coating agains damage from earth backfill of trench.

Silicone masonry paint comes as a dry powder, to be mixed with water into a thick fluid. A 25-pound box is sufficient for about 200 square feet, or a 25-foot length of wall.

Waterproofing Applications. After patching all cracks and holes, brush off loose particles with a stiff fiber or wire brush, saturate the wall with a brush or the spray of a garden hose. The first sealer coating is applied with a fiber scrub brush (not a paint brush that will quickly deteriorate). Work the paint thoroughly into the concrete pores and mortar joints. Allow it to dry overnight, then apply a second coat with a paint roller.

Repairing Wall Cracks. Epoxy cements, the most advanced patching material, can be used on in-side and outside walls. Widen the cracks with a chisel to at least ½-inch width, brush out all loose particles, and moisten. Mix a stiff mortar of the cement, shape it into a plug, and press it deeply into the crack, smoothing immediately with a trowel. The epoxy comes in two cans, the contents mixed in equal amounts to start a chemical reaction. Mix only as much quantity as can be applied within 10 minutes. A quality epoxy cement for waterproofing is ZAP, produced by Construction Chemical Corporation of Monroe, Conn., and sold in convenient quart cans.

A foundation crack can be patched even while water is pouring in. Mix Waterplug cement into a stiff mortar, pack it firmly into the crack and hold it in place until the cement has set, then level off with a trowel. After the cement hardens, coat the entire wall with epoxy sealer.

Epoxy waterproofing paint is applied on foundation wall in thick coating with bristle scrubbing brush. A second waterproofing coat is brushed on easily.

The basement floor is another source of moisture, but the mastic used for cementing down floor tiles in the finished room usually will seal the evaporation and the warmer tiles will inhibit condensation on the floor.

Wood Flooring. Many older homes have wood flooring in the basement, laid on 2 × 4 "sleepers" over the concrete. Occasional flooding of the basement soaks the wood, causing dry rot and mildew, with a resulting clammy odor. In such situations, the best remedy is to rip out and discard the wood boards, installing instead vinyl asbestos tiles cemented directly on the concrete. This alone often eliminates an objectionable odor.

Humidity Control. Adequate venting is the best method of basement humidity control, supplemented where extreme conditions exist with exhaust fans or air conditioners placed into window wells. In some excessively humid areas, it is necessary to shut the basement windows during hot daytime hours and open them at night when the outside air is cooler to exhaust moisture-laden air. An electric dehumidifier, which can draw gallons of water out of the air each day, will make a considerable contribution to basement comfort.

Sump Pumps. An automatic drain pump permanently installed in a floor pit will control occasional basement flooding from laundry machine overflow, pipe leaks, or storm sewer backup. The compact electric pumps are actuated by a float similar to that in a toilet flush tank. When water rises in the pit to a preset level, the pump automatically goes into action to discharge the water through a pipe leading outdoors. The sump is particularly useful in homes subject to frequent seepage because they are situated on land with a high water table.

An excellent supplement to the sump is a narrow channel along the rim of the basement floor, about 3 inches deep and sloped into the sump pit. Water entering the basement flows toward the sump pump, where it is promptly discharged outdoors.

Off-the-Floor Sewer Line. In many basements the sewer soil pipe is above the floor. Until recently, this required that laundry washing machines and tubs be mounted on platforms several feet above the floor so the waste water could drain into the soil line. Now automatic pumps permit installing the washer more conveniently at floor level. Similar pumps permit installation of a toilet or complete bathroom in a finished basement despite the high sewer line.

TERMITE CONTROL

Termites go for wood, so a first step in termite control is to remove all wood debris around the house, particularly dried-out bushes, wood scraps, and fireplace logs. Tree stumps must be dug out, all roots removed. Examine basement window sills and door frames; any that are in direct contact with the ground must be provided with a concrete barrier. Any accumulation of earth around a wood member—stairs, siding, milkbox chutes, and the like, is suspect as a termite tunnel and must be brushed clean.

A definite sign of termite infestation are rows of flat mud tubes along outside walls leading to a wood member. These tubes should be broken and brushed away. House beams and sills can be tested for soundness by driving an ice pick or long awl into the center of the beam—if the pick suddenly slips inward with less resistance than at the outside of the beam, there's a strong possibility that the wood has been weakened internally. Replacement of damaged framing members is very difficult because the new beams must be fitted into place without causing sag or displacement of the house frame. This work should be done only by the best professional carpenters with adequate equipment.

Chemical Treatment. The generally accepted chemical for termite control is orthodichlorobenzene (chlordane) available as a 76 percent concentrate in a petroleum base, to be diluted 1 part to 100, or 1 pint of chlordane to 12½ gallons of water. Sale of chlordane is banned in several states, however, or restricted to commercial exterminators.

Example of extensive termite damage that has reached to the surface. In most situations, the termite infestation is unseen because the insects attack the innermost parts of a beam, causing it ultimately to weaken and sag.

The diluted chemical is sprayed into a trench, at least 15 inches deep, all around the house. Drench the sides and bottom with 8 gallons of the solution for each 10 feet of trench. After backfilling the soil, spray an equal amount of the solution along the surface.

This treatment would require 1¾ gallons of the concentrated chlordane for a house approximately 20 by 30 feet. Chlordane is highly toxic and must be handled with great care, the hands protected with rubber gloves. Apply bicarbonate of soda to relieve any skin irritation from the chemical.

The area at the front door is highly vulnerable to termite attack because the banked earth under the stairs and stoop is close to or in direct contact with the wood sill under the doorway. Burrowing under a brick or stone stoop is a difficult task, particularly if the stoop has masonry sidewalls. A practical alternative is applying the antitermite treatment from above, through the access pro-

vided by removing the front door threshold, which may be of brass, aluminum, or wood. This will expose the structural house member below, most likely a large wood beam resting atop the foundation wall. Drill holes about 2 feet apart, straight down into the sill beam, to about half the thickness of the beam. Pour the chlordane or other termite control chemical into the holes, using a funnel. You can seal these holes by tapping in short pieces of dowel if the holes have been drilled to the right diameter.

This treatment provides an effective, long-lasting protection against termite infestation. There is one critical objection, however, in that the chlordane contains a crude petroleum as a vehicle, and a distinct odor like that of tar will last for some time, usually several weeks. The best time to do the project, therefore, is just before the family takes off for a holiday. But while some people find it offensive, others are very fond of the creosote odor.

FINISHING THE BASEMENT

The most basic approach to a functional basement is to paint the floor and walls, tile the ceiling, and improve the lighting. These simple steps will make the area sufficiently bright and clean, so it can be used as a playroom, workshop, and for other practical purposes.

A more complete basement conversion is a practical project that produces an attractive recreation room, with separate provisions for other requirements. The cost of this finishing will depend, of course, on the materials used, and whether the work will be done entirely by the homeowner or will include professional services for some or all parts, such as laying the floor tiles, framing the walls, applying wall panels and ceiling tiles, electrical wiring and plumbing work.

Total cost can be estimated beforehand by figuring the quantity and prices of different materials required, such as the number of 2 × 3s for partition framing and wall studs, the 1 × 3 strips for the ceiling tile supports, the wall panels, ceiling tile, floor tile, and doors. Estimates can be obtained for electric wiring and fixtures.

Planning the Project. You can do part of the project now, leaving other sections or rooms for later when leisure time and budget permit. But start with at least a tentative overall plan, providing for facilities that will be ultimately needed, so that it won't be necessary later to tear down any finished segment.

Make cardboard cutouts in proportionate sizes based on actual measurements of the various enclosed areas that you want; move these around on the overall sketch until you have the best arrangement. For the workshop, make sure there is access to the basement for bringing in lumber, and also space to use your stationary power tools, but keep in mind that when fitted with casters, a bench saw and other power tools can be moved out of the workshop into the playroom whenever greater space is needed for handling long boards and panels. It would be best to set up the workshop first, as that will help the project. Try to locate a bathroom and perhaps a guest room, where each will have at least one window. Provision for emergency exit also should be considered.

Scheduling the Project. Individual phases of the finishing project are scheduled so that each can be done in the most expeditious order. After waterproofing the foundation walls, the first step is framing the partitions and walls. Ceiling joists are furred out with 1 × 3 wood strips to which the ceiling tile will be attached. If insulation is to be placed inside the wall framing, this is done before the electric wires are strung. Next, electrical outlet boxes and fixtures are roughed in, wire cables strung through drilled holes in the studs. Built-in wall units, frames around windows, boxing in of pipes and heating ducts, and similar details are completed; then the walls are paneled, the doors hung and finally the ceiling and floor tiles installed.

RECOMMENDED MATERIALS

The lowest cost wall panelings include gypsum (plasterboard), insulation board, and hardboard, all available in 4 by 8 foot panels and variations

Room finishing starts with 2 × 3 framing for partitions and wall panels. Corner studs, one in each direction, are nailed to floor and ceiling plates. Use a level to see that the studs are plumb.

Studs are placed 16 inches apart, "on centers" (OC). This modular dimension assures that the edges of standard wall panels will meet the studs for nailing.

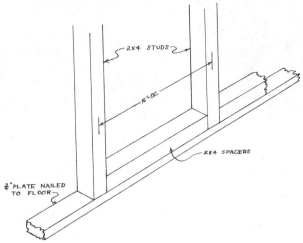

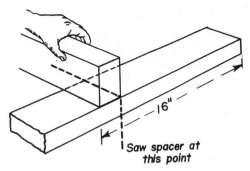

Saw spacer at this point

Spacers help position the studs correctly. The stud is held tightly against the spacer while nails are driven in at an angle to fasten the stud to the plate.

How to find 16 inches OC? Just cut a piece of 2 × 3 or 2 × 4 to 16-inch length less the thickness of the stud stock, which is about 1½ inches. Thus this spacer will be *about* 14½ inches long, and when studs are installed with the spacer between them, they will be 16 inches OC.

Partition framing follows the same procedure as for wall panels, the studs plumbed and nailed to top and bottom plates.

of that size. In basements with ceilings less than 8 feet high, savings can be achieved by buying 4 by 7 foot panels, to rest on baseboards of suitable size so the panels will reach full height. These panels, when the joints are taped, can be painted or papered.

A more attractive result is obtained with prefinished plywood panels that need no further work once they are installed. Another preferred surface for basement rooms is Marlite, a rigid hardboard panel with an exceptionally smooth plastic surface that is easy to clean and almost indestructible. These panels come in a wide range of colors and patterns, including natural wood and marble finishes that are indistinguishable from the originals they simulate. The Marlite panels are impervious to wood rot, moisture, and other adverse conditions that might exist in a basement.

Floor Coverings. For the floor, use tiles specifically rated for "below grade" or below-ground-level installation. Typical are Armstrong's vinyl-asbestos Excelon tiles, which are installed over concrete or old tiles with a mastic cement. Also suitable for basement installation is self-adhesive indoor-outdoor "grass carpet," which includes its own foam rubber backing and is especially desirable where small children may be playing on the floor.

You can doll up the grass carpet with inset cutouts of a contrasting color. As illustrated, the inset pattern is placed over the carpet, and the outline sliced with an X-Acto blade, cutting through the bottom carpet. The inset figure will then fit precisely, held in place with double-faced adhesive tape. Use your imagination and talent to design your own inserts, representing the theme of the room, or write to Armstrong Cork Company, Lancaster, Pa. 17604, for a free package of 12 patterns.

Install-It-Yourself Carpet. The material that can well make your finished basement room is colorful carpeting, in shag and other popular types, that you install yourself, directly on the concrete floor, or over present floor tiles. Epilogue carpeting by Armstrong has integral foam backing, needs no padding, comes in 6- and 12-foot widths. The carpeting is simply unrolled along any wall, trimmed to length with heavy shears. The next strip is unrolled alongside, the precisely cut edges joining perfectly and the seam retained underneath by a vinyl tape having adhesive on both sides. The taping is done by folding back the carpet edges, applying the tape to the floor, then press-

Popular shag style carpet is cut to length with heavy shears. The latex foam backing obviates need for padding, also minimizes effect of any floor irregularities.

Wall-to-wall carpeting now can be installed in below-grade basement, directly on the concrete floor or over old tiles. The do-it-yourself installation starts with rolling out carpet along one wall.

Factory-cut edges of the strips form a perfect seam, held by a special vinyl tape with adhesive on both sides. The Epilogue carpeting by Armstrong is rot-proof and mildew proof.

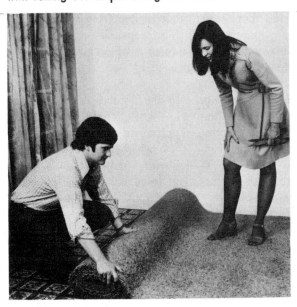

ing down the edges. Extra strips of the tape are placed along door openings and any places where the carpeting is not fitted against a wall. This carpeting also comes in 12-inch squares with an adhesive backing.

Older basement rooms that still have the dark, bleak asphalt tiles, which were the only below-ground-level floor covering of earlier years, can be rejuvenated at lowest cost with the Epilogue carpeting. Normally, changing deteriorated tiles

(Below) Place your figure pattern over the carpet and slice around it with a sharp blade. The carpet is easy to cut. Figures should be of a sharply contrasting color.

(Right above) Remove the piece of carpet and press the insert down on double-faced adhesive tape applied to the bare spot. The inset will be snug enough so that the vacuum can be used over it. The figure that has been removed can be applied to another spot of a different color.

(Right below) Room can be decorated with the insets to carry a particular design motif, such as nautical, skiing, card game, or nursery themes.

would be quite difficult and expensive as the old tiles must be torn up, the old adhesive scraped off, the floor sanded to remove surface irregularities. In addition, there is the cost of the new tiles, adhesive, and installation charges. But install-it-yourself carpeting changes this. The old tiles remain as they are—no sanding, no adhesives, no padding, no replacements. The carpet goes down in just an afternoon or evening, ready for use—bright, warm and colorful, perfect for a basement room.

OUTSIDE ENTRY

An outside staircase is essential as a fire escape route, particularly if you plan a guest room. It also permits children to enter the playroom directly from outside, and facilitates bringing in wall panels, lumber, and other large materials for the finishing project. If there is no present entry, one is installed by breaking an opening in the foundation wall, 30 or 36 inches wide, and a foot above the inside floor. A 4- by 6-foot area outside is excavated, lined with concrete blocks for the stairs, which may be of concrete or metal. The area is enclosed along the top with a concrete curb to block water entry, and fitted with steel hatch doors. The Bilco company of New Haven, Conn., manufacturer of these steel doors, also produces metal stair stringers for easy assembly with wood treads. Write for an instruction booklet.

The wall opening can be cut with a cold chisel if the wall is of cinder blocks. A poured concrete foundation, however, requires a pneumatic hammer, and that is a job for a professional contractor

An outside entrance to basement is obtained by breaking through the foundation wall for a 30-inch-wide opening. Work is done with pneumatic drill by contractor.

8/14
Area outside is lined with concrete block to grade level, stairs built of concrete, or prefabricated steel stairway installed.

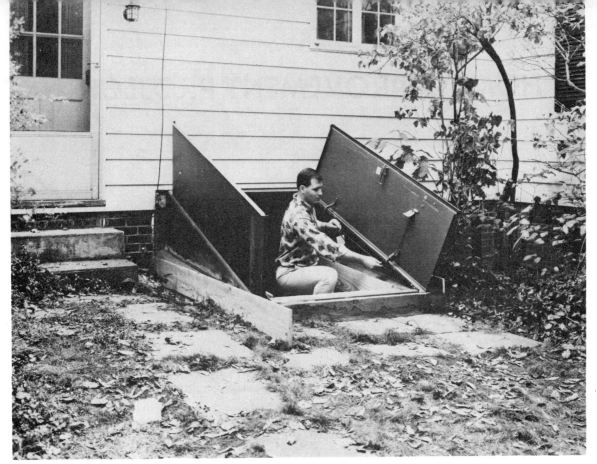

Steel hatch doors, bolted to a concrete curbing around the stair opening, are waterproof. Doors are locked from inside or outside.

who can assure that the cut is made square and neat, without damage to the adjacent wall. Locate the staircase where it won't interfere with the inside room arrangement.

KEEP IT LIGHT

An important contribution to an attractive basement recreation room is fluorescent lighting. The cool, white lights provide a uniform, glare-free brightness that transforms what might be a cavernous bleakness to a fresh, sparkling, and inviting room. Use a 2/40-watt fixture (two lamps of 40 watts each) for each 40 square feet of floor space. Supplement with 40-watt strips behind cornices along the side walls for interesting indirect light-

ing. A large full-color landscape mural on one wall, framed like a window and well-lighted, will give the room an outdoors atmosphere.

IMPROVING THE STAIRCASE

In many basements, the stairs are rickety, of minimum construction, a source of accidental stumbling. Reinforcement of the stairs often is possible, usually by adding risers and reinforcing the treads. A worthwhile expense, in some instances, may be replacement with custom-made stairs that provide greater rigidity for sure footing. Improved handrails and light switches at top and bottom also help assure comfort and safety.

9. HOME IMPROVEMENT PROJECTS

Running a home is not all care and repair to keep ahead of incipient deterioration. There are any number of initiatives and ideas, some of them quite simple and quickly put into effect, that make the home more comfortable, more economical, more attractive. We are not concerned here with decorative aspects—a very large and worthy subject by itself—but rather with practical projects, such as expanded storage space that makes so great a difference in family convenience. The various projects presented in this chapter will prove of interest and assistance in many households.

A CEDAR WARDROBE

One of the most practical additions you can provide for your home is a large cedar wardrobe in the basement for out-of-season garments to ease crowding of your everyday closets. Its location and actual dimensions will depend on available space. A cedar-lined walk-in closet, 6 by 10 feet, provides space for long double rows of garments and other seasonal items.

Aromatic, insect-repellent red cedar lining will give the wardrobe a pleasant forest fragrance in addition to helping make it mothproof. Cedar strips, ⅜-inch thick and 2 to 4 inches in width, come in bundles containing material to cover about 40 square feet of surface area. The strips are tongue-and-grooved on all four edges, so they interlock at the ends as well as the sides, all joints thus being flush and tightly sealed.

One preferred location for the closet is under the basement stairs, a space that usually is not utilized. The wardrobe, including the doorway, is framed with 2 × 4s as shown in the sketch. The ceiling receives rows of 1- by 3-inch strips, nailed across the joists, to which the cedar boards are attached. The exterior walls of the wardrobe are finished with either gypsum wallboard or ¼-inch hardboard panels, nailed over the frame.

The floor of the wardrobe may be either the same cedar or of cemented vinyl tiles. Some prefer a softer and warmer floor, for which Armstrong's below-ground level foam-backed carpeting, which you can install yourself, is perfect.

For better dustproofing and insectproofing, tack a layer of building paper with a stapling gun over the inside surface of the frame before applying the cedar boards.

The cedar boards are installed either by blind nailing into the tongues so the nails are not visible, or face nailing, which is perfectly acceptable for this project. Use 1-inch cut nails for blind nailing, 3d finishing nails for the face.

Do the walls first, then the ceiling. The cedar is installed horizontally on the walls. Start at one corner, working up from the bottom, the first

A practical extra wardrobe lined with cedar can be built under the stairs or other area of the basement. A frame is constructed of 2 × 4s, faced with gypsum wallboard, plywood, or roof decking boards. The ceiling area is furred out with 1 × 3 strips to receive the cedar.

strip placed with its grooved edge down. Put at least two nails into the first strip, about ¾ inch in from the ends; the following strips are interlocked, need only a single nail each. Each strip is tapped down, snug but not too tightly, onto the tongue of the previous course. The ends are also tongue-and-grooved, tapped closely for a tight seal. Corner pieces should be fitted as closely as possible, even though you plan to cover those

joints later with cedar or vinyl moldings. Put up cedar across the ceiling furring in the same manner, so that the entire wardrobe is lined, even the floor, unless you decide to use tile there.

A 24-inch hollow core door will serve well for this project, but cover its inside surface also with the cedar boards, this time applied with cartridge-type contact adhesive.

In addition to clothes rods, build shelves of

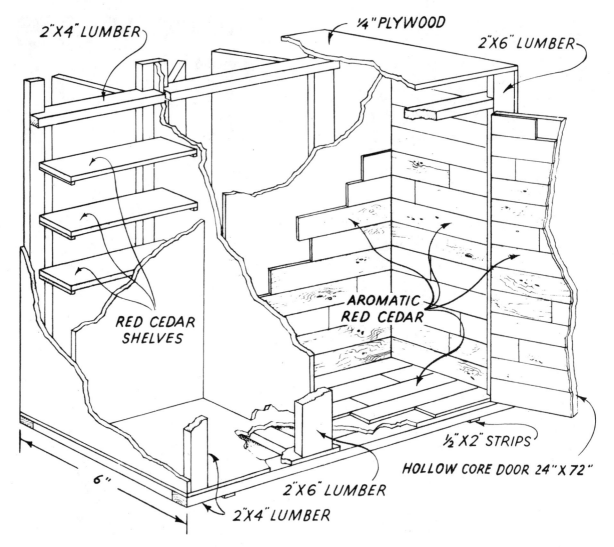

2"X4" LUMBER

¼"PLYWOOD

2"X6" LUMBER

RED CEDAR SHELVES

AROMATIC RED CEDAR

½"X2" STRIPS

HOLLOW CORE DOOR 24"X72"

6"

2"X6" LUMBER

2"X4" LUMBER

Plan for cedar closet provides sufficient width for two rows of clothes poles along the entire length of the shelves located across the ends. Closet is framed out with 2 × 4 lumber, to which the cedar boards are nailed. Install cedar on ceiling for complete enclosure.

cedar boards for sweaters and other items, and simple shoe racks. Finally cover all corner joints with moldings, paying particular attention to sealing the door edges with flexible vinyl or rubber weatherstripping. Install a magnetic catch to keep the door closed. An electric line for overhead lighting can be brought into the wardrobe easily from a basement circuit. Use BX cable or approved plastic wire, drawn along the joists, and make all terminal connections inside an approved electrical fixture box. You may also want to include an automatic light switch on the door.

The cedar lining needs no attention other than occasional dusting with a dry cloth. Do not wax, or use varnish or shellac, as that would seal in the aroma. If the aroma fades after some years, it can be renewed by light sanding or steelwooling the wood surface.

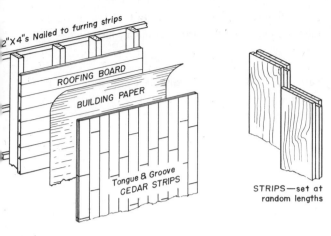

The objective is to seal the wardrobe as tightly as possible. A lining of builder's paper, placed as shown in the sketch, will help assure a dust-free closet.

Strips of red cedar, 3 to 4 inches wide, are tongue and grooved on both the sides and the ends, so random lengths are tightly joined with minimum of nailing.

Cedar strips are quickly installed on walls, ceiling, door, even the floor. Built-in shelving helps to organize storage for maximum utilization.

CLOSET STRETCHING

Looking for a space saver that makes the most of crowded closets? Sliding or bi-fold doors may be the answer—they give easy access to the full width of the closet, including the otherwise hard-to-reach far sides, when the closet front is enlarged to its full width.

Both types of doors work differently than the conventional swinging door. Bi-folds are hung in pairs; as you pull a center knob toward you, the doors double up so each pair is reduced to half its closed width and pivots completely out of the way. Sliding doors move on tracks; you must push them sideways, which may be a bit troublesome if you're accustomed to hinged swinging doors. A disadvantage of the sliding doors also is that only half the closet space is accessible at a time, since the door that is opened slides behind the closed one. Another problem is the tendency to jam when a door hanger slips off its track. Either type

(Left) Clothes closet with double bi-fold louver doors and fitted with shelves for maximum utilization.

(Left below) Much more available closet space is obtained when hinged swing door is converted with a pair of sliding doors that give access to the entire area.

of door can be the full height of the closet, making available the topmost shelves for storage of luggage and other bulky items.

Standard hardware sets for each type of door include all needed materials. Sliding doors are usually of plywood, ¾ inch to 1⅜ inches thick, of a width to overlap 1 inch when closed, and are installed with hanger sheaves that ride on rollers in an overhead track.

The track is available in lengths up to 8 feet. Bi-fold doors may be stock louvers, 1⅜ inches thick, suspended by pivot rollers from an overhead track. The bi-fold tracks come in 4-foot

Bi-fold doors: how to figure door height for existing openings.

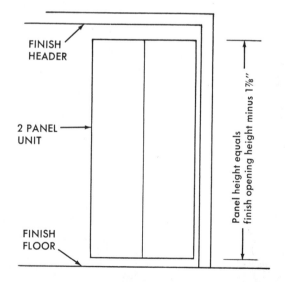

FINISH HEADER

2 PANEL UNIT

FINISH FLOOR

Panel height equals finish opening height minus 1⅞"

Allow additional clearance at floor for carpeting.

lengths; use two or more tracks to make up the required length. The doors must clear the floor by at least ½ inch.

Conversion Procedure. Enlarging the front of a closet can be done so neatly that redecorating the wall will not be necessary. Cover the floor with a drop cloth, keep an empty carton handy to dispose of the plaster debris. Follow these steps in sequence:

1. Remove the old door by driving out the hinge pins. With a wide chisel, pry off the jamb moldings, saw away the door framing studs.

Original door frame and trim are removed. Closet is opened full width, the plaster wall cut along sides, ends framed out with studs and new supporting header placed across the top.

2. Measure the distance inside the closet from the door to each end, mark these positions on the outside wall and draw vertical lines for the enlarged closet opening. Cut the plaster wall with a portable saw, using a cut-off blade. If the line is right on a stud, shift it toward the closet side and make a new cut. Saw away any intervening studs. Break out and discard the excess plaster sections.

3. Frame out the new opening at each end; put up a header of double 2 × 4s across the top, securely supported on end uprights and carefully leveled.

4. Trim the opening with standard door molding, which will cover the rough edges of the plaster.

5. Attach the door track to the header, using shims if necessary so it is perfectly level. Also install the floor guide pins, allowing just ⅛-inch clearance between both sliding doors. Two hanger sheaves are fastened at the top of each sliding

New opening is faced with molding. Measurement is taken here for the top track, which is attached to header. Hanger sheaves go on top of door, which is tilted backward for installation. Door guide pins are driven into bottom plate.

Sliding panel doors: installation clearances for overhead track.

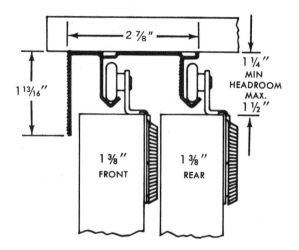

Headroom clearance for track and roller sheaves is 1½ inches to 2½ inches maximum. Install track with 1½-inch no. 10 screws.

door, pivot pins on bi-fold doors. An adjustment screw permits final detailing so the doors operate effortlessly, even though they are taller than the original one. The renovated closet may require a new clothes rod and additional shelves at the top.

WALL-TO-WALL BOOKCASE

Whether or not you're a bibliophile, you will appreciate the decorative contribution of a colorful "wall of books" that makes a room seem wider and higher, its owner more erudite. This is an interesting project, whether the cutting and grooving is done with a hand saw and router, or on a bench or radial arm saw.

The bookcase is built of 1 × 10 pine shelving. For low cost, common grade lumber is suitable, but reject any boards that are warped, split, or have loose knots. Measure the wall and make a rough sketch to determine the positions of the uprights, all equidistant but not more than 4 feet apart, and the spacing of the shelves. Vary the

shelf heights for different size books, making allowance for large special editions. Paneling the back wall with plywood or Marlite beforehand adds to the decorative effect.

All parts are precut for assembly at the spot, the shelves held in grooves cut into the ceiling-height uprights. Each shelf groove is ¼-inch deep. As all uprights except those at the ends receive double grooves at the shelf levels, only about ¼ inch of the wood thickness will remain intact, so handle carefully until the shelves are assembled. They will then be quite sturdy.

Cutting the dado grooves is the main step. With a router, use ½-inch straight bits, making two passes for a total width of ¾ inch to receive the

Board edges are trimmed with narrow molding strips, permitting use of low-cost shelving lumber.

Ceiling-height bookcase makes interesting wall treatment, provides maximum book capacity. Power saw or router cuts the shelf grooves.

shelving. (Use a piece of scrap to test the fit.) Clamp guide strips for each shelf position. On a bench saw, a dado cutter plows the groove to correct width in a single pass, a clamped spacer board serving as a jig for uniform positioning of the grooves. Grooving is done most easily on a radial or swing saw, the board resting on the table as the cutter passes across it. Turn the board over each time to make the opposite cut.

A new, inexpensive tool by Stanley, called "Electric Chisel," can be used in an ordinary portable drill to make the dado grooves and rabbet cuts. This tool requires clamped guide strips to assure straight, uniform grooves.

The uprights are slightly less than ceiling height, but the ceiling crown molding would prevent them going closely against the wall, so a triangular piece is cut from the top corner of each upright

Uprights are cut back at the top and bottom to clear the crown molding and baseboard. New molding is attached along the top to complete the installation.

and another recess made at the bottom to clear the baseboard.

As each upright is raised and plumbed with a spirit level, a couple of shelves are inserted into the grooves and the upright temporarily supported in position with nailed furring strips until the next one is set up. The final upright may need shimming at the side if the wall is not plumb, and the end shelves cut slightly longer or shorter than the others to lock in the assembly tightly.

The rest of the shelves are then tapped into their grooves. The shelf edges may be left as they are or finished with decorative molding strips. At the top, a new crown molding is applied, shaped

at the ends to fit the ceiling molding at the sides, and nailed on. If there's any doubt about the stability of the finished bookcase, put a few nails through the end uprights into the side walls, or install a few right angle brackets attached to the back wall. Apply vertical molding trim along the end uprights, for a neater finish.

SCROLLS AND FLOWERS

When you transplant your geraniums outdoors, let them blossom in style. Cast away your weathered window boxes of yesteryear; replace them with distinctively designed planters that add beauty to your home.

The graceful contours of this illustrated design give an air of lightness even to so large a planter.

Three-dimensional scroll design lends an airy grace to this window or terrace planter, in contrast to the bulky appearance of most square-edge flower boxes.

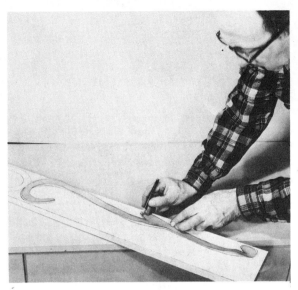

Contoured overlay is shaped with saber or jigsaw from 1 × 4 board. Cutout pattern is made for only half the figure; reverse to get opposite side.

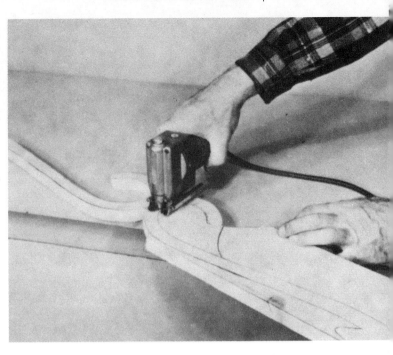

The "secret" is in the scrollshaped overlay and the tapered sides. The length of the box is made proportional to the space that it is to occupy.

The scroll figure, as seen in the photographs, loops downward at the center, curls at the sides to end with a flourish. The cutaway portion along the top is no more than 1½ inches at the deepest part. Its design is simple enough to copy. On heavy wrapping paper, make a pattern half the length of the box, less ½ inch. Start with a free-hand scroll at one end, from 3 to 4 inches in height, depending on the overall length. The line dips slightly about half the distance, then a new line is started at the top edge to merge with the first and continue to the end. There the scroll curves upward, ending flush with the top edge again. Cut out this pattern, trace it directly on a 1 × 4 board, reversing the pattern to get both sides. Cut out the overlay either in one piece or two identical pieces. Round off or bevel the sharp corners of the scroll figure so it has a softer appearance.

Now cut the parts for the box, but before assembling, outline the overlay on the box front and cut the top edge to conform. Attach the overlay with screws (brass or aluminum), then complete the box assembly.

Paint the entire box, including the inside and

Overlay is arranged on box front so that both sides of figures are equalized. Draw outline directly on wood.

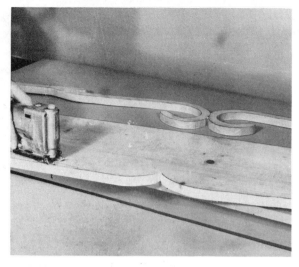

Portable saber saw is used here for shaping top edge of the box front. A hand coping saw also will do this, but more slowly.

Attach overlay to front with 1¼-inch brass screws in countersunk pilot holes. Cover heads with putty. Ends of box are sloped, attached with screws. Bottom should overlap the box sides slightly and should be drilled for draining excess water.

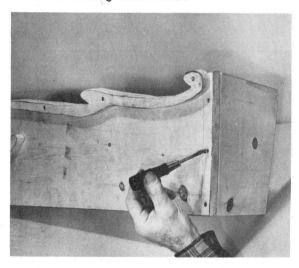

bottom. A single color is preferable in keeping with the dignity of the design. If the box is to be mounted on a wall or under a window, use a pair

of ornamental iron brackets, attach with lead or fiber anchoring plugs.

DECORATIVE CONCEALMENT

Exposed heating pipes and radiators at best are far from attractive, and often quite hideous. Certainly, they play havoc with any decorative scheme, as in the otherwise very pleasant living room of this fine, older home. The solution that

The cabinet is made entirely of stock size boards, plus two 18-inch-wide pieces of ¾-inch plywood. End grain is no problem, as the front frame covers the plywood uprights and top.

was achieved, as shown in the illustrations, may be of interest to other homemakers with similar situations.

A cabinet built along the window wall to cover the exposed radiator includes built-in space for an audio speaker and record albums. The unit is properly vented at front and top, with louvers and slots for minimum heat loss. Coordinated with the cabinet is what appears to be a post for

In place of a projecting steam radiator and exposed riser pipe, this cabinet sets the stage for an attractive decorative effect, with its lamp post at the corner and built-in audio speaker.

lamps—a lamp post, in fact—but its secret mission is to disguise the steam riser reaching to the ceiling. The small speaker cabinet at the side is an afterthought that fits into the basic theme.

This built-in unit can be constructed with basic hand tools. The boards used for the front frame and louvers are easily cut to size with a hand or saber saw; the supporting sections of ¾-inch plywood need not be perfectly square, as they are fully concealed. Even the cutouts in the cabinet top can be done with a compass saw and hand saw, starting with ½-inch drilled holes at each

Lamp post is simply two boards joined at right angles, drilled for the lamp cord which is plugged into an accessible receptacle. The "post" is fastened with hidden brackets.

Cutting the blind louver slots in the cabinet top starts with drilling ½-inch holes at each end of the marked lines. The slots, 1 inch wide, are cut quickly with a saber saw.

Large exposed steam riser pipe, completely hidden by the right-angle boards, is transformed into practical and good looking lamp installation.

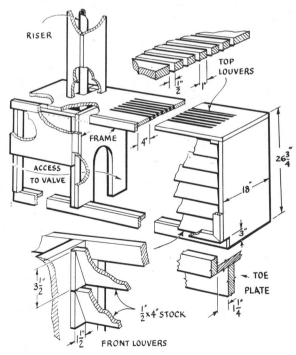

end, although the saber saw will cut the slots more quickly and neatly.

Construction details are shown in the sketch. The project starts with the 18-inch-wide plywood uprights, into which a 3-inch recess is cut in a corner of each for the toe plate. An arched opening is shaped in one upright, giving access to the radiator shutoff valve, a smaller opening in the other to reach the air valve. The front louvers, as seen in the sketch, are supported at an angle against triangular blocks attached uniformly to both uprights. The end grain of the plywood top is covered completely by the front frame, which is of solid stock.

A BULLETIN BOARD

An easy project that will prove of continuous benefit to the whole family is a bulletin board. Make it to the size that best fits the space, serving for kitchen notes, nursery displays, student assignments, and shopping memos.

Use stock wood picture frame or outside corner molding, purchased at any lumberyard. The frame corners are cut in a miter box, glued together and reinforced with corrugated fasteners at the back. A sheet of inexpensive insulation wallboard, cut to fit the frame, will be quite satisfactory for the panel, as it is soft enough to receive thumbtacks. The tack holes remain visible, however, so eventually the board will have a pockmarked appearance. When that happens, just cover with burlap for a fresh start, or resurface with cork, using 12- by 12-inch floor tiles available at any floor covering store, applied with linoleum paste.

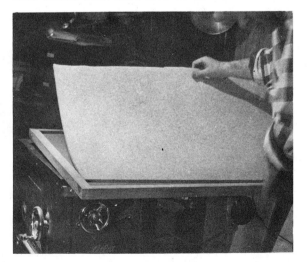

Molding has a rabbet offset along the inside edge to hold panel. Corners of frame are mitered, glued, and reinforced with corrugated fasteners.

Bulletin board is handy in kitchen, nursery, student's room. Stock molding is used for the frame to hold an insulating board panel that is soft enough for thumbtacks.

Insulation board will serve for the panel, but cork in either sheeting or 12-inch square cork floor tiles is much better, won't show tack marks.

SQUEEZING IN A DISHWASHER

The only reason that many housewives still do not have the use of a dishwasher is the problem of fitting it into a crowded kitchen. The dishwasher, 24 inches wide, goes under any kitchen counter, but obviously sacrifices scarce storage space. Even the small kitchen, however, may accommodate a free-standing "island" cabinet, which would provide a substitute pantry. Moving the sink a couple of feet to one side or another (yes, the sink can be shifted by adding extensions to the water and drain lines) may provide sufficient clearance. But dishwasher installation isn't limited to under a counter; if there is a floor-to-ceiling cabinet on the sink wall, cutting away its lower section may permit the installation there, but the front-loading type only, with water and drain connections to the sink through copper tubing or plastic pipe. Lacking these solutions, a rolling (portable) dishwasher may be stored in a convenient corridor or closet, hooked up to the sink when put to use. The dishwasher drain hose is connected to an inlet leading into a special trap that is installed under the sink.

ARBOR FOR HATS

Remember those pantograph hat racks? They weren't very ornamental, but they kept hats and caps in order for large families with many comings and goings. They're very much in demand again, perhaps joining the nostalgic trend to Tiffany lampshades. It's fun making your own copy.

The rack shown is made of 13 feet of lattice strips, ¼-inch thick and 1⅛-inches wide, a length of ½-inch dowel for the pegs. The strips are cut into four pieces, 24 inches long, and four others, 13 inches long. Mark the halfway position on each longer strip, also at 1¾ inches from each end on all strips. With a gauge, find and mark the center of the wood width at those positions for drilling.

The pegs are placed where the slats cross, as shown in the sketch. The four slats on top are drilled through for full ½-inch diameter holes into which the dowels are pressed, held by slender

Old-fashioned hat rack offers nostalgic charm while serving a practical everyday purpose. Rack is easily made of wood lattice strips and dowels.

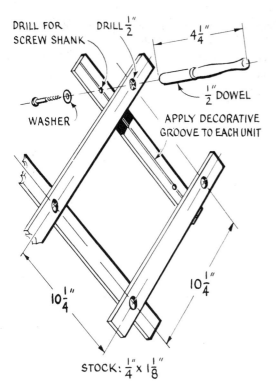

DRILL FOR SCREW SHANK

DRILL $\frac{1}{2}$"

$4\frac{1}{4}$"

$\frac{1}{2}$" DOWEL

WASHER

APPLY DECORATIVE GROOVE TO EACH UNIT

$10\frac{1}{4}$"

$10\frac{1}{4}$"

STOCK: $\frac{1}{4}$" x $1\frac{1}{8}$"

Sketch shows how rack is assembled. The dowel pegs go into ½-inch holes in the top slats, are held by screws through bottom slats. End pieces are just long enough to continue beyond the corner.

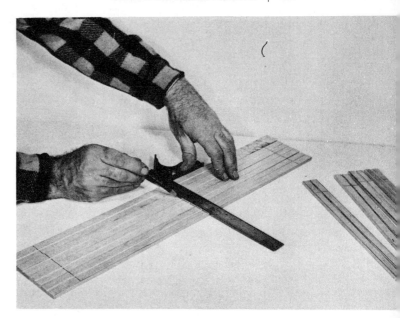

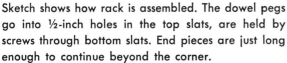

wood screws through smaller holes in the slats underneath.

Stack the strips in two piles, drill through all marked centers with a $\frac{1}{16}$-inch drill. This assures alignment of the matching parts. Now drill ½-inch holes at the middle and at each end of two long slats, and the ends of two short slats, using the pilot holes as a center guide.

Saw ten pieces of dowel to 5-inch lengths for

(Right above) Mark the middle of all longer slats, also 1¾ inches from each end on all slats for the pegs.

(Right) Half of slats are drilled for ½-inch holes, the others receive only tiny pilot holes for no. 6 screws.

Pegs are turned on a drill press. Board clamped to drill table has ½-inch hole in alignment with the drill chuck to steady the dowel while it is "turned" for decorative design.

the pegs. If you have a drill press or lathe, you can shape them for better appearance. On the drill press, drill a ½-inch hole deeply into a thick board, clamp the board to the table in alignment with the chuck. Lock a dowel into the chuck, lower the chuck so the dowel end is in the board hole. As the dowel turns, hold a small triangular or rattail file against its side to form a ring design. Repeat on the other dowels, and drill a $\frac{1}{16}$-inch hole in each for a screw.

Dowels go into larger holes, are retained by screws through no. 6 holes in bottom slats.

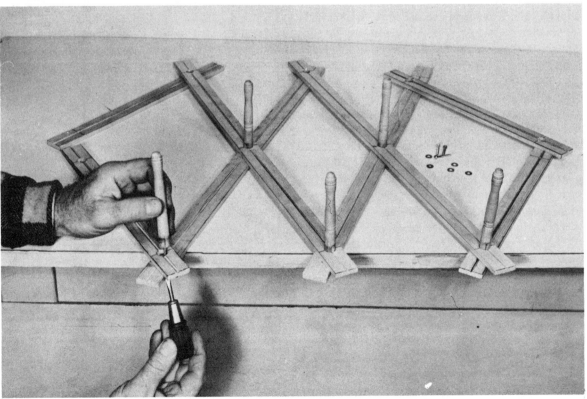

For assembly, push the dowels into the larger holes, fit the back slats in place and turn ½-inch no. 6 screws through the pre-drilled holes. Extend the rack so there is ample clearance for hats, and hang on the wall.

SCREENING A PORCH

A quick and economical way to screen an open porch uses the wrap-around method, dispensing with individual screen frames. All that's necessary is to supplement the usual support posts of the porch with uprights spaced 4 feet apart, and horizontal cross-members, as a frame for the screening.

Start by bolting down a 2 × 4 sill plate along the deck edges between the existing posts, all around the porch. Include a frame for an exterior door, if one is desired. If the porch deck is concrete, attach the sill with screws through drilled holes into masonry anchors (see Chapter 2). The uprights, of 4 × 4 lumber or double 2 × 4s bolted together, rest on the deck plate and are cut to fit under the roof support beam. Attach with right-angle metal brackets at both ends. Crossmembers of 2 × 4s are inserted between the uprights an inch less than 4 feet above the deck, and if the roof support beam is more than 8 feet above the deck, additional crossmembers are set in at the 8-foot level. Paint all framing members that have been installed.

When the paint is dry, proceed with the screening. The wrap-around method uses a continuous length of Fiberglas screening 48 inches wide. The screening can be purchased in a roll long enough to go twice around the porch (once at each 4-

Screening is started by stapling to a vertical member at one end of the wall. Place staples 1½ inches apart.

Screen cloth is held taut at each position. The 48-inch cloth covers half the height of porch framing, so two courses are required.

foot level). Thus a porch 12 by 16 feet, exposed on three sides, will have 40 linear feet, so a quantity of 80 feet is required (less the space taken by an outside door). Purchase of a 100-foot roll might be most economical, leaving a surplus for any future projects.

The screening installation starts with the lower half of the frame, a folded-over edge stapled to a far post against the house wall. Unroll the screen cloth enough to be stretched tautly around the first corner post, drive a series of staples into both crossmembers and into the corner post. Continue on to the next side to complete that level, omitting only the door opening. Repeat the process for the top course of the screening, overlapping the edges of both courses.

At the final post, allow an excess when cutting off the screening so the end can be doubled over for stapling. Wood molding strips tacked over the horizontal joints of the screening will give the appearance of individual frames and protect the staples from the weather. Installation of a standard screen door, wood or aluminum, completes the project.

HI-FI HIDEAWAY

This audio system and storage cabinet takes up no room space at all—it is installed through an opening into a closet, flush with the wall. Although the record player is 14 inches deep, the amount of space taken in the closet is only 10 inches, the remainder supplied by the thickness of the wall itself.

You may want to utilize this recessed cabinet idea also for the thinner television sets, to save on available space. Make certain first, though, that the wall you intend to open does not contain plumbing or heating pipes. You can check the plumbing lines from the basement and at the floor above—plumbing pipes are concentrated

The screen is carefully stapled to all upright and crossmember surfaces. A facing of wood molding gives the appearance of panels.

Complete audio system, including speaker box, slide-out record player and radio tuner, is built into wall niche formed by cutting into the side of closet.

Side wall of closet cut open, one wall stud removed by sawing at top and bottom. A 2 × 6 horizontal header replaces the stud.

Rear view, showing the recessed speaker and record player. Only a few inches of usable space in closet are lost.

alongside the main soil stack of the plumbing drains, usually 4 inches diameter.

Heating pipes and tubing are not likely to be a problem as they usually are in the floor or along the baseboard; if your heating system is steam, you could determine whether a riser pipe is at the location because of the warmth at that wall. Electric cable inside the wall need not be a deterrent, as it can be stapled to one side out of the way, or the cable spliced into a junction box from which a line is drawn for the audio cabinet.

The easiest and neatest way to cut the plaster wall opening is with a portable circular saw, using a non-ferrous cutoff blade. Keep empty cartons handy to discard the debris, vacuum the plaster dust before it spreads. If the cabinet width requires removal of a wall stud, frame the opening with a 2 × 6 header across the top, supported by double 2 × 4s at the sides. The cabinet shelves can be mounted on cleats attached to these supports, or on adjustable shelf standards.

The plaster edges are patched and faced with molding on which louver or other doors are hung. The section inside the closet is enclosed with plywood or wallboard panels, but includes a narrow opening or two for ventilating the heat from the hi-fi.

10. RENEWING FURNITURE

"A stitch in time saves nine" applies to furniture, too. When the glued joints of a chair or cabinet loosen, the legs and frame can twist sufficiently to split the retaining dowels or tenons, causing the furniture to completely collapse. The necessary regluing, if outside help is depended on, often is

**THIS COMPLETELY DEMOLISHED PIANO BENCH WAS RESTORED
BY THE PROCESS SHOWN IN PHOTO SERIES**

Overall staining gives a repaired piano bench a brand-new appearance. Before staining, the old surface is washed with turpentine to remove wax.

Total collapse? No, not if all parts are saved. Piano bench matches its grand piano, so was worth rebuilding.

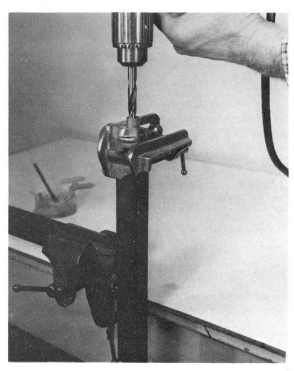

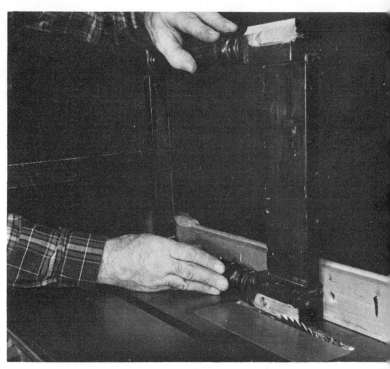

Broken dowel end is drilled out of hole, using doweling jig to keep the drill straight and avoid excessively enlarging the hole.

Split edge of leg post is cut square on power saw to permit fitting a replacement part made of new wood. Surface is rebuilt by gluing on matching wood stock, shaped to fit.

Dowel has spiral grooves to prevent air lock when dowel is driven into glue-filled hole.

Repair goes in stages as bit by bit the salvaged pieces are fitted and glued on.

quite costly—sometimes the repair comes to more than you originally paid for the furniture.

You can do the repairs yourself with a modest group of tools—a couple of pipe clamps, some C clamps, a fine-toothed dovetail saw, a drill or brace and bit, a chisel or two. To repair scratches or restore the surface finish, you will need an alcohol lamp, an assortment of shellac stick colors, a sanding pad, and a broad putty knife, all for a modest total cost.

When furniture breaks, make sure to save every piece. Parts that split along the grain are most easily glued together, made as good as new. Breaks across the grain present a more difficult condition as end-grain pieces can rarely be brought together properly. However, there are alternatives such as re-jointing by blind dowling, splines, and pins. Broken tenons and dowels can be drilled out, fitting new dowels into the joint.

The mortise and tenon, one of the oldest joints

Clamps draw the leg sections together for final assembly. Pressure must be equalized to prevent twisting. This is a critical step. Wipe off all squeezed-out glue while still fresh.

Final touchup of open spots is done with matching shellac sticks, filling indentations and spaces between glued slivers.

used in cabinetmaking, has exceptional strength because the tenon section—at the end of a rail for example—is reduced in size so that when joined into its mortise, the cut-back shoulders provide extra gluing surfaces and thus greater strength. The tenon may vary ¾ inch to 1½ inches in length.

The piano bench shown is a good example of a restoration because it was reduced to a total wreck by rollicking teenagers. This would not have happened had the bench been in solid condition, but because the leg joints had become wobbly, the tenons and braces just splintered apart. This writer was enlisted to restore the bench because it matched the grand piano and could be replaced only by making a duplicate.

PLANNING THE REPAIR

The repair starts with placing all the pieces in their appropriate arrangement so the stages of reconstruction can be planned in sequence, otherwise the final assembly may be stymied by inability to fit the parts together. Separate sections are rebuilt first, as with the leg assemblies shown. Small pieces are glued on carefully to be certain that the fit is precise. Squeezed-out glue is wiped off with a damp cloth to prevent hardening on the surface, as the glue coating would prevent uniform application of the finishing stain. The way to avoid this is to apply clamp pressure, then loosen the clamp somewhat to wipe off the squeezed-out glue with a damp cloth, and re-clamp with waxed paper under the clamp head.

Replacing Lost Pieces. If small pieces are missing, do not despair—these spaces can be patched later with pigmented wood filler or Spackle. Cracked tenon holes are glued together under clamp pressure, split tenons are sawed off and the rail ends drilled to receive a dowel which serves the purpose of the original tenon. Allow each glued part to set and harden completely—several hours for resorcinol glue, overnight for animal or resin glues—before the next part is glued on. (See Gluing, Chapter 2.) Joining a number of small parts together at one time under the same clamp is a

When regluing chairs or other furniture, apply clamp pressure uniformly in each direction to avoid twisting the frame.

Complex jointing of curved table pedestal, using some clamps for aligning the pieces, others for glue pressure. Wood blocks shaped to fit the contours are used under the clamp heads.

questionable method, as they probably won't line up precisely if there has been extensive splintering.

Applying the clamp pressure correctly is the most critical phase of the repair, since any piece that is even slightly out of position can ruin the work, and most likely cannot be separated for a new try.

REGLUING WOBBLY CHAIRS

When caught in time, a chair gluing can be quick and simple. If there is just one loose tenon, it will not be necessary to dismantle the legs. Rather, if the tenon can be pulled out just part

Place wood blocks under the clamp heads to prevent marring the finish. Pipe clamps used here are of suitable length for handling. Various lengths of pipe can be kept on hand for the removable clamps.

of its length, brush resorcinol glue on the exposed area, reset and apply clamp pressure. Sufficient glue will be drawn into the joint to do the job. Some cabinetmakers prefer to chisel or drill a thin opening into the recessed part of the tenon, then inject a quantity of glue from a pressure

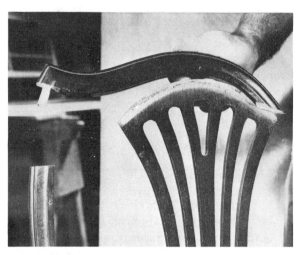

Split sections are reassembled before joining to the main body of the chair. Scrape off all old glue, sand smooth before assembling.

nozzle, allowing glue to flow into the space for a better grip, but this step is not essential and the glue may well hold even with the smaller surface. Remember that as the tenon is driven deeper, it carries some glue into the recess.

Split Dowel. When the dowel of a chair rail has broken off, the repair consists of sawing the remaining projection flush with the rail and leg joint. Drill into both sides of the joint for a new dowel, cut a replacement to a length just short of the combined hole depth. Drilling is done with an auger bit of the same diameter as the replacement dowel, usually ½ or ¾ inch. Check to see that the holes are deep enough, beveling the dowel ends slightly for easy insertion. Brush glue into both holes, insert the dowel, and apply the clamp.

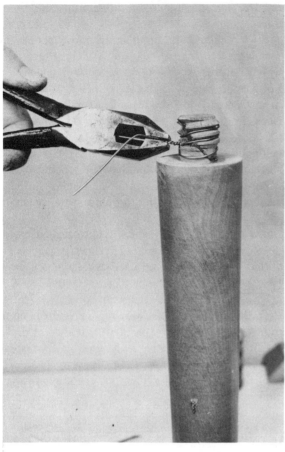

Cracked leg tenon is glued together, tightened with twisted baling wire.

With wire removed, the repaired tenon is replaced as before, good as new.

Loose Tenon. Movement of a loose tenon will enlarge the hole, so that extra efforts are needed for gluing. If the excess clearance is slight, mix fine sawdust with the glue to serve as packing, or wind silk thread around the tenon to build up its thickness. Where the hole has become too large, saw a slit through the end of the tenon, drive in a thin wedge partway—when placed into the hole, the clamp pressure will force the wedge deeper, spreading the tenon slightly for tighter fit. Be careful, however, to avoid using a wedge of such thickness that it will split the tenon. Pieces of wood veneer glued around the tenon also may serve to take up the slack.

When setting up the clamps, always insert flat pieces of wood under the clamp heads to protect the cabinet surface from compression by the clamp pressure. Where two or more clamps are used alongside, place a long board of sufficient thickness between the clamps to distribute the pressure uniformly.

Danish-Style Chairs. The seat cushion is supported in these chairs by elastic rubber straps rather than the conventional webbing or springs. The rubber eventually dries out, the straps become stretched or break. Replacing these straps, which make the chair like new again, can be done in only 15 minutes for each chair.

The 2-inch-wide strap material is sold by upholstering supply dealers, in economical rolls of 50 feet, enough for several chairs. The cost is perhaps 2 or 3 dollars a chair. The straps have either metal clips at the ends that are inserted into slots in the chair frame, or end plates with a projecting peg to be inserted into a drilled hole. The strapping is cut to length with scissors, the old metal clips transferred to the new material and squeezed tightly in a vise. Strapping also can be purchased in correct lengths, with the clips attached for $1.35 each from E. J. Evans, 630 Northwestern Ave., Los Angeles, Calif. 90004.

When installing the straps, set one clip into the far end slot, then stretch tightly in order to slip the front clip in place. All the straps should be of the same length to provide uniform slat support.

REPAIRING SCRATCHES AND DENTS

A small dent or gouge in furniture can be repaired so it is hardly visible even on close inspection. Oftimes a dent can be swelled out just by steaming or soaking, minor scratches are blended in with pigment wax on thick plastic varnish, rubbed when dry. For deeper gouges and scratches, the most effective method is the old-time "burning in" with melted stick shellac of matching color.

This work is beautifully done with a deft touch by expert furniture finishers. It is quite expensive, however, to call a finisher to your home just to cover up a mark on a table or the piano. The average homeowner can develop sufficient skill with the stick shellac, after a little practice on a discarded piece of furniture, to make satisfactory

repairs. The equipment and materials cost very little.

Stick shellack is familiar to most people as "sealing wax" in many colors, which at one time was widely used to seal documents or envelopes. For furniture repairs, the stick shellac is available in dozens of wood shades to match furniture finishes. Professionals generally keep on hand a full selection, but the homeoner should buy only the colors likely to be needed, plus the transparent shellac which comes in handy when a better match cannot be made. Matching powder stains are also needed for color padding to blend in the patch.

Dents and Gouges. Shallow dents, caused by an object dropped on the table, sometimes can be "lifted" by swelling the wood with a steam iron. Use a cotton swab, dipped in turpentine, to dissolve surface wax at the dent. Place a blotter over the dented area, use a medicine dropper to moisten the spot over the dent, then press down on the blotter with the iron. One or two short bursts of steam will apply the necessary heat. Repeat the process if the fibers have not been raised sufficiently, but don't overdo steaming as it may affect the rest of the finish.

The treatment for deeper gouges is to pack the depression with wood filler or Spackle plaster,

Small dents sometimes can be "raised" almost flush by swelling the compressed wood fibers. First remove the surface wax with cotton swab dipped in turpentine.

Cover the area with blotter or cotton gauze, soak the spot over the dent with water from a medicine dropper.

Apply heat with electric iron for short period to steam the wood fibers. Don't let the iron touch the finished wood surface.

leaving just enough depth for a surface application of stick shellac in matching color. In preparation for this process, cut away the compressed wood fibers with a narrow chisel or penknife. Pack the filling compound with a broad putty knife; before it has hardened, scrape a little off the top. Allow the filler to dry completely before applying shellac to the surface, as described below.

Stick Shellac Patching. Prepare deep scratches by washing off any wax or polish with turpentine, then scraping the surface with sandpaper or a knife point to remove the old finish. Sand the damaged surface to clean off loose wood fibers, wipe off the dust. Touch up the bare wood with color stain, which is allowed to dry.

Select the shellac stick that most closely matches the original finish. Light the alcohol lamp,

FILLING SCRATCHES OR DENTS IN FINE FURNITURE

Stick shellac comes in hundreds of shades. Selection of matching color is difficult.

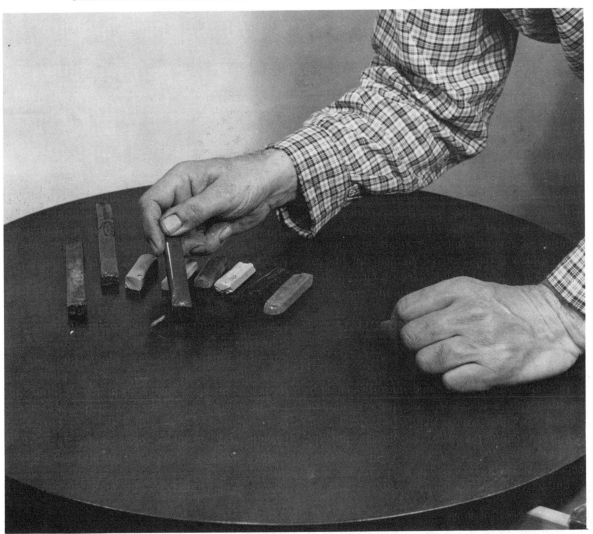

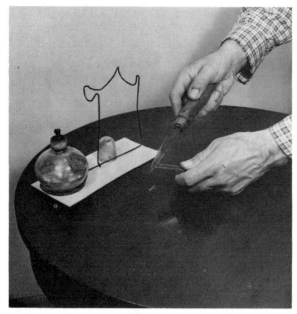

Heat the spatula over an alcohol lamp until it is hot enough so shellac will melt onto the steel blade. Do not overheat.

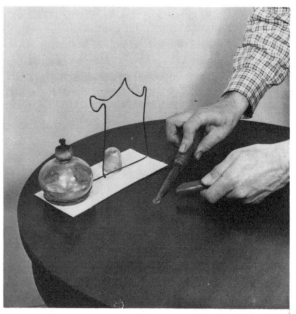

Pass spatula quickly over the flame again, then quickly turn the blade downward and draw it over the damaged area.

With pumice (rottenstone) rub repaired area to blend into the surrounding surface. Shellac should be flush.

Touch up the rubbed surface with blending color stain, applied with camel's hair brush.

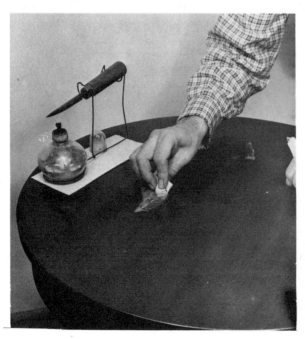

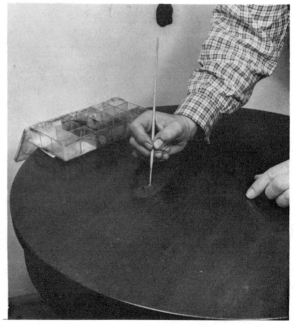

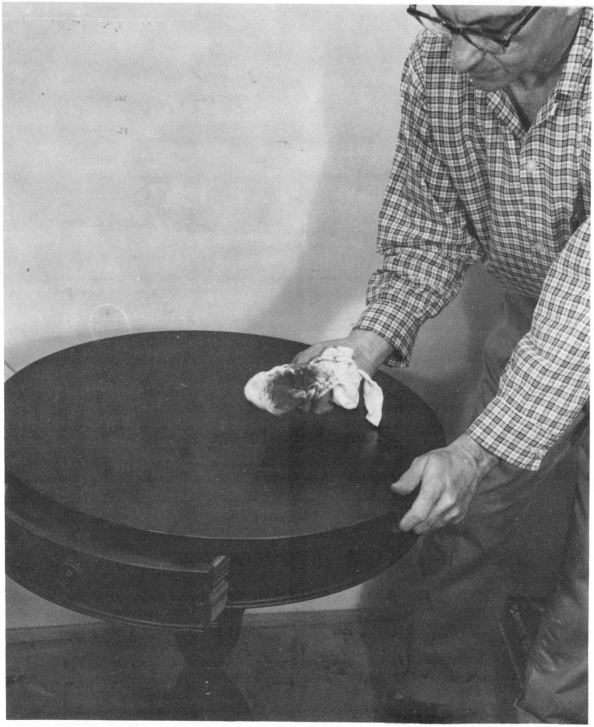

Work in color with soft cotton pad in circular strokes and an ever-widening circle. Do not rub back and forth, as that will leave a grained effect. Final polishing obscures the repaired area, brings up the patina of the table top.

heat the spatula. Touch the shellac to the spatula so that a little melts onto the blade. Pass the blade again momentarily over the flame to keep it hot (tilt the blade to concentrate the molten shellac at one edge). Immediately turn the blade and draw it quickly across the scratch to spread the shellac evenly. Examine the result. Perhaps a bit more is needed—in that case, let only a very little shellac melt onto the blade. It's not always effective to heat and lift any excess once it has hardened on the surface, so be careful not to carry too much along. It's best to fill the space in a single application, rather than building up bit by bit, though it often is necessary to add a little. The objective is to fill the scratch so it is just flush with the table surface.

For deep gouges, a simpler way is to allow some of the shellac to drip into the space (holding the spatula on its side) until it is built up almost flush, then fill the rest flush with shellac applied with the heated blade.

There are several things to watch for:

1. Do not overheat the spatula as it will cause the shellac to boil and become charred.

2. Keep the spatula perfectly clean—heat and wipe the blade frequently with a cloth.

3. Do not deposit so much shellac that it produces a raised mound—too little is better than too much.

4. Avoid spreading the shellac beyond the patch area.

The next step in the process is rubbing the patch with rottenstone or fine pumice to remove any slight surface irregularities and to feather the edges into the surrounding surface. In the course of rubbing, some of the finish alongside will be removed—that is unavoidable and even desirable, as it will help blend in the patch smoothly.

Blending. A stain of matched color is rubbed briskly into the surface with a felt pad. The stain, usually in powder form, is moistened with lacquer and applied directly to the shellac with a thin artist's brush. If, after rubbing to a high polish, the color proves too light, go over the patch again with a somewhat darker stain until the blending is satisfactory. This is an important detail, par-ticularly for the novice who will find color-matching difficult at first.

Finally, wax and polish the entire surface. A stick shellac repair will be generally not noticeable except when viewed from a particular angle. However, this is to be expected and is certainly a lot better than the original damage. The patch eventually may lift out or swell as a result of temperature changes, because the solid shellac expands and contracts at a different rate from that of the natural wood; in that event, it may need redoing.

Here's What You Need:

Stick shellac—assortment of colors
Alcohol lamp
Steel spatula—¾-inch-wide blade
Assortment of matching stains
Also standard supplies—wood filler paste, buffing cloth, sandpaper, rotten-stone or pumice powder, putty sticks, camel's hair brushes.

REMOVING OLD VARNISH

The newer plastic polishes do much to keep furniture looking its best, but despite the laudatory advertisement claims, they cannot restore the original luster to a cabinet that's wearing a time-worn, bedraggled finish. Cabinets with a single coat of varnish over penetrating stain may need only a light sanding to receive a refurbishing new finish. However, cabinets with numerous layers of varnish can be brought back to their original beauty only by stripping off the old finish down to the bare wood.

Varnish and enamel coatings are not very difficult to remove, but the process is certainly messy. Two methods are available, sanding and chemical removers—and in either case the work should be done outside or in the garage to avoid an extensive cleanup task. An electric orbital or straight line sander is fairly effective on flat surfaces, though it won't cut down enamel or hard plastic coatings as quickly as you might wish. A belt sander is

REMOVING OLD FINISH AND REFINISHING A CHEST OF DRAWERS

Complete refinishing, other than enameling, requires removal of the old finish. Use paint remover, of the non-toxic and water washable type. Lacquered furniture yields only to lacquer thinner.

Apply stain, starting at the top. Let stain penetrate for at least an hour to assure uniformity of color.

Paint removing is, at best, a messy job. Place plenty of newspapers to catch drippings. Use broad blade putty knife to remove the softened material.

Surface coating follows, in this case shellac is brushed on. Apply several thin coats, rather than trying to pile it on deeply.

After finish is removed, wash the surface thoroughly with a mineral solvent, sand any roughened areas, watch for glue spots.

Rubbing with fine steel wool is essential to remove air bubbles and smooth down the shellac.

Final polishing with fine pumice assures a smooth finish and brings out the luster.

Finished piece is functional and attractive, rescued from contemplated discard.

faster but should be used very carefully to avoid cutting uneven swaths across the surface.

Chemical paint removers do the job adequately. Of the commercial preparations that are available, some are extremely flammable, or highly toxic. Use, instead, the water-washable type, which is safer and equally effective, take proper precautions. Wear rubber gloves, avoid contact with the skin or eyes, and provide ample ventilation. Be sure to cover the area in which you will be using the chemical with canvas drop cloths or large pieces of corrugated boards from cartons. Do not depend on layers of old newspapers; splatters of the chemical may be absorbed and spot the surface underneath.

The varnish remover comes in paste or liquid form. The liquid type is suitable for horizontal surfaces, such as a desk top, but the paste form would be best for vertical surfaces.

Apply the chemical with an old paint brush, laying on a fairly generous quantity and working the liquid into all recesses. When the old finish has softened and become wrinkled, scrape off as much of the sludge as you can with a broad putty knife. Have a carton or similar disposable receptacle handy to receive the scrapings. Wash off the remainder with a wet cloth or sponge, rinsed repeatedly as the work progresses, but be careful not to allow water to collect on the surface, as it would warp the wood. Deeper areas in decorative carvings and similar places can be cleaned with a discarded toothbrush or other suitable brush with the required shape. A final sponging of the entire surface with fresh water will assure removal of all the chemical. A light sanding then with fine grit paper or steel wool will remove raised wood fibers for a clean, perfectly smooth surface to receive the new finish.

Piled-on varnish coatings can hide an unusually fine and valuable piece of cabinetry. A case in point is that of a New York executive who had purchased a small farmhouse upstate near the Canadian border as a summer home. In keeping with his intention to retain the original rustic character of his farmhouse, he attended local auction sales to acquire the needed furniture. One piece he bought was a heavy sideboard cabinet, its finish almost black with dirt and age. The numerous coats of old varnish were finally removed after considerable time and effort, to reveal a fine cabinet of French Provincial origin, about

150 years old, with delicate hand carvings and painted decorative designs. The value placed by experts in antiques exceeded the entire cost of the farmhouse that it now graces.

CASTERS

You would be surprised to learn how many casters there are in your home. They're on the nursery crib, sofa, beds, living room chairs, serving cart, portable TV stands, piano, stationary power tools, planter stands, ottomans, and other items. Like other mechanical products, casters require occasional attention. When furniture can be moved only by shoving, or your floors become marked, the casters are not rolling properly.

twice a year, lubricate both the swivel bearings and wheel shafts with a drop or two of oil.

If the casters tend to slip out when the furniture is tilted, the reason is a worn or excessively spread retainer sleeve, or socket, the part that is recessed into the furniture leg. Pry out this sleeve with a screwdriver, compress its slotted end slightly by tapping with a hammer. When replacing tap the bottom flange so the teeth around the rim sink into the wood. Insert the caster stem, pushing it in so the bulge at its top bypasses the slotted end of the socket. If the furniture hole is

Sleeve socket is driven into the hole so the toothed flange locks into bottom of leg. Sleeve is slotted and pinched together at inside end to retain the stem at the end of the caster leg.

Making up the beds is lots easier for any member of the family when beds can be rolled away from the wall on casters. Fitting other heavy furniture with casters also helps household cleaning, makes occasional shifting possible.

The most common fault is binding of the wheels by thread or lint caught in the wheel shaft. Remove with an awl or other pointed tool. Once or

Workshop tool casters are controlled by pressing on lifter bars with foot.

Furniture glides serve in place of casters. Adjustable screw permits leveling so frame is not distorted, drawers function properly.

too large to hold the socket securely, wrap masking tape around the socket for snug fit.

The rule for caster selection is soft rubber wheels on hard floors like wood or concrete for easy movement and quietness; hard wood or plastic wheels for carpeting. The larger the wheels, the easier they roll on any surface. For beds, the 1⅝-inch wheel is usually adequate, while tea

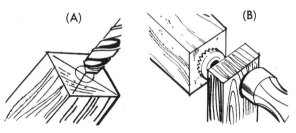

Installing furniture casters:
(A) Drill hole at center of furniture leg of same diameter as the caster socket; (B) Drive in socket by tapping on the flange, so retainer teeth sink into the wood; (C) To retain original height of the cabinet with casters, saw off section of leg equal to distance from bottom of caster wheel to the top of socket flange; (D) Socket will fit snug if wrapped with masking tape. The socket slot should be tight enough so the caster stem won't slip out.

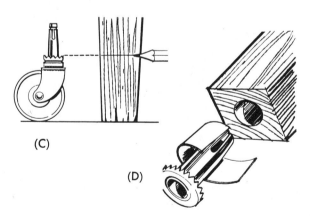

carts and nursery cribs should have the 2-inch or even 3-inch size. A locking type caster, having a friction lever on the shaft that is pressed by a toe, is important for bench saw stands to prevent movement while the saw is operated.

Installing Casters. Nearly all furniture can be equipped with casters, of which there is a type for every situation. Chairs and other furniture with legs take the stem type. Drill a hole at the center of leg bottom for the caster socket, which is inserted full length with a hammer blow on the socket flange. Press the caster stem into the socket, and the installation is complete. If it is necessary to retain the original height of the furniture, shorten the legs by sawing off a section equal to the measurement from the bottom of the caster wheel to the base of the socket.

Plate casters are installed by simply attaching the plate to the bottom panel of the cabinet with screws. Stem casters can be installed in furniture with tubular metal legs by using plastic adapter sockets to fit, or tapping wood dowels into the tube ends and drilling for the caster stem.

11. MASONRY WORK

New adhesive mortars simplify the fitting and setting of colorful slate flagstones for walks and patios. The concrete base is prepared beforehand to proper pitch, the flagstones laid flush in the adhesive mortar.

Working with cement is one of the more interesting and satisfying activities around the house, so much so that many homeowners take up masonry work as a hobby—and eventually run out of projects to do, or a place to put all the items they would like to make. Examples of this are seen in almost every neighborhood—homes in which both front and back yards are crammed with concrete fountains, benches, ponds, walks, stepping stones, and a dozen or so decorative figures molded in cement.

Be that as it may, masonry work becomes a routine item of the maintenance and repair calendar. Sidewalk slabs, the driveway, brick mortar, stoop steps, stucco walls, curbings, each at some time will need attention. A trowel in the hand, then, will be like money in the bank, staving off extensive and costly services. Small bags of mixed mortar and other special cement combinations make masonry repairs easier than ever.

Some, but not all, masonry repairs can be very strenuous to do, especially those that call for much digging, lifting, and carrying stones, moving sand and gravel, placing forms, mixing and pouring and finishing larger quantities. Even with transit-mixed concrete delivered to the site by truck, the speed with which it must be moved, poured, spread, and finished may be quite beyond the homeowner's capability, unless ample help is at hand.

Smaller projects, however, can be handled with ease if only limited batches of cement need be mixed and placed. This is true of most repairs and simpler projects, like the driveway curbing described later, which can be completed in a day or weekend.

A few tools will equip you for most masonry work. A wheelbarrow is essential to move the heavy sand, gravel, bags of cement, and excavated earth. Moderate-size batches of concrete can be mixed right in the barrow, then trundled to the site for pouring. Hand tools include a pointed trowel, rectangular finishing trowel, a large carpenter's level and a line level, several cold chisels of different shapes, and a small sledgehammer. For brick pointing, you will need also a mortar joint striker, which is a narrow bar of steel with one concave surface and one flat.

PROTECTIVE CONCRETE SEALANTS

Water penetration and traffic abrasion both cause deterioration of concrete surfaces, but application of the new epoxy sealants can provide a tough protective coating, preventing small cracks that permit water entry and freeze-up cracking, and will last almost indefinitely. An epoxy enamel such as ZAP, which is made by the Construction Chemical Corporation of Monroe, Conn. 06468, is available in a waterproofing kit containing the required materials. Two quart cans, mixed together, will cover 100 square feet. The epoxy is easily applied with a brush or roller but the surface must be properly prepared, completely clean and free of flaking paint, grease, oil, or dirt. Any crumbling masonry should first be patched and allowed to harden before applying the coating. Wire brush the area, then hose it down or use the vacuum to clean up the dust rather than simply sweeping, which would leave some residue. The coating may be applied even if the surface is

Silicone rubber is troweled over sundeck terrace in thickness of only ⅛ inch to seal leaks that had penetrated into house basement. The topping, by General Electric, is waterproof and abrasion resistant.

damp, but not soaking wet or with puddles of water.

Some manufacturers of epoxy sealants recommend washing the surface with trisodium phosphate (TSP), or better still, etching with muriatic acid solution to assure good bonding of the sealer coat.

Epoxy must be used correctly: the chemical comes in two cans, one of which contains the hardener. The mix contains an equal amount from each can. Mix only small amounts at a time, as much as would be used within a maximum of 20 minutes. Stir the mixture thoroughly until the paste is smooth, of uniform gray color, and without streaks.

Epoxy's toughness, superior adhesion, abrasion resistance, and durability make it the cement of choice for any kind of masonry repair such as plugging leaks in swimming pools and roof gutters, fastening loose shingles, recementing loose brick, and pointing up crumbled mortar. In fact, the range goes far beyond just masonry jobs, as the easily handled compound will effectively seal bell-and-spigot joints of drain pipes, cement ceramic tile and floor slates, patch leaks in boats, and can be used for cementing shelves to both inside and exterior walls. Until the two parts are mixed together, the epoxy can be safely stored for long periods.

Most of the regular manufacturers of glue produce epoxy cement brands in the various forms. Among the most noted, in addition to ZAP, are Duratite by DAP, Inc., E-POX-E by Woodhill Chemical Corp., Helor Hi-Water Concrete Adhesive by Epoxy Coatings, PC-7 by Protective Coating Company, Two-Ton by Devcon Corporation, and Holdol, a product of Masonite.

PATCHING CEMENTS

New patching compounds consisting of latex or vinyl solve many repair problems. A latex cement, mixed with water into a paste, can be troweled on as thin as 1/8 inch over an existing concrete surface; this can be useful to correct the pitch of a patio, level off a depression in a basement floor, or repair chipped surfaces of concrete

Pointed trowel applying adhesive mortar for assembling garden bench of poured concrete slabs on cement block base.

steps. These cements have such good adhesion that they have taken the place of standard cement mortar for setting slate flagstone on a rough concrete base, and for installing ceramic tile.

The vinyl patch may be used just as a water-mixed paste, or combined with portland cement for greater density to point loose brick mortar, resurface concrete steps, set tile or stone. The vinyl has excellent wearing qualities outdoors, good adhesion, and resists chipping.

A two-part latex cement serves similarly to epoxy for repair of hairline cracks in sidewalks and driveways. Mixed to a thicker consistency with the addition of portland cement, it forms a mortar of exceptional adhesion for most masonry installations. The latex can be applied in a thin layer to any flat surface by brushing or troweling, making it suitable for coating and smoothing the sides of swimming pools and most other masonry purposes. It is used also for caulking, sealing wall openings at utility entrances, and rebuilding exterior door thresholds.

SIDEWALK REPAIRS

Sidewalks seem to deteriorate more rapidly than other masonry. The chief cause probably is lifting of the slabs by tree roots. The base becomes undermined, water freezes underneath and heaves the slab, which soon cracks and sinks back unevenly into the cavity. Periodic cutting of surface roots with a hatchet can head off this development. Inadequate underslab drainage, lack of expansion joints between slabs, and poor concrete mixture are also responsible for premature deterioration of walks and driveways.

Repairs of sidewalk cracks can be quite permanent if there is no further movement or sinking of the slab. Widen and deepen the crack as much as you can with a cold chisel, brush away all debris. Moisten the concrete, sweep away any standing water that remains in the crack. Mix a stiff but plastic mortar of 1 part portland cement and 6 parts screened sand. Add a quantity of one of the high-adhesive patching cements like epoxy or vinyl. Apply the mortar first to the side walls of the crack, brushing it vigorously into the irregular surfaces, then pack the space with the rest of the mortar. Allow to stand until the cement starts to set, then trowel it smooth. After several hours, sprinkle the patch with water for better curing. If the sun is very strong, cover with boards or straw to prevent too rapid drying.

MIXING CONCRETE

The most efficient way to do masonry repairs and small concrete projects is with prepared mixes, available in sacks containing the ingredients in the right proportions ready for mixing with specified amounts of water. Small sacks of various mixtures for different purposes are sold by all hardware and masonry dealers. The sacks can be stored for long periods, always ready to use if kept sealed and dry. Concrete mixes such as Sakrete come in 10-, 45,- and 90-pound packs.

The cost of pre-packaged cement seems relatively high for such small quantities, but remember that otherwise you might have to purchase the cement in 94-pound bags and sand by the cubic yard—and what would you do with the excess if there's no convenient dry storage space? Also, with the smaller bags, you use just about what you need. The total cost then is really nominal, and they're so convenient.

For large projects, such as a patio or driveway, it may be better to buy transit-mixed concrete delivered in large tank trucks, but be prepared to pour it all into the forms immediately on delivery. Purchasing the sand and aggregate by the cubic yard, and doing the mixing yourself with a rented electric or gasoline-powered mixer, lets you do the work in more convenient stages and is more economical.

Measure quantities of material accurately when mixing concrete. A water pail usually is easy way to do this.

The ingredients for concrete are portland cement, sand, gravel or crushed stone or other aggregates, and measured proportions of water. The gravel or crushed stone for around-the-home uses should be from ¼ to ¾ inch in diameter. Cement mixed with the proper amount of water forms a paste that completely coats the sand and gravel particles. Too much water in the mix results in weaker concrete. The less water the better, as long as a workable mix is obtained.

Selecting the Mix. Most sand is more or less moist; allowance must be made for this in measuring the amount of water. Gather a handful of sand from the interior of the pile and compress it tightly; if the sand flows between the fingers, it is dry; if it compresses but falls apart upon opening the hand, it is damp; if it forms a ball which holds its shape, it is wet.

A good workable mix for patios, driveways, and most other home projects can be obtained with the following proportions of materials, based on sand in average wet condition:

    1 sack (1 cubic foot) portland cement
  2¼ cubic feet sand
    3 cubic feet aggregates (gravel or crushed stone)
    5 gallons of water

If hand tests show the sand to be nearly dry, add a half gallon of water in the mixture above; if the sand is very wet, reduce the amount of water by half a gallon. A proper mixture, when flattened by a shovel, should produce a smooth surface with no excess of water on top.

If you haven't done concrete work before, you can gain the necessary competence doing a few small projects. Meanwhile, follow these directions to avoid placing down a walk or patio that will crack up in short order because of poor mixture, improper base, lack of drainage, or insufficient thickness.

Coloring of concrete is best done in the wet mix by adding powdered pigments, in a ratio of 1 part pigment to 10 parts portland cement, the proportion modified according to depth of color desired. Pigment may also be sprinkled over freshly poured concrete, but this produces a speckled or streaked effect that may not be satisfactory.

Estimating Quantity. A fairly accurate estimate of the concrete needed is important. If the batch is too large, you would have a deuce of a time disposing of the excess. When there's too little concrete, the first pour may have set before you could mix more, and the job will go sour, having a poor joint and insufficient strength. That does not mean that you must mix all the concrete in one batch, but rather that the ingredients be right at hand, in measured quantities, so that repeated batches can be mixed quickly as required.

Each full sack holds 1 cubic foot of portland cement, weighs 94 pounds. When mixed in the proportions of 1 part cement, 2½ parts sand and 3 parts gravel, you will have 4 cubic feet of concrete. You may think that 6½ cubic feet of ingredients should produce more than 4 cubic feet of concrete, but gravel, sand, and cement combined with water take up less space than their separate measurements. There are 27 cubic feet in a cubic yard of concrete.

Using the chart shown here, you can estimate fairly closely the quantity needed for a project. A sidewalk slab, 3 by 4 feet in size and 4 inches thick, requires 4 cubic *feet* of concrete (12 square feet, ⅓ foot thick). But there are variations for which allowance must be made, for example, when a form is partly filled with large stones.

Example. A patio to be installed will measure 10 by 10 feet, which means a total surface of 100 square feet. If the cement is to be poured 3 inches, or ¼ foot, deep, a cubic foot will cover 4 square feet of surface. (It's like slicing the cube into four equal layers, placing them side by side.) In this case, 25 cubic feet of concrete or about a cubic yard will be needed to cover the 100-square-foot patio. A cubic yard contains 27 cubic feet. The computation will be easier and will allow for some waste if you buy a cubic yard of cement, instead of the actual 25 cubic feet, but be careful about accumulating an excess quantity of mixed cement.

Thickness of slab 10 by 10 feet square	Cubic yards of concrete needed (at 27 cubic feet per yard)
3 inches	.92
4 "	1.24
5 "	1.56
6 "	1.85

The quantity of concrete needed to pour patio slab 10 by 10 feet in size, to various thicknesses listed. Proportions of cement, sand, and aggregates for concrete mixture of a cubic yard are stated above. Compute total quantity, based on size of project and depth of pour.

Mixing the Material. Small batches are most conveniently mixed in a wheelbarrow. For larger jobs, a rented electric or gasoline-driven mixer will save much back-breaking effort and speed the job, making it possible to fill a form with continuous pourings. Projects such as a patio, retaining wall, or driveway can be done more easily with transit-mix concrete, but if the delivery truck cannot back up closely to the site, you will need help to move the concrete quickly in wheelbarrows.

A good mix! Concrete is sufficiently plastic for working, has no excess water as indicated when shovel is drawn across.

Forms prepared for pouring concrete for curved backyard walk. A 4-inch base of gravel and other aggregates assures good drainage.

PREPARING THE SITE

Sidewalks, patios, and other on-the-ground projects usually omit footings or curbings. The concrete is poured into wood forms, secured by stakes driven into the ground. In areas where the base is sandy and frost is no problem, the concrete can be poured directly on the soil, excavated to the required depth. In most areas, however, a subbase is necessary to assure adequate drainage so water won't collect and freeze underneath, cracking the slab. A 4- to 6-inch layer of gravel or cinders over clay or hardpan soil is usually adequate. Where experience shows that water collects at that location, some further means of drainage may be needed such as gravel-filled sump or drain tiles.

LEVELING THE FORMS

The patio must be pitched so that the water runoff is away from the house and toward a sloping part of the ground. Use a spirit level to adjust the form boards to the required height, the forms tapering down in the required direction. When the poured concrete is "struck" with a long board resting on both sides of the form, the patio surface will conform to the position of the boards. A pitch of 1 inch per 6 feet (a drop of 3 inches for an 18-foot-long patio) is usually adequate.

Divider strips (expansion joints) are necessary in large surfaces like a sidewalk or driveway, to allow for expansion and contraction of the concrete. Commercial asphalt-impregnated strips or redwood may be used, embedded in the concrete.

When the concrete is poured, spread it with a rake to fully fill the form, then place a long 2 × 4 across the form boards and with a person holding each end of the 2 × 4, work it back and forth until the concrete is level with the forms. Allow the concrete to set sufficiently, no free water at the top, before final finishing. Sweeping the partly set concrete with a stiff bristle floor brush will produce a rougher traction surface.

Curing Is Important. Newly placed concrete should not be allowed to dry out too quickly, as this results in loss of strength. Cover sidewalks, driveways, and similar flat surfaces on hot days with straw or old burlap bags, sprinkle lightly with a hose for several days for better curing.

BRICK POINTING

Brick walls deteriorate when the mortar separates from the brick or the mortar crumbles. These conditions should not be allowed to remain uncorrected since the open spaces allow rainwater entry, which presents a threat to the house framing, and loose or absent mortar soon results in splitting of individual brick.

Correction is done by "pointing," in which fresh mortar is packed into the joints. This work can be done satisfactorily by the homeowner. The masonry tools needed are a small pointed trowel, a hawk (a small board with a handle underneath to hold a supply of the mortar), a narrow-blade cold chisel and small hammer to break out the deteriorated mortar, and a striking tool, which is a bar of steel ½ or ¾ inch wide with an offset bend at the center, to compress and shape the mortar joint so it is similar to the original wall. You will also need a ladder long enough to reach the places on the wall that are to be repaired.

Use fresh packaged mortar mix, 1 part portland cement, 3 or 4 parts fine sand, adding latex or epoxy cement for good bonding. Mix a small batch, let it dry a day or two to test for color match with your present mortar joints. If there is a marked variance, add small amounts of pigment obtained from the masonry dealer, so the newly pointed mortar will not be obvious.

While testing for color, prepare the brick joints for repairs. With a cold chisel, chip out all defective mortar, not just along the front edge, but all or nearly all of the entire depth, so the new mortar can be packed in deeply. Open at least one vertical side of each joint as well as the horizontal, so you can key in the new mortar securely.

Brush out all mortar dust, then thoroughly dampen the adjacent brick with a brush, not by spraying with the garden hose, which would soak the sheathing inside the wall. Mix a small batch of mortar, using the exact amount of water stated in the package instructions, so that you have a fairly stiff mixture with no oozing liquid that can smear the brick. Set the trowel alongside the opened joint, and with the striking tool push the mortar deeply into the joint. Some of the mortar will drop away and be lost, but that is to be expected; enough will go in to fill the joint.

Fill the horizontal part of the space first, then do the vertical. With the striking tool, compress the mortar tightly, then "strike" the joint with the appropriate edge, moving the tool laterally along the cement, for the desired shape. Good results will be accomplished and the work will go much faster when you acquire the technique. Try to avoid smearing the surfaces with the soft cement.

After the mortar has set for a few hours, sprinkle lightly with water for better curing. Mortar spots on the brick surface are allowed to dry before trying to scrub them clean with a wire brush.

CUTTING MASONRY MATERIALS

Did you ever watch a skilled bricklayer at work and marvel at the ease and accuracy with which he splits a brick to size with one or two taps of his trowel? That skill would be useful when you lay patio blocks, build a brick enclosure, or set ceramic tiles in the powder room. The desired results can be accomplished in other ways, however, more slowly but just as effectively.

Masonry materials break along the line of least resistance. If the surface is scored, a sharp blow or steady pressure will break the material at the scored line.

Brick can be cleaved as you want it, if you have the knack; otherwise use this method with chisel and sledge.

Bricks. With a sharp cold chisel, score a shallow groove at both wide sides, place the chisel edge at the center of the line on one side and whack it sharply with a hammer. The brick will nearly always split neatly across the line.

Ceramic Tile. Score the surface glaze with a sharp awl or a glass cutter (preferably having a carbide wheel), using a ruler as a guide. Place the tile on the floor with a heavy nail or metal rod under the scored line. Step on one side of the tile to hold it

Ceramic tile can be broken into precise dimensions. First score the tile glaze with sharp awl point or carbide-wheel glass cutter on line of the desired break.

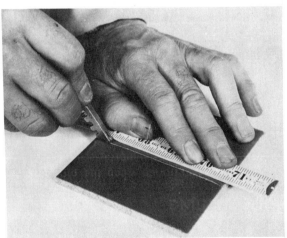

down, apply pressure on the opposite side with the other foot. The tile will cleave along the line. Narrow trimming is done, and irregular shapes cut, with nippers (end-cutting pliers), a small piece being chipped off at a time. Hold the tile in one hand, close the nippers to get a "bite" that will break off a small piece. Don't squeeze the nippers so tightly that the tile will shatter, rather snap the nippers downward in a breaking motion. Smooth the edges, if needed, with a carborundum stone.

Place large nail under the scored line and step on the tile. It will break on the line if even pressure is applied. More effective cutters can be rented from the dealer.

Mosaic tile is chipped rather than cut with end-cutter pliers. This method is used also for shaping ceramic tile around pipes and other obstructions.

Concrete Blocks. Use the same method described for brick, cutting a groove top and bottom, but place the block on earth or grass for the cleavage blow rather than a hard surface so the impact more readily follows the direction of the grooves.

Concrete and cinder block can be broken with adze using the chisel point. Nail-puller end of carpenter's hammer also serves this purpose.

Clay Drain Pipe. Place the terra cotta pipe on soft earth to prevent cracking. With a sharp chisel, score a deep line all around while slowly rotating the pipe. Continue around until the pipe parts.

Slate Flagstone. Slate is cut commercially to various straight-line shapes on a swing-type power saw with an abrasive cutoff blade, made of nylon mesh impregnated with silicon carbide grit. Irregularly shaped flagstone slate can be trimmed roughly, hammering against a straight solid edge such as heavy angle iron. Mark the trim line with chalk or crayon, place the slate over the corner of the inverted angle iron. Strike off small chips to prevent splitting beyond the line. If a large section is to be broken, strike a series of light blows back and forth along the line until the slate crushes and separates. Tap the edge with a hammer to reduce any sharp projections of the stone. Mostly, flagstone is placed so that irregular edges fit together in the best possible arrangement, the gaps simply packed with mortar.

(Left above) Drain tile pipe also can be cut neatly with series of cold chisel blows, repeated all around until the pipe parts along the scored line.

(Left below) Break is completed without damage to rest of pipe. Square-cut end permits joining pipe into its fitting.

(Below) Most masonry materials, including clay drainage tile, can be cut with a circular saw using a reinforced cutoff wheel of resin-bonded grit. This method is particularly useful for cutting neatly into a brick wall to install an air conditioner.

DRIVEWAY CURBING

When the lawn alongside the driveway is defaced by the car riding beyond the runways, consider putting in a curb along one or both sides. This will help guide the car even in the dark, without overriding the lawn.

The curbing may be of poured concrete, precast concrete sections 3 feet long, or old cobblestones set into a mortar base. The curbing should extend only 4 or 5 inches above the level of the driveway, with a cross-section thickness of 4 inches. A depth of 12 inches for the base trench will be ample to protect against cracking or heaving, because the curbing is narrow.

Excavate the trench with a narrow spade, following a string stretched along the line to keep it straight. The earth that is removed is placed into a wheelbarrow so it won't damage the grass. When the trench is completed, place wood forms along the sides, supported by stakes driven into the ground, the top edges of the boards at equal height so the surface can be finished level.

Use concrete mixed 1 part cement, 3 parts sand, 5 parts gravel. Spread a 2-inch layer of gravel at the bottom of the trench, pour the concrete into the forms up to the top, use a steel float to smooth the top. After a few hours, dampen the concrete and continue to sprinkle the next few days for better curing. Wait a day or two before breaking out the wood forms.

WIDENING YOUR DRIVEWAY APRON

Driveway aprons often are built too narrow, making it difficult to turn onto the concrete runway, the tires bumping over the street curbing. The apron should be at least 8 feet wide, preferably 9 feet for greater convenience. If it is too narrow, extending the apron about a foot at each side, or at least on the side where you most frequently turn, is a fairly simple project. The street curbing is broken away at that spot with a chisel, and the newly exposed end trimmed to a gradual slope. In some areas, a permit must be obtained to break the curbing. The concrete poured to form the added section of apron should be contoured neatly to conform with the original lines of the apron.

12. OUTDOOR MAINTENANCE

Outdoor maintenance is concerned to a large extent with keeping the house sealed against rain, wind, insects, and cold. Wall joints need to be caulked, loose shingles cemented down and missing ones replaced, flashings resealed, roof gutters kept clear of leaves, and downspout drain pans kept at the proper pitch so water won't form puddles alongside the walls.

CAULKING

Aside from routine painting of siding and trim, the chief weapon for weatherproofing is the simple caulking gun, which has remained virtually unchanged since development of the ratchet-pressure cartridge model. Caulking compounds, however, have been greatly improved: vinyl silicones are more flexible, adhesive, durable, easier to apply. In addition to the regular latex caulks, special-purpose types now are formulated for aluminum siding and gutters, roof shingles and flashings, brick mortar joints, cement and stucco cracks, foundation walls, and sealing of utility entrances.

One form of the compound (Mortite) comes in rope-like strands for easy application around drafty windows and doors. The electric gluing gun described in Chapter 2 applies a heat-softened compound to small areas that are difficult to seal

All joints around windows, siding panels, and door frames require sealing with caulking compound. Annual checkups to replace cracked and separated caulks are advisable, although some applications may last years.

with the caulking gun. Compounds are mostly white, but are available also in gray, black, and metallic aluminum. At least one siding manufac-

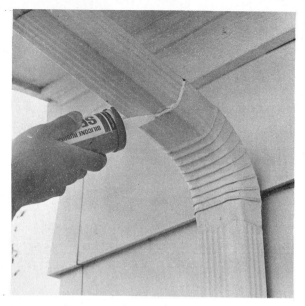

Gutter sealing compound applied to slip couplings, end caps, and other joints will prevent leaks into the eaves and behind siding.

Synthetic rubber is base of sealant used for caulking dissimilar surfaces, such as the joints at patio and house wall, coping stones, stucco, and entrance stoop.

turer (Insulite) offers caulking compound in colors to match the siding.

Using the Gun. Caulking compounds come in paper cartridges that slip into an applicator "gun." Pressing the ratchet trigger forces the compound through a spout, like spaghetti. Caulking is done by running this spout tightly along the joint, keeping the trigger under pressure.

Load the gun by twisting the ratchet rod to pull it all the way back, permitting insertion of the cartridge with the spout extending through the front hole. Pull the trigger until the pressure plate at the back just touches the cartridge. With scissors or knife, clip off about ½-inch from the plastic spout to provide an adequate opening. The size of this opening determines the rate at which the compound will flow. Make this cut at a moderate bevel, as the gun will be held at an angle so that you can watch the application. The gun is now ready for use.

Always carry a dry cloth or soft brush with you to dust off the surface; dust will interfere with good adhesion. The best time for caulking is a dry, warm day, when the compound will flow most smoothly. After a rain, delay caulking long enough to be certain the wall joints are perfectly dry.

The objective is to lay on a uniform, continuous bead of compound. It need not be a heavy strip; in fact, a thin, flat layer is preferred as it will adhere better and be less likely to crack than a heavy one. Press the spout at the start of a joint, pull the trigger and hold it with a moderate pressure while you move the gun along steadily. Any faltering will cause the compound to pile up heavily at one spot, so keep the spout moving along. Pull the trigger another notch when more pressure is needed. When you come to the end of the run, quickly twist the ratchet rod arm and pull it back to release the pressure, thus stopping the flow of compound. Wall openings wider than ¼-inch should be packed first with compound applied with a knife, allowed to set a day or so to form a skin, then covered with a bead of compound.

Laying down a perfect bead is quite a trick, so don't get discouraged with results at the start. A little practice will make it go much more smoothly. After putting down the first perfect bead, you can exclaim "I've got it!" and from then on it will somehow go much better. A window or door frame can be caulked all around in five minutes or less after you've acquired the skill.

Special Mortarfix compound can be applied for repair of any size joint without sagging or running, replacing loose mortar as in chimney repair to retain full draft capability.

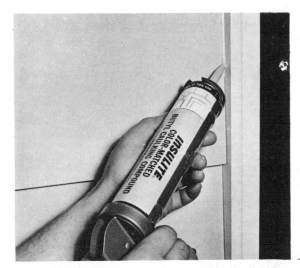

Elastic general purpose compound seals wall siding panels, air conditioner casings, and other projections through the walls. Some siding manufacturers supply compounds that match the siding color.

Water can seep under the frames of roof ventilators. Caulk along the edges with special rubber-base compound, such as the Dow Corning black Sealant.

Places to Caulk. Start by caulking the complete frame of every window and door; next do the joints where the wall siding meets the chimney and the decorative front entrance. Check, and reseal if necessary, the flashings at the chimney and eaves, using special roof sealant. Repair any cracks in stucco walls, the driveway runways, and window sills. Epoxy cement and other patching compounds also come in cartridge form, applied like regular caulking compound. Seal end caps and assembly joints in gutters and downspouts with a thick coating of metallic compound. Finally, plug all wall openings for utility lines—

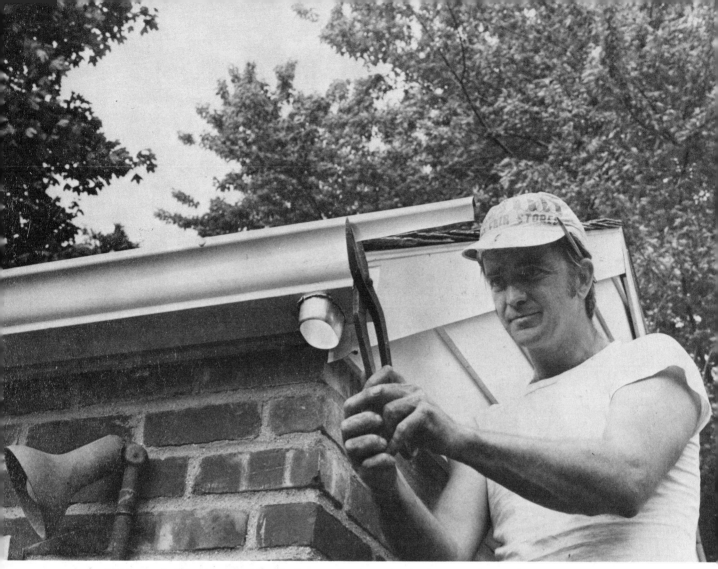

New aluminum gutter, fitted with drop outlet, is cut with shears to required size. End caps are glued on.

telephone wires, hose faucet, gas pipe, etc.—with elastic putty.

HOUSE SIDING AND TRIM

Regular inspection of exterior walls and trim and prompt correction of any defects will keep your house in sparkling, tip-top condition. Look for cracked, loose, or missing shingles, split clapboard, gaps in wall joints around window and door frames, rotted wood trim, loosened flashings, sagging lintels, rusted window drip caps. Asbestos-cement shingles are brittle and subject to cracking; aluminum siding can become dented, its corner joints separated; clapboard may split or become rotted, its paint blistered by vapor penetration.

Cleaning the Siding. Tree sap stains during the early spring, soot stains, or soiling caused by birds can be washed down with the garden hose. Use a soft brush, such as the kind made for car washing, on a long pole, to scrub the siding. Aluminum and plastic wall siding, as well as wood, can be washed in this manner. Be careful,

Aluminum gutters may bend out of line under heavy snow load. Reinforce with additional gutter brackets; check that the pitch flows toward the downspout outlet. In some areas, Chromalux heating coils are needed to prevent ice dams on roof.

however, to avoid spraying the water from below directly into vented openings in the underside edge of metal siding panels.

Brick walls can be scrubbed with a solution of trisodium phosphate (TSP) in water, but keep the chemical away from painted trim and window and door frames, to avoid streaking the paint. White streaking of brick walls is treated with muriatic acid, a corrosive chemical diluted with 6 to 10 parts water, in an earthenware or glass container. Pour the acid into the water, *not* the

water into the acid. Wear rubber gloves and goggles, avoid splattering on the skin. Handle the acid solution with respect.

Repairing Clapboard. Minor splits in clapboard siding may be repaired with wood filler, which is sanded smooth when dry and painted. Boards that are soft and spongy, showing signs of dry rot, should be replaced. The ends of clapboard are particularly susceptible to rotting if unpainted, or gaps at the joints not promptly caulked. You can't properly patch just the ends of these boards—the entire board should be replaced.

When removing an individual board, a narrow section that is overlapped about an inch by the higher course must first be split away from the rest. All remaining pieces are then chipped out, the retaining nails clipped or pulled, including the overlapped strip at the top. Slip the new board into place, tapping it deeply enough behind the overlapping board so that the new board is perfectly aligned with its course. Nail through the face of the board into the sheathing inside the wall or the studs.

Before installation, apply a coat of primer to the new board, with particular attention to the end grain, then a final painting to match the existing wall. Countersink the nailheads, cover with caulking compound or putty.

REPLACING ASBESTOS SHINGLES

Asbestos shingles (also known as mineral wool) are fairly brittle and tend to crack. A damaged shingle can be broken out, but it will be necessary also to remove the two original nails that are under the overlapped portion of the shingle above.

Use a thin chisel or similar tool to split and remove the upper part of the damaged shingle. Insert a long flat chisel under the overlapped section, tap gently on the nails in an attempt to shear them off, or at least bend them flat out of the way. Be careful not to crack the upper shingle. The new shingle then can slip into the space easily, but its predrilled holes will not be in the right place—you can't drive the nails because of the overlap shingle on the next course. Instead, drill two new holes, just below the course line, using a carbide bit. It may be possible to obtain enameled nails to match the wall color, but in any event they won't be visible. Use a counterset or similar tool when driving the nails, so you won't accidentally crack the upper shingle, but don't drive the nails too tightly. Make sure that the inserted shingle is straight and flush with the others in its course.

The chief difficulty, actually, will be finding a replacement shingle that will match the present wall as closely as possible. Even if you've saved some of the original batch, they will vary somewhat in shade if the wall is more than a year old, unless the replacement shingle has been left exposed to the sunlight during that period. Otherwise, the new shingle will be quite obvious and there isn't much that can be done except to hope that it takes on the weathered appearance as quickly as possible. It is not unusual to spot such walls with half a dozen or more replaced shingles, each of a different shade, presenting a patchwork appearance.

An alternative to complete reshingling is refacing with aluminum or vinyl siding. The clapboard styling will give the home a new and more attractive look while providing the other advantages of the modern siding, including elimination of the need to repaint for ten years or more.

WOOD SHINGLES

Badly warped or split shingles should be replaced, as they allow water to penetrate and remain at the back, causing dampness and further deterioration. The old shingle is removed by splitting it with cuts in the end grain so that narrow strips can be pulled out one by one, clearing the overlap of the higher shingles. With a long hacksaw blade inserted underneath the higher shingle, try to cut the original nails. If this can't be done, insert the new shingle and tap the bottom edge with a hammer, then withdraw the shingle and look for the marks made by the nails along the top edge. With a saw, cut slots at those positions to clear the nails, to the depth equal to the nail holes on the original pieces of shingle. Now drive the new shingle into place and fasten with a nail at the lower edge, countersinking the nail head for coating with caulking compound.

Another way to install a replacement shingle uses one or two thin brass or copper strips, one end of which is bent into a flat U shape. The strips are inserted into the vacated shingle space and manipulated so the U bend catches on the edge of the upper shingle. The new shingle is inserted and the lower end of the metal strip is bent tightly underneath, thus holding it in place.

FLAT ROOF REPAIRS

Bubble, bubble, toil, and trouble. That refrain sooner or later becomes quite familiar to the homeowner with flat roofs over a den or other room extension.

When your seasonal inspection of the roof reveals a blister or two in the roofing material, don't ignore this harbinger of imminent leakage. The blister means that, for one reason or another, the heavy felt covering has separated from the roof deck and will eventually allow rainwater to seep underneath.

The situation calls for a bit of roof surgery. Slice the area around the blister on three sides to form a flap that can be lifted. Allow the exposed roof deck, usually found to be damp, to dry thoroughly, then coat the exposed area with special roofing mastic, the kind used on flashings, and cement the flap back into place. Press the flap tightly with a hand roller; seal the flap edges all around with more roofing compound to complete the repair.

But there is an important in-between step—that is, to find the reason for the blister. In some cases it resulted merely because the cement didn't stick when the roof covering was originally put down. If that is so, there should be no further problem. Most likely though, water has penetrated at some other location, possibly a loose flashing on a nearby wall or chimney joint.

The source may be difficult to locate. One way is to walk along the roof between the blister and the flashings to see if you can locate a spongy trail. Softness of the roof covering, with a cushiony resilience, indicates separation of the cement bond. This trail may meander in every direction, but you should be able to follow it to the fault that caused the damage.

Repair of a flashing is done with the same cement mastic. Pry the flashing slightly away from the wall with a broad knife, pack in a quantity of the cement, then tap the metal back in place with a mallet or by hammering on a wood block. Don't hit the flashing directly with a hammer as it will dent the metal unevenly, and prevent proper sealing.

After the cement has hardened, coat the flashing

A bubble in a flat roof calls for prompt repair. Slice open three sides of the blister. Lift the flap gently to avoid cracking. It is best to do this in warm weather when the material is more pliable. Dry out any moisture underneath, then spread roofing cement and flatten firmly with a hand roller. Apply cement to seal the edges.

edges with thick roofing compound. While you're at it, reinforce the nearby flashings and valley runners. An excess of sealer compound can't hurt, but apply it neatly wherever it can be seen from below.

THE CRAWL SPACE

Wood joists and floor boards are affected by moisture coming up through uncovered ground. A test for ground moisture may be made with a piece of rubber matting several feet square, laid over the earth for a day or so. If the earth beneath is damp when you remove the cover, that is evidence of subsoil moisture that permeates the confined crawl space, affecting the framing. Permanent correction of this condition involves pouring a slab of concrete over a watersealing membrane of plastic sheeting. Also effective is covering the earth with roll roofing (55-pound grade or heavier) overlapping each row at least 6 inches. Heavy grade plastic membrane sheeting, available from building and masonry supply dealers, also will be satisfactory in place of the roofing material. Adequate ventilation, essential for an enclosed crawl space, can be provided by inserting a number of small metal louver vents into the walls of the crawl space enclosure.

CARE OF CANVAS AWNINGS

Proper storage will extend the life of canvas awnings possibly for several seasons. Before seasonal removal, brush the canvas to remove all sand and grit, then wash down with soapy water. Rinse thoroughly to remove all traces of soap, allow the canvas to dry completely, then spray with Lysol or a similar disinfectant as a precaution against mildew.

When taking down the awning, avoid straining any part. Fold neatly without compacting the creases, wrap in heavy kraft paper or polyethylene sheeting (you can buy these 12 feet wide and to any length) and store the awning in a dry, well-aired place. A high shelf in the garage is usually the preferred spot for storage. Tie the ends of the wrapping securely, and avoid placing heavy articles atop the stored awning.

When replacing the awning on its frame, unfold it completely on the lawn before raising it in place. Look for any rips or weak spots, make needed repairs at once with canvas patches. Cut the patch so it extends at least an inch on both sides of the rip. Brush heavy grade rubber (contact) cement on both the canvas and patch, allow to dry about 10 minutes, then put on the patch and roll it, applying pressure for good contact. Double patches—both outside and inside—are advisable for adequate strength.

Check the tie laces, replace any that are torn or frayed, also oil the pulleys. If the canvas appears thin in spots or the color is faded, a reinforcement coating of Toplife by CAH Industries, or Luxall by National Manufacturing Company, can preserve the awning for at least another season. Apply with a brush like paint, covering as uniformly as possible.

RESURFACING BLACKTOP DRIVEWAY

Puddle-catching depressions in asphalt driveways are not only annoying, they set the stage for eventual cracks and other damage, besides being a source of mosquito breeding. Patching is done quickly with prepared asphalt compounds. A hot, sunny day is best so the material can be spread more easily, although an "all-weather" mix that is said to be workable at any temperature is available. The mix, in 80- and 100-pound bags, is dumped right at the repair spot. Rake it out evenly, just a bit higher than the surrounding surface, then tamp down with a rake or roll it out if you have a lawn roller. Another way to compress the compound into small holes or depressions is to roll your car over it a few times. An 80-pound sack will cover an area of 7 square feet, 1-inch thick.

To rejuvenate a worn asphalt driveway or patio, and for protection against further damage, coat it with special blacktop sealer, available at building supply and masonry yards. Made with an asphalt base emulsion in several colors, it will contribute greatly to the appearance of your grounds. The sealer compound is applied with a wide floor brush.

KEEP YOUR FENCES UP

A fence is no stronger than the posts that hold it up. The first sign of a sagging post should bring prompt action; otherwise the weight of unsupported fence may cause other posts to topple and require complete rebuilding. A post may tip due to softening of the soil around it, needing just tamping of the earth. More likely, however, the lower section of a post has become rotted—then it is the rails rather than the post that hold up the fence for a while.

A temporary repair may be made by driving flat wood sections deeply on two sides of the post. Cedar wood is preferred, possibly from a leftover fence picket. The supporting stave is placed directly against the old post, and driven with a sledge as far as it can go, with at least a foot of length remaining above ground. Nail the staves to the old post section for reinforcement.

More permanent replacement of rotted posts is, of course, much better. Remove the linkage rails and pull the old post out of the ground. If the bottom is rotted and broken, pry up the stump with a pinch bar.

With a "clam digger" tool, extend the hole depth to at least 24 inches. Get a can large enough to receive the end of the post—a round gallon-size anti-freeze can for example, with one end cut away, can take up to a 4 × 4 post.

Fill the can part way with cement, drop it into the hole, and force the post into the can. Plumb the post with a spirit level, support it with stones, and pour additional cement. After the concrete sets, back-fill the hole, tamping the earth tightly. Wait a few days until the concrete has fully hardened before renailing the fence rails. The post will last much longer if the lower section is treated with preservative such as Woodlife, by Dow Chemical; Penta, product of U.S. Plywood Corporation; Woodie by Savogran Company; or Staintox, by Miller Purcell Company.

13. LOCKS, BURGLAR AND FIRE ALARMS

Prompted by the widespread incidence of residential burglaries, including an increasing wave of daytime intrusions, homeowners and apartment residents are giving closer attention to their security provisions. Stronger doors, better locks, an efficient alarm system, elimination of vulnerable entryways including reinforcement of windows, and personal alertness to avoid danger, are all essential. The more formidable your defenses, the safer your family will be, of course.

Many homeowners, because of inexperience with

This advanced entry lock by Schlage has restraining bar on the spring-loaded latch, a deadbolt with full 1-inch throw, and recessed keyway for the outside cylinder.

security measures, put their reliance on intriguing gadgets, while overlooking basic conditions that leave the home easy prey to prowlers. There's no objection to pickproof locks, for example, although lock-picking requires considerable skill and is rare in residential burglaries. Secure installation of a sturdy lock is more important. But a lock is no stronger than the door frame that it grips. No lock will be very effective if the jamb is so fragile that it splinters and the door opens at a strong shove.

An alarm system offers a considerable deterrent to burglary, and just as important, it can contribute substantially to personal security. But many items sold as burglar alarms are hopelessly inadequate. Another factor is that many of the more dependable and sophisticated electronic systems are so highly efficient that some families just can't adapt to living with them. Following are some practical suggestions that you may utilize to improve your home protection.

HINTS FOR IMPROVING HOME PROTECTION

Control of Your Keys. Locks are of doubtful reliability if any of your keys are in unknown hands. When you move to a new home or apartment, there's no knowing whether any of the keys are floating around in the hands of unknown persons. A wise precaution is to change the locks or their cylinders when moving into new quarters. Then keep close check on all keys so you'll know who has them and if any are missing. Instructions on changing cylinders follow later in this chapter.

Master keys in apartment houses are ostensibly under the control of the superintendent, but outsiders may get temporary possession to make duplicates, and then every apartment is vulnerable to intrusion and burglary. Apartment house owners insist, with justification, that the master key is essential so that the apartment can be entered quickly in an emergency, such as fire or a water leak.

Here's one way to comply with the rule and still win your point: Install your own lock or separate cylinder, but agree to provide the super with a key to your own lock. Place this key in a sealed envelope with your signature on the flap. Whenever it has been necessary to use the key, you are to be notified and can seal the key again in a new envelope. If your apartment is entered and burglarized, the super must show that your key is still sealed—if not, he would be subject to suspicion.

Access Through Glass Invites Trouble. Glass panes in or adjacent to an exterior door negate the lock's purpose, as it is easy for a prowler to break the glass, reach in, and open the lock. The two solutions to this are: (1) replace the glass with burglarproof clear plastic sheeting such as GE Lexan, or (2) install a double-cylinder deadbolt having a key cylinder on the inside as well as the outside. When the night bolt is thrown, hang up the inside key on a hook that is out of reach from outside through a broken glass.

Key tags should not bear name or address for return. It is better that lost keys be without identification and lost for good, than worry about a possible intruder using them weeks or months later. Better still, change the cylinder whenever a key is unaccountably missing.

An emergency house key is a good idea, but never cache it in the usual places, over the door frame or on a hook inside the garage. Instead, select a completely unexpected and hidden place.

Replacement for window and door glass, Lexan plastic sheeting is burglarproof, cannot be smashed with a hammer. The plastic, shown here with paper coating, is clear as glass, easily cut with ordinary saw.

Window gratings are favored by many as the most dependable protection against intruders, particularly on lower floor windows. When making such an installation, don't block your escape route for quick exit in emergencies such as fire.

A good way is to tape or wire the key to a tree branch or under a fence rail, where it will not be visible to prowlers, but available when needed for the family.

Keyed-alike locks for all exterior doors help reduce the number of keys that you must carry and watch out for, thus minimize the chances of loss. Your locksmith can quickly reset the pins on all your cylinder locks so that a single key will serve the entire house.

Curing Dangerous Sticky Locks. After long use, a cylinder may become so worn or gummy that the lock can be opened without a key, just by turning the keyway with a small screwdriver or even a coin. Accumulation of grit, or the gum that forms when a lock is lubricated with oil, causes the pin tumblers to stick in open position.

Extensive wearing of the pins, on the other hand, may make turning the cylinder plug so difficult that the key breaks. Spraying a degreasing solvent into the keyway will correct this condition. When the solvent is thoroughly dry, apply graphite, either in powdered form blown in from an applicator tube, or the fluid type such as Lock-Ease.

A Barrier to Jimmying. One common cause of door vulnerability is an excessive gap between the closed door and its jamb, permitting the blade end of a pry bar (the burglar's "jimmy") to be inserted into the open space. Even a small pry bar or a heavy screwdriver can force a door open by springing the lock bolt out of its strike plate on the jamb. The average bolt moves only ½-inch toward its plate, and if there's a gap of ¼ inch or more between the door edge and the strike plate, obviously there's very little of the bolt itself holding the door. A closer fitting door, a night bolt with a "throw" (movement) of ¾-inch or more, and a solidly fastened strike plate, are all essential for door security.

Apartment doors in high-crime areas can be guarded against jimmying by attaching a length of angle iron with screws along the outside door frame so that the angle flange covers the latch side of the door. Double locks add considerably to safety. Apartment owners who formerly prohibited

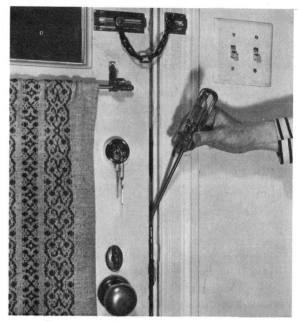

Excessive gap at door jamb, illustrated by the heavy screwdriver inserted into the space, makes the door subject to jimmying.

Illustrating how the leverage of a prybar that is fitted into a gap at the jamb can splinter a door apart. A loose door that does not close tightly against its stop molding is subject to such attack.

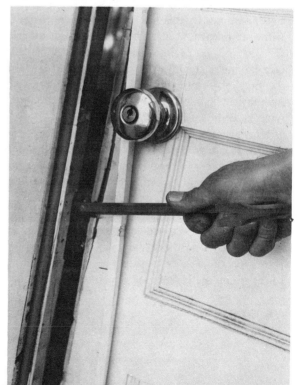

such extra installations are now lifting this re-striction, but require a copy of the new key, which can be handled as suggested previously.

If the Latch Doesn't Catch. When a latch or dead-bolt does not engage fully into its strike plate, the cause is misalignment of the latch to its plate, usually owing to slight sagging of the door. Directions for correcting this condition have been given in Chapter 3, page 57. An alternative method is to obtain a new strike plate in which the screw holes are spaced farther apart, enlarging the recess cut into the jamb with a chisel to receive the new plate. A badly decayed jamb, however, makes useless any number of locks you put on the door. The solution is to repair the door frame, a difficult and costly but necessary effort.

Identification Markings. Would you be able to positively identify your typewriter if it were re-covered after a burglary Or your radio? While you possibly would recognize your possessions, that would not help police to recover your prop-erty if it had been pawned, or stand up as evidence in court. Police in many areas have instituted a campaign urging residents to inscribe an iden-tifying mark on valuables. Initials or any special insignia would serve; better still, the use of Social Security numbers would be most helpful in tracing the ownership of items recovered from question-able hands.

The markings can be done with a manual scriber which has a diamond or carbide point, or a minia-ture drill. An electric engraving tool, which weighs only 10 ounces and will make permanent mark-ings on metal tools, glass, plastic, wood and stone, is listed for $8.49 in the catalogue of J. C. Whitney & Company, 1919 Archer Ave., Chicago, Ill. 60616.

TIGHTENING AND CHANGING CYLINDERS

In mortise locks, the round cylinders are se-cured by two very thin screws which enter from the edge side of the lock to engage grooves in the body of the cylinder. When these screws are loose,

Cylinder of mortised locks is secured by two long setscrews through edge of door. When setscrews are loosened, the cylinder can be turned out and locking bolt withdrawn easily with the fingers.

the entire cylinder can be turned out from outside the door. The opening exposes the interior lock bolt mechanism, which can then be moved with a finger to open the door.

These cylinder retainer screws may loosen in time, allowing the entire cylinder to turn, rather than just the key plug, and one day you may find yourself locked out because the key won't work. In that case, use a screwdriver in the keyway to turn out the cylinder completely, permitting opera-tion of the latch from outside.

A more dangerous possibility to be avoided is that some delivery man, kept waiting at the open door, may very quickly loosen those screws so that, at any time, the cylinder can be removed to gain entrance. Keep these retainer screws tight, the cylinder keyway in vertical position so that the screws are squarely seated in the cylinder grooves. A useful and practical protection is easily pro-vided by a special brass collar that covers the cylinder rim so it cannot be gripped and turned by pliers. This collar can be purchased at nominal cost from any locksmith.

Cylinder barrel is threaded for turning into the lock body. A protective collar on cylinder prevents gripping by pliers to force it out.

Conversion kit for replacing old-fashioned mortised lock with a dependable cylindrical lockset. Kit includes two trim plates, latch cover, and strike plate. Only two auger bits and screwdriver are needed for installation.

INSTALLING A LOCKSET

In many homes, the kitchen and back doors, and the one leading to the basement, often have an almost primitive mortise lock with a simple spring latch, opened by turning the knob, inside or out. The door is locked only when the bolt is turned with a key—and usually this is a typical "skeleton" key, the kind that can be purchased anywhere for a dime, and fits every lock of its type! There is a way to replace this lock with one of the modern cylindrical locksets in which the spring latch can be set to lock automatically when the door is closed. Another important advantage of the better locksets is that the spring latch is backed up by a short retainer bar—when the latch is locked, it cannot be pushed back, thus defeating the old celluloid strip trick often used by burglars. The new lock also handsomely updates the door's appearance.

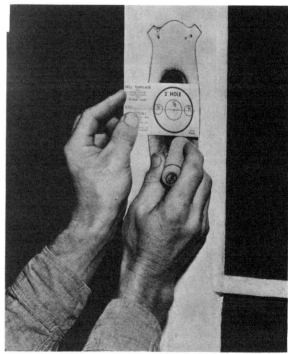

Template locates position for boring a ⅞-inch and two 7/16-inch holes. Instructions given here are for installation of the Kwikset "400" line lockset.

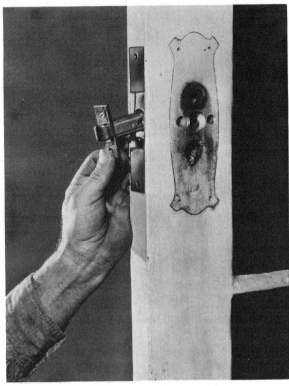

Install latch in existing mortise, attach with screws provided.

Slip lock shaft onto exterior trim plate. Depress the latch so its prongs interlock with the lock body.

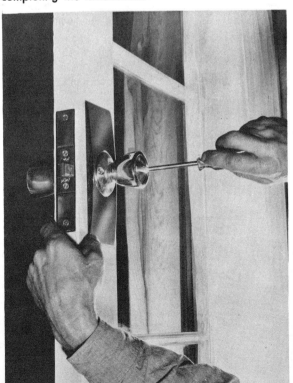

Interior trim plate and knob are assembled on the lock shaft. Two screws are turned into the inside plate, completing the installation.

Modern hardware transforms appearance of the door. No remnant of the old borings that marred the door is visible.

Steps for Converting into Modern Lockset

1

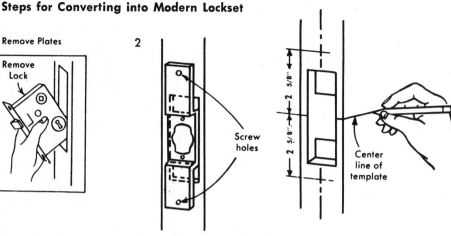

Remove Screws

Remove Knob

Remove Plates

Remove Lock

Remove the old mortise lock. Loosen knob setscrews, turn out knobs, pull out the spindle. Remove the face plates and screws on the door edge holding the lock in place, then force the lock out of the mortise with a screwdriver.

2

Screw holes

Center line of template

Center the new latch plate over the opening in the door edge, mark the screw holes, then draw a line at the center position, midway between the holes.

3

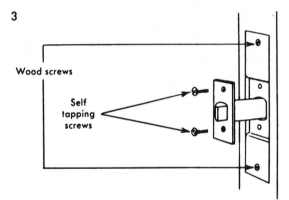

Wood screws

Self tapping screws

Install the latch plate on the door edge, chiseling out sufficient wood to a depth of $\frac{1}{16}$ inch so that it is flush. Fasten with two screws.

4

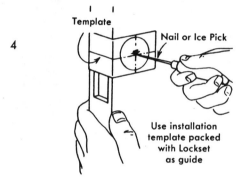

Template

Nail or Ice Pick

Use installation template packed with Lockset as guide

Locate the template that comes with the lockset on the center line of the door edge; mark the position for drilling the face of the door. Bore the hole to size specified for your lock, which most often is 2⅜ inches. An expansive bit, auger, or hole saw will drill the large hole.

5

When boring the cylinder hole, back up the hole with wood at the opposite side, or drill partway from both sides, so the drill does not splinter through.

A round plate on the inside of the door is attached with two screws into the lock body. The large rosette plate is then put on the spindle, and finally the inside knob is snapped on to complete the assembly.

BORE HOLE

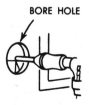

6

Install the strike plate on the door jamb.

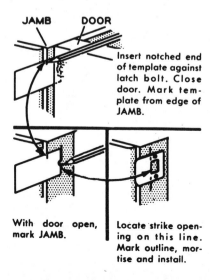

JAMB   DOOR

Insert notched end of template against latch bolt. Close door. Mark template from edge of JAMB.

With door open, mark JAMB.

Locate strike opening on this line. Mark outline, mortise and install.

This lockset installation in an old door is made possible by a special conversion set which includes decorative metal plates that cover the previous keyhole drilling on both sides and edge of the door. With the new lockset, you know that every time anyone leaves, the door is automatically on "lock." This is important particularly in the daytime when children and others come and go frequently, yet the door must not remain unlocked as an easy entry for an intruder. The installation procedure, fully illustrated by the charts and photographs, can be done by the homeowner.

Only one hole, 2⅜-inch diameter, need be bored into the face of the door. An installation tool kit, including the necessary drill and jig for locating the hole centers, can be borrowed without charge from Sears, Roebuck. A deposit is required, refunded on return of the kit. The lockset knobs are disassembled by sliding back the covering plate below the knob and compressing a hidden catch

Cross-section of lockset, showing attachment of rosette plates that cover the lock body, which is recessed into the door. The small solid bar alongside the spring latch prevents depressing the latch by pushing in on the end.

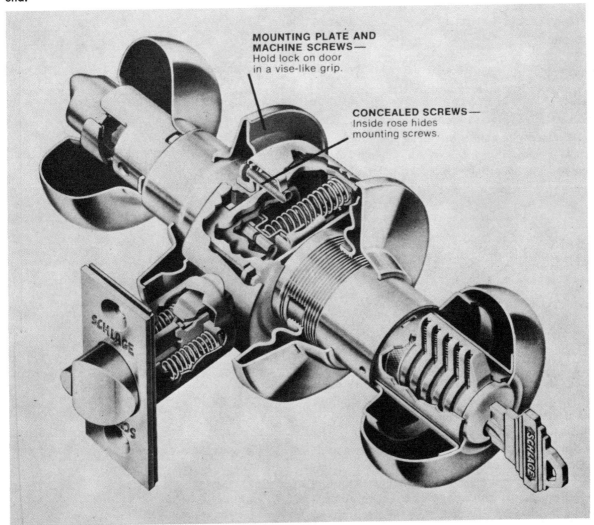

MOUNTING PLATE AND MACHINE SCREWS—
Hold lock on door in a vise-like grip.

CONCEALED SCREWS—
Inside rose hides mounting screws.

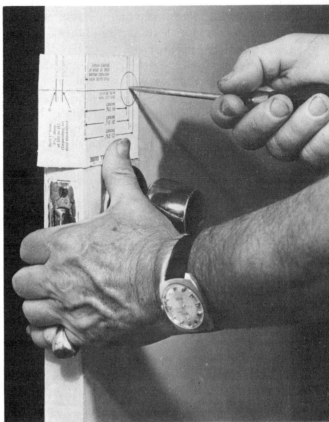

Typical lockset has attractive **rosette plates** that cover the lock body. This one is by Yale. Inside knob is snapped onto the spring retainer.

with an awl. The knob will slip off its shaft, permitting installation in the newly drilled holes.

INSTALLING A DEADBOLT

A mortised deadbolt lock with single or double cylinders is an effective addition to home security. There is a difference between the deadbolt and a latch—latches are beveled to slip into the strike plate by spring pressure. The deadbolt, in contrast, has a square end and is "thrown" to lock the door by manually turning a thumb knob or key. The deadbolt can be opened from the outside only if it has a key cylinder.

Two holes must be bored for the installation—one through the inside door face for the thumb knob, another into the door edge for inserting the

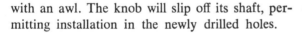

(Left) An additional deadlock on inside door from the garage or basement enhances security. Cardboard template supplied with lock is folded on line representing door width, placed over edge of door and marked in two places as indicated for drilling.

(Left below) Face of door is drilled first, partway through if lock is to have only a thumbscrew on inside, all the way through for a key cylinder to open from the other side. Clamp wood at back to prevent splintering the door panel. Use a hole saw of correct size or an expansive bit.

(Below) Drill through the door face into the larger opening from the edge. Drilling must be straight and true so latch from edge lines up.

(Right) Insert the latch, mark outline of its plate on door edge for mortising.

Latch can now be inserted, will fit flush.

Final assembly consists of inserting the bolt handle and turning in retainer screws. Locate the strike plate position, lining it up with the bolt. Drill hole to sufficient depth so bolt enters completely.

lock mechanism. A third hole on the outside door face is necessary if it will have a key cylinder. A template supplied with the lock shows the positions for drilling. Drill first through the door edge. A smaller hole is drilled on the inside door face for the turnscrew. This hole goes only to a depth that just reaches the larger boring from the door edge, but if the lock has an outside key cylinder, the additional cylinder hole will be indicated on the template. Deadbolt locks come also with double cylinders, so that a key is used on the inside as well, instead of a knob.

Insert the bolt mechanism from the edge, mark the outline of its attachment plate, remove the bolt and mortise the door edge with a chisel sufficiently to recess the plate flush. Mortise also the

jamb for recessing and attaching the flat metal strike plate. Insert the bolt from the edge, engage the turnscrew stem into the bolt, and attach the plate with screws.

EXTRA SECURITY LOCKS

Residences and apartments in some areas that are particularly exposed to burglary require extra security barriers that are more effective than the conventional locks. One such is the Fox Police Lock, consisting of a heavy steel bar that wedges against the door at an angle, and is an effective defense against jimmying. This lock, which has an

Fox police lock includes a heavy steel rod that wedges at an angle from the floor to the lock, which is positioned at a height of approximately 4 feet.

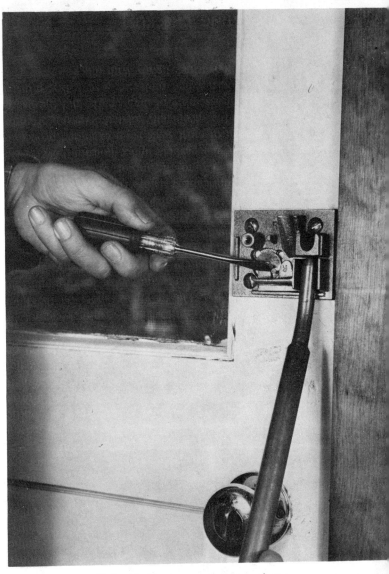

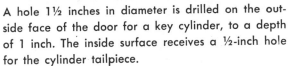

A hole 1½ inches in diameter is drilled on the outside face of the door for a key cylinder, to a depth of 1 inch. The inside surface receives a ½-inch hole for the cylinder tailpiece.

The lock is installed with heavy screws; the rod, set into a floor cup, wedges against a solid casting at top.

outside key cylinder, is quite easy to install with ordinary tools—no mortising is necessary. The installation includes attaching a metal plate on the floor about 2 feet from the door for the bar rest. The lock is mounted on the door surface with heavy screws. When the door is closed, the bar wedges at an angle against a metal barrier in the lock. When the key turns the lock cylinder, this barrier moves aside and the bar slides upward inside a loop, permitting the door to be opened wide enough to enter. The bar can be easily lifted out so the door can be opened fully, or placed out of

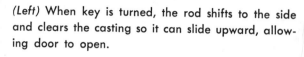

(*Left*) When key is turned, the rod shifts to the side and clears the casting so it can slide upward, allowing door to open.

(*Left below*) Cover removed to show how rod shifts to the side and can move upward when the door is opened.

(*Below*) Rugged surface lock with double vertical bolts. This model has key cylinders on both inside and outside the door to guard against entry by breaking glass and opening the lock from the inside. Shown is Sears, Roebuck model.

the way—and out of sight—when the family is at home. The installation and action of the Fox lock are shown in the illustrations.

Surface-mounted Segal and Eagle locks, which have double vertical bolts, can resist aggressive attack if solidly mounted on a sound door. A similar lock is the Abloy, made in Finland, which has an extra deep deadbolt and a uniquely shaped key that would be extremely difficult to duplicate.

LOOSE DOORKNOBS

A small setscrew in the narrow collar of the knob tends to loosen, allowing the knob to spin ineffectively. When tightening the setscrew, make sure that it engages a flat side of the square spindle, otherwise it will become loose again. The way to determine whether it is correct is to turn out the screw partway, then twist the knob slightly back and forth while tightening the screw—you'll be able to tell when the screw is firmly seated.

BATHROOM DOORS

An emergency keyway is provided so that bathroom doors can be unlocked from the outside. This situation may arise when a sick or elderly person becomes panicked; or the door is inadvertently shut while the locking button is in the closed position. An emergency key, or any narrow-blade screwdriver that fits into the outside keyway, will turn the door latch.

PATIO DOORS

Sliding glass patio doors can be lifted out of their tracks if a door is forced just an inch or so beyond the end channel. Protection against this is provided by either a spring-type bolt attached to the side jamb which engages the closed door, as illustrated, or by a "katy bar," which is an aluminum bar of the right length, hinged inside the end channel. When this bar is dropped, it prevents even slight movement of the doors.

Aluminum bar, hinged inside the channel of glass patio doors, is dropped into horizontal position to prevent movement of door. The bar must precisely fit the door span.

Another type of patio door lock is a spring-activated bolt attached to the frame so bolt slips into hole drilled in door.

WINDOW LATCHES

A locking-type window latch, although of limited value, does provide some additional protection. The latch may be attached to both sashes of double-hung windows, or one side of the latch may be screwed to the lower sash, the other to the window frame. A spring-type latch may be preferred, as it offers some flexibility for leaving the window partially open, automatically gripping the sash at any position.

(Above) Lock for double-hung window is installed by drilling hole in sash for plunger.

(Left) Lock body is attached with screws either to lower sash or to the window frame. Key is kept on convenient hook, out of reach.

(Below) Casement window opener with lock, replaces standard handles, is easily installed.

BURGLAR ALARMS

Modern technology has developed new equipment and numerous devices to make burglar alarms more efficient and dependable. One big advantage of a home alarm system is that you find out right away, when you try to set the alarm, whether a window or door has been left open. The

Typical burglar alarm panel containing the terminals for low-voltage wires from individual detectors, and automatic switchover from house current to battery in event power fails. Line leads from panel to alarm bell. This is a combination burglary-fire panel made by Alarm Devices Manufacturing Co., Syosset, N.Y.

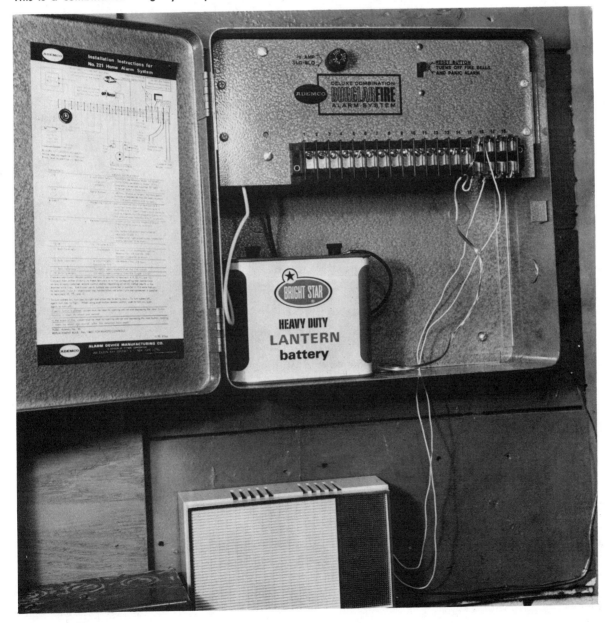

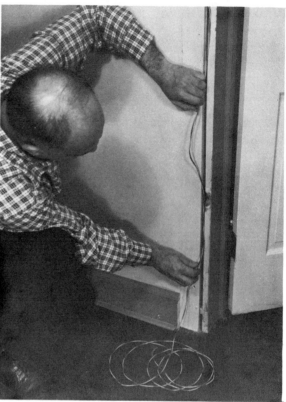

Door detector button is installed by drilling ¾-inch hole in the hinge side of the jamb. The terminals are at the back, attached by tightening the screws.

The aim always is to conceal the wiring as much as is possible. Removing the clamshell molding at the door frame is one way, permits wire to be drawn through space inside.

chief benefit, perhaps, is the feeling of security it offers, the knowledge that you won't be caught unawares if an intruder manages to break into your home.

How a Burglar Alarm Works. The basic component of the alarm system is the detector, an electric switch that reacts when an entry is made or attempted. There are many types of detectors that can be set up so they are activated when a door or window is opened, a glass broken, a screen ripped, or stair stepped upon, a window shade raised, or someone walks across a room.

The detector is connected by low-voltage bell wire to the power source, either a battery or transformer, and to the alarm bell or horn. Opening the door turns on the alarm. But won't the alarm shut off if the door is closed immediately? The answer would be yes, were it not for a simple device called a Constant Ringing Drop (C.R.D.). Once the alarm is sounded, the bell will keep ringing until it is disconnected with a key or a hidden switch.

Installing Door Detectors. The most simple and dependable door detector is a small push button with very flat brass flange. The button is set into a ¾-inch hole drilled into the hinged side of the door jamb. When the door is closed, the button is depressed; opening the door releases the button, and the switch makes electric contact, just the opposite to the bell button on your front door. In this installation, the wires leading to the alarm bell are concealed by drawing them through the space inside the door frame. If this method involves some difficulty there are other types of door detectors that can be installed more simply, including a surface leaf switch.

Wherever possible, burglar alarm wiring should be totally concealed. The low-voltage wires can

Another way, if there is a recess at the side of the frame, is to drill a small hole all the way through, lead the wire down the outside, and tack it into the recess.

Lifting the door saddle permits running the wire underneath it and down through a hole into the basement.

Often the wire can be fished down through the door frame, using a wire fish tape, or "snake," then carrying the wire under the door saddle.

The door detector button has very thin flange, fits almost flush with the jamb when fastened with screws. Contact is made when the door opens, allowing the button to emerge and closing the switch.

be safely, and legally, strung anywhere—(except in the same conduit with high voltage wires) through the walls, inside closets, along baseboard shoe moldings, and on basement and attic joists. Where surface installation cannot be avoided, use clear (almost colorless) plastic-coated wire that will be hardly visible when strung along base-boards and door frames. Burglar alarm wire is about the same size as bell wire, no. 20 or 22.

Constant Ringing Drop. This device, about the size and appearance of a small buzzer, has an electromagnetic coil that sends current directly to the alarm bell when a detector switch is actuated, by-passing the detector circuit. Thus the bell will continue ringing, even though the door has been shut instantly, until it is disconnected by pulling a separate switch and resetting the C.R.D.

The illustrations show various types of door and window detectors, and diagrams for installing an alarm system, including the C.R.D.

Window Detectors. For double-hung windows, the most practical detector is the magnetic switch, which consists of two separate parts, each fully

Circuit diagram of the basic "open" residence alarm system. One transformer lead wire goes directly to the alarm bell, the other is connected to the Constant Ringing Drop. The circuit wires from the detectors are connected to the C.R.D. and the bell. A single wire leads from the third terminal of the C.R.D. to the bell.

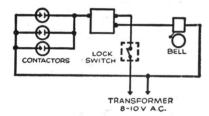

CONTACTORS   LOCK SWITCH   BELL

TRANSFORMER
8-10 V A.C.

Magnetic window detector, installed with magnetic half on the sash, the switch part attached to the window frame or nearby wall.

The Constant Ringing Drop keeps the alarm ringing even if door is closed instantly. Device has three terminals. When detector sends signal, an electro-magnet closes a switch and rings the alarm, bypassing the detector.

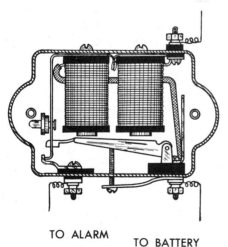

TO DETECTORS

TO ALARM   TO BATTERY

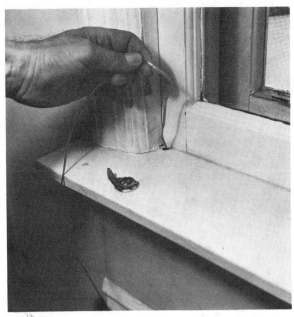

Thin wire for window detector is concealed inside wall below the window. This concealed wiring is done by first fishing the wire tape through to the floor below, then attaching the wire to the end of the tape so it can be drawn through.

Another example of concealing wire to window detector. The frame is drilled through so wire can be brought to outside and tacked along the outside frame. An extra long electrician's drill is used.

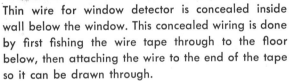

Molding along ceiling is removed to conceal alarm wire.

Wire is stapled along the ceiling line, to be covered by replaced molding. This work was done in finished recreation room.

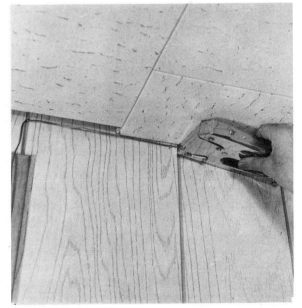

enclosed in plastic. The magnetic part of the switch is attached to the sash; the switch itself is affixed to the window frame. The magnet holds the switch in "normal" position, either open or closed, depending on the type of system. (There is a basic difference between an "open" and "closed" system

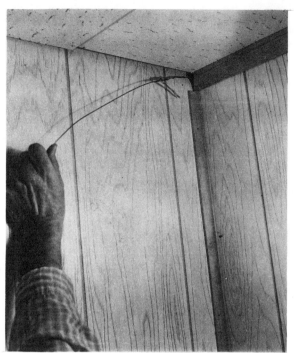

Steel tape is fished through corner hole, then wire is attached to be pulled through.

Corner drilled to carry the wire into closet in adjacent room. Only ¼-inch hole need be drilled for the fish tape.

—in the former, the alarm is sounded when the detector switch is closed, sending current to the bell; in the "closed" system, current flows constantly through the system, and any break in the current by actuating a detector switch will set off the alarm. Most homeowner-installed systems are the more simple open type.

Wire Traps. A most adaptable form of detector, the trap consists of a wire placed across a door or window, at the foot of a staircase, the entry to a room, or on a window shade. When the wire is disturbed, a clip at its end pulls out of the switch in which it has been held by spring contacts, sending a signal to the alarm panel. Wire traps are

perhaps the easiest detectors to install, and they will serve for locations where other detectors would not be suitable.

Other Detectors. Various types of devices have been developed to meet almost every possible situation, including flexible cord switches for door transoms, garage doors, and similar fixtures with extensive movement; leaf switches for casement windows, and vibration detectors to defeat efforts to break through walls. One type of detector that will serve in most locations is the switch mat. This is a very thin mat with closely spaced internal wires that make contact when anyone steps on the mat. It can be placed under windows, at doorways, on stairs, even under regular carpeting. The illustrations show the method for wiring the mat into an alarm unit.

Another simple and completely self-contained alarm is the photoelectric unit, in which a light beam is focused on a receiver. If the beam is broken momentarily by anyone passing by, the receiver contacts close and sound the alarm. An interesting improvement on the photocell is a miniature version that looks like a typical electrical receptacle installed into the wall. The light beam is bounced off a reflector on the opposite wall to the receiver switch. This unit is sold by the Alarm Devices Manufacturing Company of Syosset, N.Y.

Installing Your System. The basic components include a 6-volt transformer or lantern battery, an alarm bell, individual detector switches at doors and windows, and a C.R.D., all connected with no. 20 or no. 22 bell wire. A commercial panel box will simplify the installation as it has labeled terminals for making all connections, and a metal door that can be locked to prevent tampering. The wiring diagrams and photographs show the installation and connection of the system.

FIRE ALARM

Installation of a fire alarm is similar to that of the burglar alarm, except for the difference in detectors, and a fire horn rather than the bell. Small thermal switches are attached to the ceilings.

Fire alarm system is essentially the same as the burglar alarm, but its detectors are thermostats, rated to close the circuit and sound an alarm at 130 degrees. Any number of detectors may be included in the system.

The detectors, small and white, are almost invisible on the ceiling. They are attached with two screws, the wires drawn up through the ceiling to the attic.

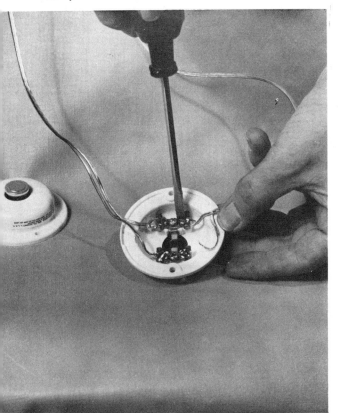

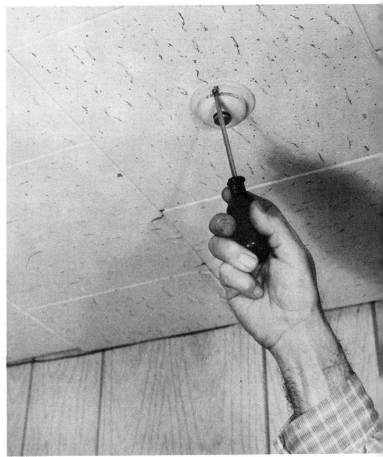

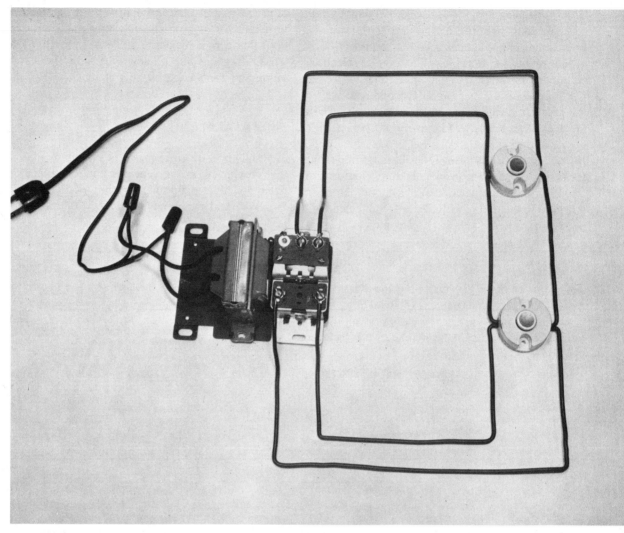

Fire alarm detectors are wired in parallel, any one detector able to close the circuit. Shown here is a transformer that can be plugged into any receptacle, with the low-voltage wires brought around to the detectors. The actual alarm system would also include a fire horn. A Constant Ringing Drop is not necessary, as the circuit remains closed, and horn sounds, until the detector cools.

A single detector provides protection over a space of 400 square feet, but that is so only when the detector is in the center of the space, as its distance of coverage (d) is 10 feet in each direction. A detector at the corner of a room protects only the area 10 feet from its position.

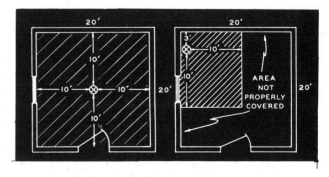

The thermostats, of white plastic that blends well with the ceiling so they are hardly noticeable, are all of the "open circuit" type, that is, the current flows through the wires only when any thermostat switch closes. Wiring is quite easy in ranch-type houses where there is access to the ceilings from the attic—thus, the thermostat detector is attached to the ceiling, its wires drawn up through a tiny hole drilled in the ceiling, and brought down through a closet to the control panel.

In two-story houses, the wires can be snaked through the ceiling to the nearest closet. The thermal detectors are set to close contact at 135 degrees, except for those that are located at the furnace, near the kitchen stove, or in the attic, which are set for 190 degrees. A useful addition to the fire system is a smoke detector, located at the head of a stairway or in the corridor of the bedrooms, and wired the same way into the control panel.

14. KEEP APPLIANCES HUMMING

Quite a few people are convinced that the way to fix a balky appliance is to "give it a hard kick." The funny thing is that this often achieves its purpose—by temporarily restoring the electrical contact at some loose terminal connection or broken wire. This energetic treatment, though, leaves the fault uncorrected; the trouble soon recurs, sometimes with a more serious short circuit and burned-out parts. Millions of dollars worth of serviceable appliances are consigned to the junk heap each year that needed only a new electric cord or tightening of a terminal nut to restore them to good condition.

The homeowner who isn't awed by mechanical or electrical devices, and learns how to keep them in working condition, is way ahead on all counts. Despite the family's dependence on sophisticated home equipment, there'll seldom be need for him to rely on outside repairmen, and he'll reap considerable savings by avoiding such service calls.

Most appliance failures result from an electrical fault—a worn-out receptacle that does not make firm contact with the cord prongs, a frayed insulation, a terminal clip that has slipped its moorings, a burned-out switch, and more often than is realized, a blown fuse resulting from a circuit overload and not from any deficiency in the appliance itself.

Other appliance breakdowns may result from malfunction of a single mechanical part, such as a loose fan belt, inoperative water inlet valve, a clogged pump, or a burned-out motor. These repairs require an adjustment or parts replacement; both procedures are within the capability of the handyman homeowner.

Occasionally, however, the breakdown involves a complex assembly like the transmission of a washing machine or the compressor of a refrigerator, that can be repaired only in a shop by experienced mechanics using special tools. This often raises the question whether such an extensive repair is worth while. If the machine is quite old and its parts guarantee period has expired, the cost of overhauling may be out of proportion to its expected remaining years of service, or to the cost of a brand-new appliance. It's almost an axiom that, as with an automobile, one big repair job leads to another, the equipment so far gone that extensive repairs mean throwing good money after bad.

Repairing appliances isn't the mystery that it is believed to be by many. There is a definite approach that narrows down the possible causes of a breakdown, then locates the actual fault. Methods of electrical testing and details of certain mechanical procedures are given here. However, specific step-by-step assembly and replacement instructions for each part would, of course, be impossible, since they differ for each of the many makes and models.

The information supplied applies to all types

of home appliances and is intended to provide a basic understanding so that the homeowner can make his own intelligent appraisal, diagnose the trouble, and proceed with those minor repairs that are within his capacity.

The best approach to any appliance repair is to have the assembly diagram and parts list at hand. Most manufacturers issue such diagrams or service manuals. One publishing company that issues specific service manuals for various major appliances is Master Publications, 1660 Euclid Street, Santa Monica, Calif. 90404. These service manuals are sold also by repair parts dealers.

WHERE TO BUY PARTS

The larger appliance manufacturers have branches in various localities where parts can be purchased over the counter or ordered by mail. In every community, additionally, there are independent dealers who carry parts for all makes. They are listed in the telephone directory under "Supplies and Parts" for specific appliance groups —washers and dryers; refrigerators and freezers; air conditioners; heating plants and stoves, and so on. Electronic and plumbing supply stores also carry many of the items needed for home appliance repairs. These places are quite knowledgeable about "interchanges," that is, certain parts that fit numerous makes and models, because many brands contain components from a single source. Electronics and radio shops, like Lafayette, Allied, and Radio Shack, supply the special wire and terminal connectors that are needed. When you go for a replacement part, have the model number of the machine, and if possible bring along the original part so it can be matched. If unable to obtain the parts you need, write for sources to the Association of Home Appliance Manufacturers, 20 North Wacker Drive, Chicago, Illinois 60606.

TOOLS NEEDED

Complete servicing of all appliances would require an extensive collection of tools, including some that are designed for a specific make and model. The tools listed below, however, have been selected to serve for the limited range of repairs likely to be done by the owner.

Screwdrivers: assortment of sizes in standard and Phillips types, including offset and stubby sizes.

Pliers: Slip-joint, lineman's, needlenose, wire stripper, and wire crimping pliers.

Hammer: Light ballpeen.

Wrenches: Set each of open end and socket wrenches, the latter with ratchet arm, ¼- to ⅞-inch sizes; adjustable and Stillson 8-inch wrenches, and set of Allen hex wrenches.

Drop lamp.

Drift punch and awl.

Hose spring pliers, for washing machine and dishwasher hose-clamps.

Neon continuity tester is used to check electrical current at various units of the appliance. The neon lights up when the contact points are made on a live circuit.

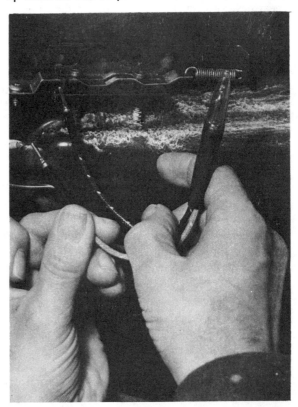

Hub puller, for dislodging motor pulleys and lubricant seals.

Testers: Continuity test light or neon tester (described in Chapter 5), and an ohmmeter or Amprobe for extended electrical checking.

LUBRICATION

Premature deterioration of appliances sometimes is due to lack of lubrication or improper lubrication. Although most motors, air conditioner compressors, washer transmissions, and some other assemblies have permanent sealed-in lubrication and should not need any attention, other parts that are subject to constant motion, vibration, or stress will wear rapidly or become noisy unless oiled periodically. Lubrication pointers are given in Chapter 2.

Belt dressing, a special kind of wax, is used on belts of clothes dryers, washing machines, attic fans, and vacuum cleaners. Attic fans need a drop or two of oil before each season on the fan shaft bearings, also the motor bearings if they are not the sealed type. But be careful not to get oil on the belt.

Even sealed motors and assemblies cannot be totally ignored. Oil or grease spots on the floor indicate that the lubricant seal is leaking and that the parts ultimately will be running dry and will burn out unless the seal is restored.

Additionally, grease released into a washing machine tub by a leaking agitator seal will cause permanent staining of linens and clothes.

Some lubricant seals are rubber collars that are tightly fitted onto the motor or machine shafts; others are flat gaskets under housing covers. Replacement of most seals is an extended procedure shown in the specifically related diagram, often requiring disassembly of many parts and the use of special tools. When replacing a seal, first moisten the bearing surface lightly with oil.

OPERATING CHECKLIST

Certain conditions must be provided for satisfactory performance of appliances.

On the Level. Stationary appliances must stand level, on a solid base or floor, to operate with minimum vibration and stress. Washing machines must be balanced so that the tub agitator won't tilt or the machine "walk" during the spin cycle. Machines with spring-mounted mechanisms must be leveled just like any other. Adjust the screw-type bolts under the cabinet, checking the cabinet with a carpenter's spirit level.

Correct Voltage. The electric circuit wires and the fuses of the circuit into which the appliance is plugged must be of recommended size to carry the current drain of the appliance. Also see that the extension cord is exactly the same size as the wiring. Most small and portable appliances can be used on a 20-ampere circuit of no. 12 wire and a 20-ampere fuse. Major appliances and tools should have individual circuits with no other receptacles into which other equipment can be plugged, unless only one appliance is ever used at a time (for example, a power saw and a drill press), but this does not apply to portable drills, vacuum cleaners, and similar "small" appliances. Some motorized equipment with heavy starting current loads, like air conditioners, need delayed action fuses (discussed in Chapter 5). Appliances with heating elements, such as a clothes dryer, may be listed for operation only on 240-volt, 30-ampere circuits, requiring no. 10 wire.

Give It Air. Refrigerators do their job by dissipating into the room the heat which had been absorbed during the cooling process. Don't crowd the rear of the cabinet, which contains the compressor and condenser tubing, against the wall. A refrigerator should not be completely enclosed unless it has been designed for such installation, has a condenser fan and ample provision for air circulation.

Keep It Clean. Dirt and other clogging material affect both performance and durability. Vacuum clean the rear of the refrigerator periodically to remove dust and lint from the condenser tubing, thus facilitating the heat transfer. Empty the lint trap of the clothes dryer each time it is used, and check also the exhaust tubing occasionally to remove any accumulation. Shake out the toaster frequently to remove crumbs that may become carbonized. The vacuum cleaner is harder to use when its wheels become snagged by lint and carpet fuzz, or the hose clogged with paper chips. Dirt-matted filters on furnaces and air conditioners reduce efficiency, raise costs, overburden the machines.

Grounding. Except for appliances equipped with a 3-wire grounding cord plugged into a grounded receptacle, every stationary appliance must be grounded with a wire of adequate size, attached to a water line or heating pipe with a special grounding clamp. Refer to Chapter 5 for further details.

Vacuum cleaner failure is nearly always caused by a clogged hose or an overloaded dust bag. Inserting a flexible coiled wire, such as the common drain auger, will release a surprising quantity of dust and carpet fibers that have been blocked by some crumpled paper or similar object.

Special grounding clamp for attaching the ground wire from a washer or other stationary appliance assures good and continued contact. Simply wrapping the grounding wire around a water pipe is unreliable.

REPAIR PROCEDURES

Every appliance has both an electrical system and a mechanical system; washing machines and dishwashers also have a water system. Since electrical switches control the mechanical action, the electrical details are checked out first when there is trouble. These steps start with determining whether there is current to the machine, then the internal electrical connections are checked out and tests made for a short circuit. When it is obvious that the electrical controls are functioning, this step is bypassed and the mechanical cause is diagnosed, the suspected part removed for testing, and repaired or replaced. The water system, a common cause of trouble, involves the connecting faucets and hoses, inlet and water mixing valves, and the discharge pump. Additionally, the clothes dryer and dishwasher, and certain small appliances like the hair dryer, have heating elements with their own thermostat controls.

The most useful single piece of equipment for trouble-shooting an appliance failure, as for all other repair work, is the drop lamp. This puts the light where you need it to make an effective inspection, and guides disassembly of parts that you undertake. Seeing what you're doing is a prime rule for any service work.

Frayed Line Cord. Visual examination of the cord may detect a frayed insulation and exposed bare wire; either can be the cause of a short circuit. A perforation in the cord insulation indicates a

Typical cause of appliance failure is a short circuit caused by fraying of the wire insulation, as shown. Check wires under retainer clamps which may be responsible for the condition.

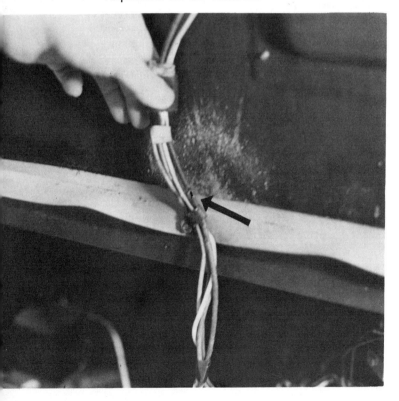

broken wire, and should be tested out. Another point of failure may be loose connections either at the cord prong or inside the appliance. (See Chapter 5.) The internal connections can be inspected only after removal of the cover or shell of the appliance. Always disconnect the line cord before opening any appliance.

Wire Replacements. In appliances, the wires are attached to the terminals of the timer, motor, and other parts by means of solderless connectors. These are mostly flat metal strips shaped to slide onto "shoe" terminals. The wires have differently colored insulation, making it easier to trace and connect them to the correct terminals. Timers of washing machines and dishwashers, for example, have color coded terminals, marked R for red, B for black, Y for yellow, G for green. Thus, installing a new timer means merely slipping each wire onto the terminal shoe marked for that color insulation.

When a frayed wire must be replaced, the new one should be of the same gauge, and the insulation of the same color, as the one that is to be discarded. If the original wire has terminal connector lugs, these are put on the replacement. The connectors cost just a few cents each, can be purchased in small lots at any electronic supply store. Use terminal connectors of the right size for the wires that will be attached, stripping the wire end to the indicated length, ⅜ or ½ inch, to fit.

The connector lugs are secured to the wire by crimping, which is done with a special tool that serves also as a wire stripper and bolt cutter. You might think that the crimping can be done with ordinary pliers, but that would not properly secure the lug on the wire. The crimping tool costs between $2.50 and $5.00, can be obtained at hardware and electronic supply stores like Allied Radio and Lafayette Electronics dealers.

The Timer. In the washing machine, dryer, and dishwasher, the various functions of the machine are controlled by a timer. This device consists of a clock-type motor that turns a cam, a small eccentrically shaped plastic wheel. As the cam turns, various high and low spots signal different

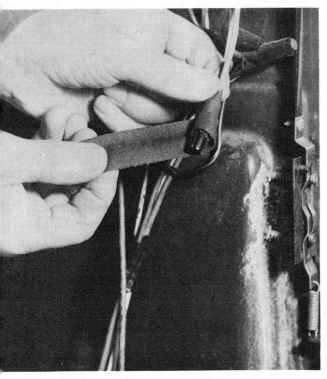

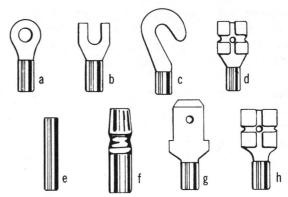

Solderless terminals provide sure grip for wire connections, have permanently attached insulation sleeves for protection against short circuits. Crimping of the terminal with a special pliers assures a positive wire connection. The types illustrated are (A) ring tongue, (B) spade tongue, (C) hooked tongue, (D) female tab socket, (E) butt connector, (F) snap terminal, (G and H) male and female tabs.

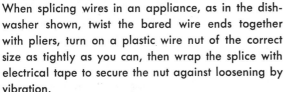

When splicing wires in an appliance, as in the dishwasher shown, twist the bared wire ends together with pliers, turn on a plastic wire nut of the correct size as tightly as you can, then wrap the splice with electrical tape to secure the nut against loosening by vibration.

switches as (in a washing machine) to open or close the water inlet valve, start the washing agitator, then the pump, the rinsing, and finally the spin dry cycle. Some additional functions are added in luxury machines that control the water temperature—hot, warm, or cold—by letting in a selected volume of hot and cold water.

WASHING MACHINES

But the washing machine is more complex than that. Water flows into the machine at different rates of pressure, so there must be safeguards against flooding; a separate float or pressure switch watches that the tub does not overfill. And the agitator must not start until there is sufficient water in the tub, otherwise the clothes would be damaged, so the float switch intercepts the timer impulse to the agitator until the water is at a specific level. The spin directive from the timer also will be countermanded until all the water has been pumped out, otherwise the motor will be under critical strain. And above all these, a door switch cuts off all action when the lid is opened, as a safety measure.

A line test for any of the washer parts—inlet valves, pump, motor, or others—obviously then must be coordinated not only with the related timer position, but also the overriding safety switch, including the one on the door which so often is forgotten when troubleshooting.

Electrical function may be affected by a mechanical condition, as when the motor cannot turn because the washer tub is jammed by clothes caught in the casing, or in a dishwasher by a spoon jamming the impeller. When checking the motor, turn its pulley to make sure that it is free. An odor of burned insulation usually, but not always, is a sign that the motor windings have burned out. The odor may have been caused by a slipping belt when a part is jammed. A motor that hums or clicks but does not start possibly is blocked by a clogged pump, too heavy a load, a lint-plugged exhaust line, or other difficulty.

Removing the Motor. When there is doubt about the condition of a motor, inlet valve, or other part, it is usually better to remove the part from the machine for testing. The motor is comparatively easy to remove from a washer or dryer by loosening the motor mounting bolts and removing the belt. In Norge dryers, the motor is released simply by pulling out a rod on which the motor swings by spring tension against the belt.

Clearing Jammed Washer Pump. Remove electric cord from plug, drain tub water by lowering the drain hose into the floor trap or a pail. Tilt the machine forward so you can reach the back, providing some support to hold the machine securely in position such as a low bench covered with a blanket to protect the finish. Remove the back panel by taking out the self-threading screws all around. The pump is round and has two hose connections. Remove the pump inlet hose. The obstruction can now be cleared and the hose replaced. A special pliers is used to release the hose retainer clamps.

Removing Tub Motor. Tilt washer on a secure, padded support to obtain clearance at back. Remove the back panel. The motor is near the bottom of the tub and can be taken out together with the clutch. Remove bolts of the flexible fabric coupling. Loosen the four motor mounting nuts and push the motor toward the transmission to disengage the V-belt from the motor pulley. Release the wire connectors from the motor terminal box, remove the motor support nuts, and lift out the motor. A bench test, touching the terminals with live wire ends, will immediately show whether the motor is in working condition.

Transmissions. Removing and rebuilding a washer transmission should be attempted only by persons with extensive mechanical experience and an adequate workshop, guided by a service manual illustrating the mechanism and the rebuilding procedure. Replacement with a new or rebuilt transmission is usually the best solution, a job for an experienced serviceman.

CLOTHES DRYERS

Slow Drying. A clogged lint screen prevents venting of moist air. If the heating coils are functioning and the lint trap is clean, check the venting hose for an obstruction by accumulated lint at a bend, or a sticky baffle plate on the outside wall. Too many wet clothes will overload the machine, require too long a drying time. Limit the loads to the weight recommended by manufacturer for that particular machine. A voltage drop, or too-small wires in either the power cable or the extension cord, can be responsible for inadequate heat, and therefore slow drying.

No Heat. The cause may be a burned-out heat selector switch, a faulty thermostat, or a break in the heating coil. A 240-volt dryer has two fuses, one for each leg of the circuit, so while the motor may start, one side of the line may be "out" if a fuse has blown. Check the fuses or circuit breakers. Further checking necessitates removing the back panel of the machine to test the electrical continuity to the thermostats, then the heating element. Note: If you test the electrical continuity with the line cord plugged in, take all necessary precautions against shock. Do not stand on a damp floor, wear gloves (preferably rubber gloves), avoid contact with water pipes or other conductors. Continuity can be tested more safely with an Amprobe using battery current, the main power disconnected.

The condition of the heating elements can be inspected visually. Look for a break in the coil, or sagging of the heating wires which results when a coil is burned out, or two coils are in contact. While it is possible to repair a break in these wires, replacement of the unit is easy and inexpensive. The heating element is mounted on a wire frame, removed by turning out the retainer screws and disconnecting the wire leads. A burned-out heat selector switch can be removed from the timer assembly and replaced individually.

Overheating. Dryers have two or more thermal switches, or thermostats, to cut out the heater if temperature gets above 200 degrees. These are important for safety and should never be bypassed by direct hookup to the heating element. The thermostats are usually round and flat, about 2 inches in diameter. The circuit diagram on the machine will show their location. The thermostats are self-restoring; that is, they make contact again when the temperature drops to allowable setting. A defective thermostat may fail to cut out the coils, permitting excessive heat so that the clothes are too hot to touch.

Motor Won't Start. Make sure the tub turns freely. If fuse, line cord, and "on" switch check out, remove back panel of machine. Disconnect the tub belt by pulling the motor against its springs. Try the motor shaft, which should turn smoothly. An odor of burned insulation indicates damage to the motor, which should be taken out by pulling a pivot pin or removing the mounting bolts. Try starting the motor out of the machine by connecting direct wire leads. If motor is dead, have it checked at a motor shop before replacement, as repairs may be minor. Rewinding of motor wiring is an alternative possibility, but usually the cost is equal to that of a new motor.

Drum Doesn't Turn. First check by hand that drum turns freely. The trouble may be a torn or loose motor belt, broken tension spring, or a sheared motor pulley pin. If belt is torn, take it along when getting a replacement, to duplicate the size. The motor pulley will not turn the drum belt if the tension spring has slipped off or is

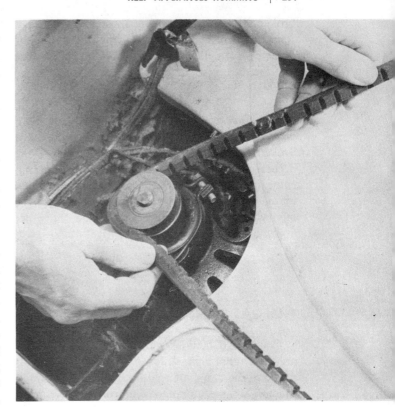

The motor in most dryers turns the tumbler drum by means of a notched belt. Pushing the motor forward to relieve the spring pressure permits removal of the belt from the motor and drum pulleys.

A torn or worn belt is often the cause of poor dryer operation. Take the old belt along to your appliance parts dealer for exact replacement.

broken. If drum is jammed, most likely cause is some garment caught between the drum and the dryer case. Remove screws at back panel to raise the top cover so exterior of the drum can be reached.

Timer. Failure of machine to shut off automatically at the end of a drying period is due to a broken link in the timer assembly. Remove the decorative covering plate at the front of the machine for access to the timer. Test the operation of the timing device, particularly the link to the off switch. A new linkage belt inside the timer may correct the condition.

THE GAS RANGE

Common difficulties with gas ranges and ovens are faulty pilot light, yellow flame, popping sounds at the burners, unbalanced door springs, and malfunction of the automatic controls. Only limited maintenance of gas appliances is advisable; avoid tampering with the gas supply lines and connections. Such repairs should be left to experienced servicemen who make careful tests for gas leaks.

Gas reaches the pilot light through a separate thin tubing. A screw at the coupling adjusts the size of the flame, which should be small and steady, preferably blue, although many stoves do not have pilot light air adjustments. Failure of the pilot to light the burners, or a tendency of the flame to go out, nearly always is due to a clogged burner cap. Clean by brushing, or inserting a soft fine wire into the cap. Air currents from a nearby window may also be responsible, and would require some form of shield for the pilot light. Increasing the gas flow is rarely necessary.

The oven pilot is linked to a safety valve, which prevents gas flow to the burner if the pilot is not lighted. Cleaning the pilot orifice by brushing should be the only effort. A gas odor at the oven, other than from an unlighted pilot, may indicate a valve or gas line leak. Call the gas company for a serviceman, leave the oven door and windows open until the leak has been checked. Gas leaks are detected by a special instrument, but it also is done by smearing soapy water over the pipe connection and watching for any sign of bubbling.

Air adjustment corrects a yellow flame at the burner. Loosen the screw at the air inlet shutter at the burner base or the slotted plate on the burner housing. After a steady blue flame is obtained, retighten the shutter screw carefully. Air adjustment also eliminates the popping that occurs when interrupted gas flow is relighted. The accuracy of oven temperature controls can be checked with an oven thermometer. A setscrew on the dial permits resetting to adjust for any differential.

The oven door springs, located behind the oven lining or inside the door itself, sometimes snap off at the hooked end. A short link of heavy steel wire shaped into hooks at each end will extend the broken spring if you can't get a duplicate. Access behind the oven lining may be difficult, but the spring usually can be fished out sufficiently to attach the link. Springs inside the door itself are more easily replaced by removing the door cover panel, which is assembled by a series of sheet metal screws.

ELECTRIC IRONS

Iron Won't Heat. The principal source of this trouble is in the cord, either a broken wire or burned contacts at the inside terminals. If the cord appears in good condition, remove the temperature setting knob to inspect the connections to the heating element. The knob is held with a small setscrew, requiring an Allen hex wrench. A shorted heating element may mean that a new sole plate will have to be put on. The other alternatives are a stuck thermostat or melted fuse, which can be replaced.

Scale buildup from minerals in hard water may plug the steam vents. Clean the holes with fine wire. Vinegar left in the tank overnight will loosen some of the scale so it can be drained or tapped out.

VACUUM CLEANERS

The vacuum cleaner is essentially a fan. The air forced out at the exhaust end creates a vacuum that sucks air, and with it dust and dirt, at the vacuum hose. The stronger the suction, the more efficient the cleaning. This principle is the same regardless of the type of cleaner—tank, upright, lightweight, workshop canister models, and even the central vacuums with their remote motors and dust collectors. The main element of the vacuum is, then, the motor that moves the air, and in the upright type, drives a carpet brush and even provides traction for the machine.

Decreased efficiency of the cleaner most likely is due to either a clogged air hose or a leak at the hose connectors. An overloaded dust collector bag can cut air flow all the way to zero, as will a piece of crumpled paper in the hose. A cloth bag can be cleaned best by beating it like a rug to loosen embedded dirt. (Replaceable paper bags are more efficient.) Check the hose connections (bent ends prevent proper joining) and fitted parts of the cleaner's housing. Hold a piece of tissue at suspected places to test for leaks.

When the vacuum cleaner won't start, don't take anything apart until you've checked out the most likely cause: the line cord. The cord, heavy as it may be, is subject to kinking and a broken wire is quite common. The switch, operated by foot pressure in the tank type, at least, is the second most common cause of vacuum failure. The switch is on one line only—the second wire goes directly to the motor, so to check the switch, use the neon tester or a short piece of wire bare at both ends to jump across the two terminals. If the motor starts, the switch is definitely the cause of breakdown and should be replaced. Access to the switch varies with the different types and makes, but usually requires removal of the housing plate at the motor end.

The vacuum motor is a universal type, which means it has brushes. These may be found jammed in their holders. Just freeing the brushes so they respond to spring pressure will correct a lagging motor. Brushes that are considerably worn can be replaced by just slipping them out of their retainer springs.

If the armature of the motor is coated with a black residue as a result of arcing, which is caused by poor contact of the brushes, light sanding can rejuvenate it. After replacing the brushes, hold a piece of fine sandpaper against the armature, with the motor running, for a moment or so until the metal is bright. Fold the sandpaper to the width of the commutator so that the thickness of the paper provides some pressure, but do not use any tools on the running motor. However, if the motor won't start at all, the field coils are burned out and replacement of the motor will be necessary.

DISHWASHERS

Dishwashers are similar to, but much simpler than, washing machines. There is a timer that controls the wash cycles; a water intake valve and discharge pump; wash, rinse, and dry cycles. Many dishwashers also have heating coils to boost water temperature. Flooding is prevented by an overfill pressure switch.

The timer is most often responsible for malfunction, probably because it is the only part of the machine that is subject to user control and abuse. Adjustment of the timer is not feasible, and replacement of the entire unit the only course. The timer terminals are coded for wire replacement so there's no problem about installation of a new unit, provided the correct insulation colors have been retained for all connections.

The dishwasher is located at the sink, so there should be special concern about properly grounding this machine. If any shocks are felt while the machine is operating, there evidently is an inadequate ground contact, either at the machine itself because the ground contact surface is rusted, or at the water pipe to which the grounding wire is clamped. A shock that occurs when the machine is off indicates that the polarity is switched, the machine ground serving as the neutral wire of the circuit. Check the circuit leads and reverse for proper connection, making sure that there is no current leakage at the terminals, or contact of a frayed wire with the cabinet.

Water Valves. The water inlet valve is controlled by a solenoid coil switch that sometimes jams in open or closed position. A check for electrical continuity is necessary—this can be done with an ohmmeter without removing the solenoid. Disconnect the power wires from the coil, touch the ohmmeter leads to the terminals. The solenoid is defective if it does not show a reading. The solenoid is removed by loosening the two water tube connections and the retainer screws.

Dishwasher motors are somewhat difficult to remove because of the narrow clearance under the tub. Access is from the front of the machine after removing a cover plate at the bottom. In some makes, the motor has a split shaft—a rod inserted from above through the tub opening is turned into a threaded hole in the motor shaft. The impeller goes on the top end of this rod, locked in place by a nut. The side of the lower shaft is drilled so that a drift pin or nail can be inserted to hold the shaft while the upper rod is turned out.

A plunger-type switch disconnects the power when the dishwasher door or lid is opened. If the motor or pump continue to work after the door is opened, this switch is defective. Conversely, a burned-out or disconnected door switch may be responsible for failure of the washer to start. A quick test can be made by jumping the switch terminals with a test light when the dial is at wash position, but expect a spray of water should the machine start. Replacement of the switch involves removal of the inner door panel.

AUTOMATIC ICE MAKERS

Failure to produce ice, or too little ice, usually is caused by a clogged water line or high temperature setting. Lower to 10 degrees or less. Make sure that the valve is open, the water flowing. If the ice cubes are too small or too large, adjust the water switch and check the inlet valve for possible sticking. Hollow cubes indicate defective cycling and may require replacement of the thermostats. When left in the bin too long, cubes will get an odor from stored food in the refrigerator. Discard any that have been stored more than two weeks, and keep food containers tighty cov-

ered. Discoloring of ice resulting from minerals in the water or tarnished water tubing often may be corrected with filters.

SINK GRINDERS

Jamming of the grinder blades by a spoon or other metal object dropping into the drain opening may occur with certain types of grinders. Provision is made for releasing the jammed blades, using a large Allen hex wrench that fits into a socket at the bottom of the grinder. The wrench is forced back and forth, manually operating the cutter blades until the jamming object is worked loose and can be removed through the top.

An inoperative switch is difficult to trace, unless the switch is a separate toggle type mounted on the sink cabinet and can be tested with a jumper wire. A built-in automatic switch requires removal of the grinder unit for testing.

Leaking at the sink trap connection nearly always results from a loose slip-joint nut, or unsealed threads at the nut (see Chapter 6). Turn out the nut and examine. If threads are damaged, or the nut is distorted out of round, replace. When installing the nut, coat the threads with Loctite sealant to prevent leaks.

ATTIC FANS

Decreased efficiency of the fan is usually due to a slipping motor belt. Shift the motor mounts so there is just enough tension on the belt, and apply a belt dressing compound. Replace a frayed or excessively stretched belt, also make sure that the motor pulley is in direct alignment with the fan pulley, to avoid belt distortion.

Routine maintenance, at least annually, includes cleaning or washing of the fan blades to remove accumulated grime. Check the motor wiring, replace if insulation is oil soaked or shows signs of deterioration. Lubricate the fan and motor bearings with just 2 or 3 drops of oil—avoid overlubricating. Make sure the motor mounting bolts are tight; check the fan housing and louvers, tighten where necessary to eliminate rattling.

LAUNDRY TUBS

Leaks or water seepage from a cracked concrete or ceramic laundry tub can be repaired with epoxy cement. Dry the tub completely before applying the cement, which is described more fully in the section on gluing (Chapter 2). The repair sometimes can be done with a stiff mortar made of 1 part portland cement and 2 parts fine sand. Open the crack as wide as possible with a chisel and pack the groove tightly, smoothing the surface. Cure the patch with a sprinkling of water several times for the first few days, then coat with epoxy cement paint.

EFFECT OF DIMOUTS

Power shortages in recent years have resulted in occasional dimouts during which the utility companies reduce the voltage, sometimes as much as 10 percent. How does this affect your equipment and what can you do to avoid damage?

Motors in stationary equipment, such as those in the furnace, refrigerator, air conditioner and washer are subject to damage, since their constant speed under the condition of a voltage drop causes excessive current draw, thus building up heat that can burn out the wire insulation. Universal motors on portable appliances like drills, vacuum cleaners, and sanders, however, stall when the voltage is below rated current load. Heaters and electronic equipment like the radio and record player are not adversely affected, but the television may go out of sync or lose picture quality. A voltage regulator will correct the TV problem.

Shutting down the air conditioner, freezer, and refrigerator during the dimout, which usually lasts only a few hours at peak current demand, will protect the equipment from possible damage and help ease the power shortage. Both freezer and refrigerator temperatures will remain at satisfactory levels if opening the door is restricted to a minimum.

TROUBLESHOOTING CHECKLIST

The probable causes of service failure for small appliances (toasters, irons, percolators, blenders, grills, and the like) are listed in the order of frequency as experienced by servicemen.

1. Loose wire connections or defective cord.
2. No power—fuse blown.
3. Faulty thermostat (on appliances with heating elements).
4. Switch contacts inoperative.
5. Timer out of sync or not functioning.
6. Faulty water inlet valve or pump switch.
7. Mechanical adjustment.
8. Heating element shorted or thermostat not working.
9. Water tubes clogged.
10. Drain pump inoperative.

15. FAMILY SAFETY

The number of appliances, power tools, and other equipment in the home increases dramatically year by year, so that some homes have as many items of electrical and mechanical equipment (though of smaller size) as a factory. The list ranges from electric blankets, can openers, and hair dryers to major items like power mowers, snowblowers, and garden tractors, besides the washers, dryers, TVs and air conditioners that are in almost every home today.

Although much of this equipment is fully automatic and designed with built-in safety factors, the casual use of such equipment ignores certain hazards. A refrigerator can become a death trap if a child manages to climb in and the door is closed; serious injuries have resulted from crashing through large glass patio doors that lack visibility stickers. Portable auxiliary electric heaters are fire hazards if they have wobbly legs, or are carelessly placed directly on wood floors.

The following safety cautions can guide you in protecting your family against needless accidents.

SAFETY CHECKLIST

Chemicals. Insecticides and other dangerous chemicals like drain cleaners, bleaches, and furniture polishes should be kept in tightly sealed containers on high shelves, not in the undersink cabinet if there are small children in the home.

Furniture. Test heavy furniture and tall, free-standing lamps for wobbles that can cause an upset. Correct any imbalance of cabinet legs. See also "Outdoor Furniture," below.

Glass Patio Doors. Apply decals so the door is readily seen. Do not place small area rugs that may slide and cause falls against the glass.

Guns. Whatever the type of gun, even battered antiques, keep them securely locked away, never loaded, the key carefully controlled.

Medicine Cabinets. They should be well-lighted to prevent errors, with all medicines in approved containers that cannot be opened by small children. Make it a practice to discard all prescriptions that are no longer current and needed.

Clotheslines. Both outdoors and in the basement, the lines should be high enough so they can't cause injury in the dark. Remove low clotheslines promptly when not in use.

Outdoor Furniture. Store lawn and patio furniture in good time, well before wintry blasts can lift and hurl lightweight chairs around. Be sure to wash rustic furniture and spray it with an insecticide before bringing any items into the house where insect eggs can hatch in the indoor warmth.

3. Keep children and pets out of the area. Do not allow children to operate or ride the mower—it is not a toy cart.

4. Wear proper clothing, not shorts or sandals. Never go barefoot while operating a power mower.

5. Keep hands and feet clear of the discharge chute.

6. Before making any repairs or adjustments, always stop the engine and disconnect the spark-plug.

7. Never refuel a hot or running engine. Keep gasoline in approved cans, tightly capped. Never store gasoline inside the home; limited quantities for lawn equipment may be kept in the garage or outside in approved containers.

8. Steer tractors and riding mowers straight up and down slopes, instead of across them, to avoid capsizing; walk-behind mowers, on the contrary, are steered laterally across the face of the slope. Always look behind when backing a tractor.

Shelves. Falling objects cause many serious accidents. Store items in closets well back on the

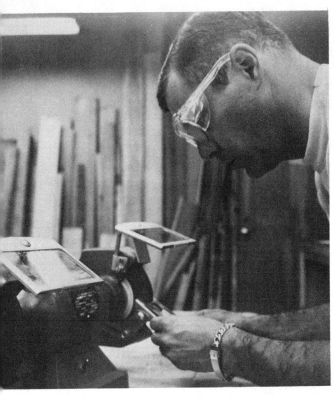

This home handyman is wisely using eyeglasses and keeping guard in place while using power tools. However, he has goofed by wearing a loose-fitting bracelet that could catch in moving parts.

Power Equipment. With more than 27 million power mowers and garden tractors in use, numerous accidents have occurred from contact with moving parts, objects being picked up and thrown by the mower blades, gasoline fires, and other situations resulting from improper operation. The Outdoor Power Equipment Institute, which established design standards, has formulated a list of rules for safe operating:

1. Keep power mower in top condition; study the operating manual to become familiar with the mower's construction and operation.

2. Rake lawn before mowing to remove twigs, stones, and other debris; keep lawn hose coiled and out of the way; make sure that sprinkler heads retract properly.

By letting children play where he is using an electric hedge clipper, this father is courting injury to them and himself.

The wrong way to use a walk-behind power mower on a slope. Instead, it should be pushed across the face of the slope from one side to the other.

shelf. A pressing iron can tumble down, pointed end foremost, if the cord trails loose; keep the cord coiled on the shelf. Bookcase shelves—the type mounted on wall standards—should be adequately supported, not overloaded with heavy objects such as audio sets and record albums.

Stairs. Be sure that stair handrails are firmly secured. Stairways should be amply lighted at both top and bottom with handy 3-way switches at each landing, always be free of obstructions, frayed or torn carpeting, or worn mats on the treads.

Swimming Pool. A non-slip surface around the rim of the pool is essential. It should preferably be of textured concrete or unglazed quarry tile. All electric wiring at the pool must be the approved, waterproof type, fully grounded and out of the reach of bathers. Overhead lights should be located so there's no chance of any lamp or wire falling into the water.

Swings, Play. The swing frame must be plumb and squarely on the ground, secured with stakes so there's no chance of capsizing. Check chain or rope supports for strength. See that there's sufficient space between adjacent swings so they do not collide.

Ladders. Caution in the presence of ladders is more common sense than superstition. Here is a checklist for ladder safety:

Keep ladders clean, free from dirt and grease, and in good condition. Rebuild or discard ladders that have broken steps, loose spreaders, or sagging rails. When using stepladders, always lock the spreaders in fully open position; do not place a stepladder (or any ladder) in a doorway where it can be knocked over or impede passage. Never stand on the top step of a stepladder or try to reach more than an arm's length—move the ladder when necessary.

Proper positioning of extension ladders requires that the base of the ladder be a distance from the wall equal to one-fourth the height of the ladder. Thus you need a 20-foot ladder to reach a 15-foot height, as the ladder base will be placed 5 feet from the wall for proper support. When carrying a metal ladder, watch out for overhead electric lines, avoid contact.

FIRE SAFETY

There should be no need to argue the importance of fire safety in the home. Still, fire prevention is not adequately observed, hazards are ignored, elementary safety rules neglected.

The principal causes of home fires are: (1) defective and misused electrical and heating equipment, (2) accumulated papers and rubbish, and (3) careless smoking. The three causes accounted for 45 percent of all fires in 1971. More than half a million of these fires occurred in private dwellings, taking a toll of 6,600 lives and causing a physical loss of almost a billion dollars.

How do you protect yourself and family against fire? Here are suggestions for a permanent program:

No Rubbish. Eliminate or reduce as far as possible the quantity of flammable materials around the home. Discard newspapers and magazines, unused furniture, lumber scraps, and the like. Keep needed papers in metal boxes or file cabinets. In the workshop, empty sawdust containers promptly.

Careless Smokers. Empty ash trays only into a metal container, not the waste basket. If a cigarette is dropped, don't give up until it is located, and you're positive that it has not left a smouldering fire in upholstery or carpeting. Never smoke in bed.

Keep Bedroom Doors Closed. More fire casualties result from smoke and fumes than from the flames. Should a fire start, the margin of time provided by closed bedroom doors may save lives. Provide escape routes such as a rope ladder for each room that is on a high floor.

Fire Extinguishers. Don't depend on a fire extinguisher—it's not likely to be handy when you need it, and most likely won't be effective except on a small fire caught at the very start. Loss of time fighting the fire rather than in turning in an alarm may be dangerous.

Furnace and Heaters. Proper maintenance of boiler or furnace includes regular adjustment, and cleaning of the pilot light, fuel lines, wiring, flue and chimney, and control instruments. Smoke pipe sections must be tightly fitted, sealed with asbestos cement. Individual space heaters must be mounted on a fireproof base, such as slate, ceramic tile, or concrete; a sheet metal base is not safe if the metal is in contact with a flammable surface. All heaters except the electrical types must be vented to the outdoors.

Alarm Box Location. Post a card with the location of the nearest alarm box, so that the entire family is familiar with it; do not depend on the telephone alone for sending a fire alarm.

Home Alarm System. A practical fire alarm system, including a smoke detector, is a valuable adjunct to fire safety. The system requires no attention other than occasional testing by pressing a button to make sure the power source is on.

Kitchen Practices. Awareness of the potential for fires from cooking equipment will go far to reduce or eliminate hazards. Flammable objects should be kept away from the stove, nearby window curtains that might be blown over the flame by a gust from the window should be retained by tie-backs, matches kept in closed metal containers, exhaust fan and filters washed regularly to remove accumulated grease.

Christmas Trees. Select a freshly cut tree, no more than a week old, dispose of it promptly by New Year, or before if the needles become dry and crisp. Use only UL approved lights, properly wired, and turned off when the family retires at night.

Storing Paints and Solvents. Oil-based paints and varnishes contain volatile solvents that are toxic and flammable. Once opened, the containers cannot be perfectly sealed. When stored in the home, limit the quantity and keep them in well-aired locations such as open basement shelves rather than in a small cabinet. An air duct leading outside is a desirable installation. Water-based latex paints are not flammable.

Store turpentine, varnoline, alcohol, and similar solvents in metal or plastic containers rather than glass bottles. If the glass were to drop and shatter, the spreading fluid could become ignited and roar into an uncontrollable flash fire. If necessary to have these solvents on hand, limit the quantity to a pint or less.

16. INSURANCE AND LEGAL PROBLEMS

KNOW WHAT PROTECTION YOU'RE BUYING

Homeowners generally are quite lax, even lackadaisical, about their insurance. It's a highly complex subject and it would take more than just a little attention to learn all you need to know for your purposes, but the homeowner should at least be very clear about what protection he has—and doesn't have.

The oft-heard expression, "You get only what you pay for," doesn't apply to insurance because you may be getting a lot of fancy but useless coverage, while leaving yourself wide open for a staggering loss on some grave hazard that was omitted or excluded from your coverage.

Most policies carry the notice "Read Your Policy Carefully" or some such reminder, printed in the largest type on the policy. But the policies are, of course, written by the company's legal staff and it would take a skilled lawyer or insurance expert to interpret the text. This is not to imply that insurers deliberately seek to befuddle and mislead their policyholders—some companies have made sincere efforts to simplify the wording of their policies and eliminate the "fine print." Also, policies must conform to the standards of state regulatory bodies. Still, you're not in a position to negotiate the policy's terms or terminology; it's

take it or leave it, and in these days of widespread rejections and cancellations of whole neighborhoods, without reason or apology, you're probably glad to get it. But you can seek to place your policies with those companies having the highest ratings for fair treatment (one of the places where comparisons are listed is *Consumer Reports*), and to select the options and amounts of insurance that give you ample protection.

Large commercial firms retain insurance consultants who know their way around and see to it that all hazards are covered while overlapping insurance is eliminated. The individual homeowner, however, relies essentially on the recommendations of his broker—who is really an agent of the insurance companies and is paid by them. There rests the prime key to a reasonable insurance program. The homeowner must select an agent who is thoroughly knowledgeable on insurance matters, of the highest integrity, and has well-established insurance underwriter connections.

There are many options available in most types of insurance, particularly in the homeowner policy. The amount carried is an essential factor, as more fully explained later, but it would be wasteful to pay for excessive or duplicated coverage. Also, some policies provide for extremely unlikely situations, while limiting or excluding many essential details.

The good agent, then, is one who will review your particular situation, learn about specific circumstances, and draw up a reasonable program that provides the broadest protection. Don't expect him to provide for every contingency or for maximum amounts. Insurance is expensive and the line must be drawn somewhere. The best you can expect is that you are covered, at minimum cost, to avoid catastrophic losses.

HOMEOWNER INSURANCE

While you're unlikely to acquire knowledge about all the ramifications of personal and homeowner insurance by studying a few books or poring over the policies, there are some essential details that you should know and keep in mind.

It is very important that you look over all your policies periodically—at least once a year is certainly a minimum—including life insurance, for possible expiration dates, conversion options, changes in beneficiaries, dividend accumulations, or loan values. The following information on home insurance is supplied to cover certain details about which many homeowners are unaware.

What Is Co-Insurance? When a home increases in value, the fire insurance coverage provided by your policy drops by the same proportion, unless you've increased the amount of insurance to keep up with the higher price. Expressed another way: if the cost of rebuilding your home has doubled, your old insurance would cover only half the amount of any loss, partial or total.

The reason is the 80 percent co-insurance clause in all home fire policies. Fire claims are computed on the proportion that the amount of insurance carried bears to the *current replacement cost* of the *entire house,* except that if the insurance equals at least 80 percent of the current cost, then the payment is in full up to the face amount of the policy.

This anomaly can best be explained by an example: A home purchased 10 years ago for $25,000 was insured for $15,000 (a proper amount covering original cost of house, less plot and foundation). At the time of a fire causing $12,000 damage, the actual replacement cost of the home itself was $45,000. Thus the insurance is about 33 percent and payment for the loss would be only one-third of the $12,000 loss, or $4,000, usually with a further deduction for depreciation. If the policy had been for $36,000 (80 percent of $45,000) the owner would have been reimbursed in full for the $12,000 loss, and some companies would not make any depreciation deduction.

In determining whether the 80 percent amount has been met, the value of the land and the cost of excavations, underground pipes, wiring and drains, and foundation wall or piers are disregarded.

The owner who wants to maintain full coverage faces the difficulty of determining the amount of insurance to carry, since the 80 percent coverage relates to replacement costs, not market value, *at the time of loss.* A broker is in no better position than the owner to determine the correct amount. Written estimates from building contractors, or professional appraisers, may be the only way properly to determine the amount of insurance to be carried, and this appraisal should be reviewed annually.

Other Insurance. The homeowner's policy may include insurance for the home and garage buildings, household contents (furniture, clothing, equipment), public liability, theft, loss away from home, and other hazards as stipulated and for which premiums are charged. Household contents are covered for an amount in proportion to the overall house insurance, usually 40 percent. Thus, if the home insurance is $40,000, the furniture and other possessions would be automatically insured for $16,000. The latter amount can be increased by payment of extra premium.

Extended Insurance. Not all homeowner policies are alike, nor do they provide the same degree of coverage. The extended risk policy, for an additional premium, liberalizes the coverage to include certain other hazards, while the "all risk" insurance goes a bit further, but still contains many exclusions, such as loss from overflowing faucets, flooding of various kinds, and "friendly" fires, such as the fireplace or heater. It is important that you study the policy, although you can't eliminate the standard exclusions.

Another desirable coverage is that of "living expenses," which pays a stipulated amount for extra expenses in hotel rooms or rented apartment while a home is being rebuilt.

Thefts. Protection against burglary and other theft losses, including holdups, has been steadily eroded. Recovery for cash theft has been limited to $250 in most policies. Items like jewelry, furs, art, coin collections, and other valuables are insured only when listed individually in a special "floater" policy, the value of each item confirmed by expert appraisal.

Liability and Property Damage. Coverage for accidents on your property, or injuries suffered as a result of your action, such as hitting someone with your golf ball, is included in the homeowner's policy, in an amount selected by the policyholder for public liability contingencies. This amount should be adequate, not only in relation to the homeowner's assets, but enough to cover the size of any possible suit. In an injury case, the plaintiff can sue for $100,000 or more. If the amount of liability insurance is small, say $10,000, the company can step aside by consenting to pay that amount, and leave you holding the bag for a judgment of the remainder. Carrying $100,000 or even $300,000 will protect you all the way, putting it up to the insurance company to carry the fight in its own interest. The small additional premium is worth while since legal costs can be enormous, even when you win the case. It's to your advantage to let the company provide the defense all the way.

The liability coverage would include injuries suffered by a domestic servant or baby sitter, but may not apply to an independent contractor doing work around the house, such as a painter or gardener. Check your policy in this regard. Also, be sure that any concern or craftsman with whom you contract for work on your premises carries workmen's compensation insurance for the protection of his workmen, and public liability insurance for injury to passersby or other persons.

SPECIAL INSURANCE

Do you have a swimming pool? Read your policy to see whether pool accidents are covered. If in doubt, get a written opinion from the company. Boat owners, or those who rent and haul a boat on vacation jaunts, should check the extent of coverage provided by their policies. Some insurance covers boats only of a certain size, specifies the horsepower limit of the motors, also contains provisions regarding boat trailers. Another important protection that may be included in the homeowner policy is that of credit-card fraud, covering unauthorized use of lost cards, also loss due to forged bank checks. A policy may even include reimbursement if you're stuck with counterfeit money.

TIPS TO POLICYHOLDERS

Homeowners can protect their interests by keeping up-to-date records on their household possessions, including purchase receipts, descriptions of the articles, serial numbers of cameras and similar items, and appraisals if the items have current value beyond cost, as in the case of paintings or porcelains. Photographs of individual pieces, and of whole rooms, will be helpful in establishing a claim. In the event of loss, if there is any dispute regarding the extent of damage, retaining a professional fire adjuster may be helpful because you will be informed of rights that would otherwise be overlooked.

A recalcitrant company may compel throwing a dispute into arbitration, but an amicable settlement, if at all possible, is to be preferred.

In this difficult period when losses tend to soar beyond any previous concept, and insurance companies become ever more selective in issuing new policies while arbitrarily canceling previous policyholders who present a claim, or even without such justification, the homeowner is well advised to make every effort to avoid casualty losses by careful fire prevention and alert cautions against other casualties. The less you have to do with your insurance company, aside from paying the premiums, the better for both.

BUYING AND SELLING A HOME

There's many a slip in real estate transactions. When accepting a deposit, or signing a contract for sale, it is wise to include a stipulation in writing that any brokerage commission will be considered earned and payable only if title actually passes. Otherwise, if for any reason the deal falls through, you may be obliged to pay a commission that could be larger than the deposit that you received.

Buying a Home. The purchase nearly always starts with signing a contract, followed after an interval with taking title and possession of the premises. But it is the contract that is the determining step, and many buyers go about it too lightly, sometimes signing a printed form contract with the attitude that it is "standard," and that a lawyer's services are needed only for the title closing. But there is nothing standard about a real estate purchase. Each transaction has many individual factors—and plenty of possible pitfalls. It is at the contract signing that the attorney's services are most necessary, since the contract spells out not only the terms of the purchase, but also many other essential details such as the option to withdraw if a mortgage cannot be obtained at a specified rate of interest, a specific date for transfer of title and possession of the premises. Other details may be the right to subsequent inspection, stipulations regarding the physical condition of the property, and what appliances and materials are part of the purchase. Perhaps the purchase is made because the buyer intends certain alterations or particular use of the premises to suit his requirements. An example is a physician who plans to set up an office in the home, and would need a zoning change in order to hang out a shingle—in that case, the contract might well specify cancelation and refund of the deposit if the zone modification is not approved within a certain time.

At the time of taking title, the attorneys representing buyer and seller have important individual roles. The plot survey must be checked fastidiously with the mortgage and title descriptions, the title policies examined for any exceptions, tax bills confirmed as to current payment, then adjustments made for deferred and prepaid charges. Real estate law takes into account every kind of situation that has been encountered; you wouldn't want to learn, years later, that there is an easement across your property, that the title is clouded by the interest of an unknown heir who surprisingly turns up, or that your boundaries are in question. A competent lawyer, responsible for the transaction from contract on, will see to it that your home ownership is free of legal complications.

DEALING WITH A HOME CONTRACTOR

Making the Contract. Dealing with a reputable local roofer, mason, tile layer, and other craftsman on a specific job most often is uncomplicated and perfectly satisfactory. A large renovation or construction job is another matter, involving considerable money and complex requirements, and can lead to unexpected difficulties. Most home contractors are competent and dependable; many others, unfortunately, are inept, disorganized, poorly financed, and you may not find out about that until after a job is started. You owe it to your peace of mind and financial protection to obtain the services of an attorney before making a firm commitment or signing any contract. Some possible pitfalls are discussed here:

An extensive remodeling project or alteration should be set forth in a written contract, describing precisely the work to be performed, the materials to be used, and the time and manner in which the work is to be done. If you have an architect's plans and specifications, these should be included or identified in the contract. The contractor is required to obtain all necessary permits, and prove that he carries insurance for workman's injury, public liability, and property damage (for example, if the wind dislodges a scaffold plank). In certain cases, a completion bond is desirable, permitting you to have work finished by someone else if the contractor becomes bankrupt or fails to do the job satisfactorily or on time.

An essential part of a renovation contract is

scheduling times of payment—possibly certain proportions of the total at certain phases of the job, with final payment subject to obtaining a certificate of occupancy or other certification that the work is satisfactory. In large jobs, part of the work usually is let out to people in other trades (electricians, carpenters, masons, etc.) and if their bills are not paid, they can levy liens or attachments against your home, even if not hired by you. The contract should specify the means for settling such disputes, possibly including escrow funds to be held by an attorney for a certain length of time, subject to an arbitration ruling or other disposition of any claim.

17. HOME MAINTENANCE CALENDAR

A blustery winter night is not a comfortable time for clambering up a ladder to lash a tree limb that is swinging against the roof, nor is it very pleasant trying to clear a clogged downspout during a driving rainstorm. Such emergency situations, which always seem to occur at the worst possible times, could have been avoided by routine maintenance.

Some homeowners, probably the vast majority, tend to leave things as they are until the need for immediate repair becomes obvious, even urgent. Others prefer a more orderly approach, pursuing a specific maintenance routine at specified times. While the calendar chart that follows will be most helpful to the methodical person in his efforts to keep the home always in ship-shape condition, as a reminder for inspections to head off potential difficulties, it may also serve to encourage others to perform those tasks which, done promptly, can prevent trouble and discomfort.

In scheduling the various tasks listed, the seasonal requirements were aligned with convenient times from the standpoint of outdoors weather and available leisure. The list does not, of course, include all possible malfunctions, but represents only a routine maintenance program to prevent breakdowns.

JANUARY

Heater. Check boiler water level weekly, refill as needed to halfway mark on gauge. Vacuum clean forced air registers; replace furnace filter. Drain expansion tank in hot water heating systems.

Tools. Sharpen workshop tools and knives, lubricate and protect against moisture.

Appliances. Check electric cords and wall receptacles, replace as needed.

Batteries. Semi-annual replacement of dry cell batteries for burglar alarm, door bells, intercom (if these devices are not powered from a transformer).

FEBRUARY

Attic. Make a thorough inspection for damp spots indicating leaks, seepage from roof gutters, or condensation. Examine snow-covered roof for signs of heat leaks, detected by rapid melting in spots.

Termites. Look for swarming of winged insects in basement. Suspected damage can be tested by driving ice pick into wood beams.

Foundation Leaks. Plug and coat cracks or openings.

MARCH

Heater. Check boiler water level; replace hot air filter.

Hinges. Tighten hinge screws in all doors; lubricate pins.

Garage Doors. Lubricate hinges, rollers, and tracks.

Windows. Replace any cracked panes; ease stuck sash; reputty and paint as needed.

Roof. Clear gutters and downspouts of debris; check for pitch of gutters that may have been altered by snow load; reinforce as necessary. Look for loose flashings and missing shingles.

APRIL

Storm Sash. Remove storm sash from windows, and store. Adjust door windcheck spring and closure.

Heating System. Wash or vacuum clean wall registers; replace filter. In steam or hot water system, brush down and vacuum the boiler tubes and chimney box to remove soot (unless boiler is serviced regularly). Flush boiler with cleaner compound, add rust inhibitor, refill.

Garage Door. Lubricate hardware.

Lawn Hose. Connect to hydrant, open inside valve.

Garden Tools. Clean, paint, lubricate. Sharpen clippers and other cutting tools.

MAY

Attic Fan. Have fan ready to work when you need it. Clean the blades, check belt tension, lubricate fan and motor bearings. Tighten support frame and louver screws.

Lawn Sprinkler. Test sprinkler operation and timer clock; brush away dirt mounds at sprinkler heads, and test each.

Screens. Replace window and storm door screens.

Garden. Rake up winter debris; turn over earth at shrubs.

Awning. Install; replace worn pulleys and cords.

JUNE

Attic. Check vent louvers and attic fan for bird nests.

Lawn Mower. Clean, adjust, and lubricate. Power mowers may need engine overhaul.

Lawn Furniture. Wash, repair, and paint, as needed.

Air Conditioners. Install stored window units. Caulk housings of through-the-wall installations. Wash or change filters.

Roof. During a heavy rain, inspect the runoff from each downspout, watch for dripping or overflow from gutters.

JULY

Windows. Ease up sticking sash; replace cracked panes, reputty as needed.

Air Conditioners. Wash or replace filters.

Mildew. Ventilate and clean with Clorox any area infested with mildew, apply fungicide.

Batteries. Semi-annual replacement of burglar alarm and bell batteries.

House Siding. Inspect for protruding nailheads and cracked asbestos shingles. Replace loose nails with a larger size, recessing and puttying the heads.

AUGUST

Roof. Remove leaves from gutters, clean wire cage at downspout, check positions of splash pans.

Walls. Inspect brick and stucco walls for crumbled mortar, point up as necessary.

Driveway, Patio. Patch concrete cracks; chop out surfacing tree roots; fill or patch depressions in blacktop driveway.

Air Conditioners. Wash or replace filters.

Kitchen Exhaust Fan. Wash filters, clean grease off motor housing.

Lubricate. Casters, door hinges, locks.

Insects. Eliminate, by spraying, wasp nests in louvers or under eaves.

SEPTEMBER

Roof. Clear leaves from gutters and downspouts; check pitch of gutters.

Heating. Fill boiler water to halfway mark on gauge. Bleed excess water from expansion tank in hot water system; bleed air from radiators. Open steam radiator valves all the way; replace defective air valves. Tape holes in warm air ducts.

Caulking. Inspect and caulk all exterior door and window frames, and wall joints. Repair joints of window wells to the house walls.

Painting. Paint exterior trim, window and door frames.

Air Conditioner. Wash or change filters.

Forgetting to clean out leaves and debris from roof gutters in the fall can result in ice dam like the one shown. Thawed water backs up under shingles, can cause considerable damage inside the house.

OCTOBER

Lawn Furniture. Store furniture and garden tools.

Roof. Check shingles and flashings, clean leaves from gutters.

Fences. Reinforce or replace weakened fence posts. Paint after shrubbery is pruned.

Drains. Clean sand from driveway and garage drains.

Screens. Remove and store screens, replace with storm sash.

Awnings. Take down, repair, wash and store.

NOVEMBER

Lawn Hydrant and Sprinklers. Shut water line valve, disconnect and store coiled garden hose; disconnect sprinkler timer.

Storm Doors. Check and adjust door closure and windstop chain; adjust clearance of sill strip.

Weatherstripping. Apply weatherstripping where necessary; clear and adjust door saddles.

Trees, Shrubs. Prune dead branches, remove large limbs that are near walls or extend over the roof.

DECEMBER

Furniture. This is a good time to reglue wobbly chairs, make other interior repairs.

Window Wells. Clear out debris, soften earth at bottom with pitchfork for quick drainage.

Snow Shovels. Apply light coating of wax or non-stick aerosol. Tune up power snowblower.

Heating Plant. Clean and change humidifier filter, check water flow to pan; check boiler water level. Replace leaking radiator vent valves.

18. MORE INFORMATION

Catalogues provide valuable information to the homeowner. In addition to detailed specifications of the various models and types of materials, which assist you in making the best selections in your purchases, catalogues contain useful data on designs, dimensions, installation procedures, cleaning, and maintenance. Many manufacturers also supply helpful brochures, booklets, specification sheets, and experience reports on their products. This literature is usually available without charge by writing to the company, stating model number and year.

Government and research institutions issue booklets covering every possible subject of interest to the entire family. You can obtain a list of publications relative to any problem by writing to the Superintendent of Documents, U.S. Government Printing Office, Washington, D.C. 20402. Many people are not aware of the assistance available from industry or trade associations in almost every field of building materials. Some of the better known organizations are the American Gas Association, concerned with gas appliances and equipment; the Tile Council of America, comprising manufacturers of ceramic and quarry tile; the National Board of Fire Underwriters, which supervises the National Electrical Code and publishes fire records; the Wallcoverings Council, the National Paint, Varnish and Lacquer Association, and many others. The address of any association may be obtained by writing to a company in the particular field. The specific catalogues and booklets listed below can be obtained by writing to the addresses stated.

Acrylic Sheeting. Safety glazing with acrylic sheeting in storm doors and shower doors, and in windows for burglar protection, is discussed in a brochure available free from Rohm & Haas Co., Independence Mall West, Philadelphia, Pa. 19105.

Aerosols. Where and how to use them for care of wood paneling, Formica counter tops, and other finishing and cleaning purposes. Free set of consumer booklets from Magic American Chemical Corp., 14215 Caine Avenue, Cleveland, Ohio 44128.

Air Conditioning, Central. Details of equipment and the required ductwork for various installations. Free booklet from Air Conditioning Institute, 1815 Fort Myer Drive, Arlington, Va. 22209.

Air Conditioners and Electric Heating. Details on selection, proper installation and maintenance. Booklet free from Commercial Customer Department, Potomic Electric Power Co., 512 10th St. N.W., Washington, D.C. 20004.

Aluminum items. "Care of Aluminum" booklet gives information on care and cleaning of aluminum siding, gutters, windows, doors, and storm sash, even aluminum pots and boating equipment. Price 25 cents. Write to the Aluminum Association, 750 Third Avenue, New York, N.Y. 10017.

Automotive Parts and Accessories. Wide range of rebuilt motors, replacement parts, and accessories listed in free 185-page catalogue from J. C. Whitney & Co., 1917 Archer Avenue, Chicago, Ill. 60616.

Burglar and Fire Alarms. An 82-page catalogue, including the newest systems with circuit diagrams and valuable installation advice, is free from Mountain West Supply Co., 4215 North 16 Street, Phoenix, Ariz. 85016.

Caulking Compounds. Leaflets describing various types of compounds, with instructions on caulking operations, available free from Stay-Tite Products, Cleveland, Ohio 44104.

Electric Code. National Electrical Code and National Fire Code. Copies may be purchased at moderate prices from the National Fire Protection Association, 60 Batterymarch Street, Boston, Mass. 02110. Write for descriptive listing of the publications and their prices.

Electrical Devices. "Wiring Devices Handbook" describes switches, receptacles, plugs, and other electrical devices, with data on making installations and connections. Available free from Circle F Industries, Box 591, Trenton, N.J. 08604.

Electronic Parts. Extensive listings of electronic and radio parts, tools, and accessories, together with many other items that are required around the home such as speaker wires, burglar alarm materials, and electronic connectors, plus related tools, are contained in free 468-page catalogue from Lafayette Radio & Electronics, 111 Jericho Turnpike, Syosset, N.Y. 11791.

A similar 552-page catalogue may be obtained without charge from Allied Radio, 100 N. Western Avenue, Chicago, Ill. 60680. Titled "Electronics for Everyone," it contains complete listings of electronic parts and devices, plastic boxes, musical instruments, hobby kits, radio receivers, and thousands of other items for the home.

Fans, Attic and Window. An informative 12-page booklet, free from Lau Incorporated, Conaire Division, 2207 Home Avenue, Dayton, Ohio 45407.

Fiberglass Sheets. Corrugated, various uses and instructions on installation, free from Owens-Corning Fiberglas Co., Home Products Division, Toledo, Ohio 43681.

Heating Cables, Anti-Freeze. For water pipe, rain gutters, driveways, walks. Booklet on Chromalox heating cables, with information on applications and installations, available free from Chromalox Division, Emerson Electric Co., 8100 Florissant Ave., St. Louis, Mo. 63136.

Home Improvement. The 48-page "Home Improvement Catalogue" illustrates doors, windows, siding, awnings, shutters, garage door openers, many other items. From Sears, Roebuck & Co., Philadelphia, Pa. 19133. Catalogue #39W 7400. Free.

Laminating Plastic Sheeting. Consoweld Corp., Wisconsin Rapids, Wis. 54494 supplies a comprehensive booklet on laminating plastic sheeting for home purposes and commercial shops.

Lawn Sprinklers, Underground. Installation instructions and descriptions of the various sprinkler heads, control equipment, and suggested lawn layouts, free from Rain Jet Corp., 301 South Flower Street, Burbank, Calif. 91503.

Masonry Fasteners. A booklet showing various types of masonry anchors, hollow wall fasteners, and drilling devices for these materials is available from the Arrow Expansion Bolt Company, P.O. Box 388, Marion, Ohio 43302. A useful chart shows the safe working load for each type and size of fastener.

Masonry Panels. Description and installation methods of "man-made masonry panels" called Roxite, manufactured by the Masonite Corp., included in leaflets available free by writing to Selz, Seabolt & Associates, 221 N. La Salle Street, Chicago, Ill. 60601.

Moisture, Excessive. Booklet issued by W. R. Meadows, Inc., 5 Kimball Street, Elgin, Ill., discusses problems caused by excessive vapor in home, and means for controlling the humidity level. The free booklet presents data on use of "premolded membrane" as a vapor seal for all types of construction. Another, excellent, 72-page manual for homeowners and builders on how to control moisture in homes is available free from the National Mineral Wool Association, 1270 Avenue of the Americas, New York, N.Y. 10020.

Painting. "Painting Walls, Ceilings and Trim" and "How to Paint the Outside of Your Home" are free brochures containing useful information on preparation, tools, safeguards, and technical tips for home painting projects. From Benjamin Moore & Co., Montvale, New Jersey, or from local branches in Boston, Jacksonville, Pittsburgh, Cleveland, Chicago, Houston, St. Louis, Los Angeles, Montreal, Toronto, Vancouver, etc.

"Specifications Information for General Painting" is an informative 16-page booklet listing the various types of paint, their formulation and recommended uses on wood, plaster, masonry, and metals. Free from Pittsburgh Paints, PPG Industries, 1 Gateway Center, Pittsburgh, Pa. 15222.

Paint Peeling. The causes and correction of paint peeling, blistering, and other failures of house siding paint are discussed in an interesting booklet, "Paint Peeling," available free from Sears, Roebuck & Co., Philadelphia, Pa. 19133. The publication explains problems of moisture condensation and faults in home construction, also shows types of ventilation louvers and how to install them.

Security. "How Do I Protect My Home?" describes locks, bolts, door chains, and security alarms, with data on installation. Free from Stanley Works, New Britain, Conn.

Shopping Guide. A helpful 100-page catalogue, entitled "Home Shopping Guide," illustrates more than 2,500 consumer items for the home, including housewares, appliances, remodeling materials, plumbing and electrical fixtures, and farm necessities. Available free at local Our Own Hardware dealers, or for 50 cents from Our Own Hardware Co., Burnsville, Minn.

Tiles, Floor. Pamphlet containing practical instructions for laying floor tiles of every type—including the self-adhesive Touch Down tiles—free from Kentile Floors, Inc., Brooklyn, N.Y. 11215. Includes details on preparation of the *underfloor* and correcting unfavorable conditions. A separate leaflet, "Fashions in Floors," shows attractive designs and color combinations; also gives hints on using vinyl tiles outdoors on patios, porches, pool decks.

Tools and Workshop Accessories. Illustrated 70-page catalogue specializing in small tools for fine or miniature work, together with exceptional items like labeling tape, measuring microscope, compressed air hose, and camera repair parts. Free from National Camera, Inc., Englewood, Colo. 80110.

Tools, Hard-to-Find. A useful information source for the homeowner is a fascinating 64-page catalogue showing workshop tools of every description, including exceptional items not available at most local hardware dealers, also garden tools, equipment for sportsmen and the outdoorsman, plus unusual gifts. It is available free from the Brookstone Company, Brookstone Building, Peterborough, N.H. 03458.

Tools, Power. The illustrated "Toolcraft Power Tool Handbook" shows basic shop procedures for effective use of power tools by the homeowner. Tells how to build a workshop, with operating hints on circular saws, sanders, jointer, lathe, even shop vacuums, with a section on blades, belts, lubricants. Booklet has 41 pages, price 35 cents from ToolcraftCorp, 700 Plainfield Avenue, Springfield, Mass. 01107.

INDEX

ABOUT THE AUTHOR

Combining his long experience as newspaper reporter and editor with a lifelong interest in mechanics and woodworking, author Ralph Treves built a successful career as writer on home and workshop subjects. After some years at McGraw-Hill as crafts editor, he produced the weekly Handyman feature for the *Philadelphia Inquirer* and *Los Angeles Times,* in addition to eight books, hundreds of articles for the national mechanics and shelter magazines, and numerous instruction booklets on manual skills and tool use. His articles have been published in *Popular Science* magazine, *Popular Mechanics, Workbench, Better Homes & Gardens, Time-Life Books, Successful Farming, Mechanics Illustrated, Science and Mechanics,* and others.

Ralph Treves, a member of the National Association of Science Writers and the American Newspaper Guild, is currently president of the National Association of Home Workshop Writers. He and his wife, Estelle, have a spacious home in a suburban area of New York City that includes a fully equipped workshop where Mr. Treves continues to pursue his fascinating profession.